Essential Linux Commands

100 Linux commands every system administrator should know

Paul Olushile

BIRMINGHAM—MUMBAI

Essential Linux Commands

Group Product Manager: Pavan Ramchandani
Publishing Product Manager: Neha Sharma
Book Project Manager: Ashwin Kharwa
Senior Editor: Athikho Sapuni Rishana
Technical Editor: Arjun Varma
Copy Editor: Safis Editing
Proofreader: Safis Editing
Indexer: Manju Arasan
Production Designer: Joshua Misquitta
Marketing Coordinators: Marylou De Mello and Shruthi Shetty

First published: November 2023
Production reference: 1081123

Published by Packt Publishing Ltd.
Grosvenor House
11 St Paul's Square
Birmingham
B3 1RB, UK

ISBN 978-1-80323-903-3
www.packtpub.com

To my wife, Anthonia, for being my loving partner throughout our joint life journey.

– Paul Olushile

Contributors

About the author

Paul Olushile is a penetration tester at First City Monument Bank, specializing in Linux administration and cybersecurity. With a strong track record of securing digital environments and a passion for Linux, Paul has a proven ability to identify vulnerabilities and protect against cyber threats. His career has been defined by a relentless pursuit of knowledge and expertise in the field. He has consistently demonstrated proficiency in network security, ethical hacking, and system hardening. He is dedicated to enhancing digital resilience, promoting secure practices, and fostering a culture of vigilance against cyber threats.

I want to thank the people who have been close to me and supported me, especially my wife, Anthonia, and my mom.

About the reviewers

Himanshu Sharma has 2 decades of experience in designing, architecting, and developing cloud and network software. He had worked for some of the biggest companies, such as Brocade and Juniper, and start-ups, such as Netskope. Currently, he works with Netskope as a principal engineer, responsible for Netskope's security service offering. He designed, architected, and developed Netskope's Advanced Threat Protection service from the ground up. He has a keen interest and experience in developing scalable cloud services with cutting-edge technologies. His favorite hobbies are skiing and playing video games.

I would like to thank my wife, Puja, who gave me lots of support, and my two loving and beautiful daughters, Navya and Jaanvi.

Also, I want to thank my brother, Sudhanshu, for always having my back, and my parents for all their sacrifices to get me where I am today.

Alan Lacerda, commonly recognized by the alias **ifundef**, is a seasoned Security Engineer, underlined by two decades of rigorous experience in network, operating systems, and software development. As a polymath of technology, his journey spans roles from being a Network Analyst to shaping solutions using diverse programming languages such as Java, Python, and Golang. His prowess has magnified as a penetration tester and, in recent years, as the mastermind behind a comprehensive malware toolkit. This cutting-edge resource serves security assessments to prominent corporations across the North American landscape. He holds the titles of CRTO, OSCP, eWPT, CRTP, DCPT, CCNA and LPIC.

To my irreplaceable wife, Naiane. This journey, every word written and every insight shared, belongs to you. It is not an exaggeration to say that without you, the knowledge I possess today would remain undiscovered.

I am deeply conscious that my role as a reviewer for this book is a testament to our shared journey. From the core of my being, thank you, Naiane. My achievements are but a reflection of your love and belief.

Table of Contents

3

Part 2: Frequently Used Commands - Part 1

4

5

6

Filesystem Mount and Manipulation Commands   105

Part 3: Frequently Used Commands - Part 2

7

File Content and Conversion Commands   121

8

Linux SWAP Commands   133

9

Linux Monitoring and Debugging Commands   139

10

Linux IPTABLES and Network Commands   159

11

File Transfer, Downloading, and Managing Log Files   169

Part 4: Linux Security and the Cloud

12

Exploring Linux Security   181

13

Linux in the Cloud   193

Index   219

Other Books You May Enjoy   228

Preface

Hello there! In our rapidly changing world of technology, it is essential to learn and understand the Linux command-line interface. The Linux **operating system (OS)**, known for its robustness, versatility, and open source nature, has become an integral part of modern computing.

Essential Linux Commands is your gateway to this dynamic world of command-line proficiency. Whether you're a seasoned system administrator, a developer, or simply someone eager to explore the power of Linux, this book offers a comprehensive and accessible guide to the fundamental tools that make Linux tick.

Linux commands are the unsung heroes, silently but efficiently performing tasks ranging from managing files to configuring networks, securing systems, and optimizing performance. Each command is a valuable tool in your arsenal, capable of simplifying complex operations and automating routine chores.

As our digital landscape continues to transform, understanding Linux commands becomes a fundamental skill. With this book, you'll not only acquire the technical knowledge to navigate the Linux environment but also the confidence to tackle real-world challenges.

The beauty of Linux commands lies in their universal applicability. They are equally relevant to individuals working on personal projects and professionals overseeing complex enterprise-level infrastructure. The knowledge gained from this book will empower you to efficiently manage and manipulate Linux-based systems.

The book provides in-depth explanations, practical examples, and valuable insights, ensuring that you gain both the technical proficiency and the practical wisdom needed to excel in the world of Linux.

Just as the world of Linux commands continues to grow and evolve, this book is designed to grow with you, offering an essential foundation for Linux mastery.

So, as we embark on this journey through *Essential Linux Commands*, prepare to unlock the full potential of Linux and transform the way you interact with the digital world. Whether you're venturing into Linux for the first time or seeking to enhance your existing skills, this book is your key to becoming a proficient Linux command-line user.

Who this book is for

This book is designed for a diverse audience of technology enthusiasts, professionals, and learners. It caters to a range of individuals who can benefit from a comprehensive guide to Linux command-line proficiency:

- **Linux enthusiasts**: If you're passionate about Linux and want to deepen your understanding of its command-line interface, this book provides a wealth of knowledge to further your expertise.

- **Developers**: Whether you're a software developer, web developer, or programmer, understanding Linux commands is invaluable for your work. This book helps you harness the power of the command line to improve your productivity.

- **IT professionals**: If you work in the IT industry, this book offers insights into Linux commands that can enhance your problem-solving capabilities and broaden your skill set.

- **Students and aspiring professionals**: If you're studying computer science or pursuing a career in IT, this book serves as a foundational resource to help you grasp the fundamentals of Linux commands.

- **Anyone curious about Linux**: If you've been curious about Linux and want to explore its command-line capabilities, this book is a user-friendly starting point.

What this book covers

Chapter 1, Getting a CentOS Server Up and Running, provides a comprehensive guide to the initial setup of a CentOS server, offering essential insights and practical steps for a seamless start. It covers key aspects such as downloading the OS installation file, downloading and setting up a hypervisor, package installation commands, and information commands.

Chapter 2, Linux User and Group Commands, provides valuable insights and hands-on guidance for using commands such as `useradd`, `userdel`, and `usermod`, as well as mastering file, directory, and permission commands. Additionally, it covers the `groupdel`, `groupmod`, `groupadd`, and `grpck` commands, along with the `pwck`, `chage`, and `passwd` commands. To enhance your Linux skills further, this chapter also delves into the `find`, `locate`, and `whereis` commands.

Chapter 3, File Compression and Archival Commands, provides a comprehensive guide to essential commands to manage and compress files and archives. It equips you with the knowledge and practical skills needed to efficiently work with file compression and archival tools. The chapter covers commands such as `gunzip` and `gzip` for compression, `tar`, `rar`, and `unrar` for archiving, `zip` and `unzip` for creating and extracting archives, as well as commands such as `bunzip2` and `bzip2`.

Chapter 4, Format and Disk Space Commands, offers a comprehensive guide to essential commands to manage disk formatting and optimize disk space in a Linux environment. It equips you with the knowledge and practical skills needed to efficiently work with disk formatting and space management tools. It explores the history and evolution of disk formatting and partitioning in Linux, providing step-by-step instructions to create partitions. It also covers essential commands such as `fdisk`, lsblk, df, and du to analyze and manage disk space, as well as commands to display package space such as dpkg and rpm. Additionally, the chapter delves into commands such as mkfs, mke2fs, and fdformat.

Chapter 5, Linux Permissions Commands, provides a comprehensive guide to managing and optimizing file permissions in a Linux environment. It equips you with the knowledge and practical skills necessary to efficiently work with Linux permission commands. It also explores the significance of permission commands and different types of permissions, and delves into commands such as chmod, chown, chgrp, and umask. Additionally, it covers the utilization of absolute paths in commands and introduces the use of sudo for executing commands with elevated privileges.

Chapter 6, Filesystem Mount and Manipulation Commands, equips you with the knowledge and practical skills needed to efficiently manage filesystems, perform mounting, and manipulate files in a Linux environment. It explores essential Linux mount commands, covering the mount and umount commands to mount and unmount filesystems. Additionally, it introduces the fuser command and delves into file manipulation, using commands such as cat and grep, enabling you to work with files and directories effectively in a Linux environment.

Chapter 7, File Content and Conversion Commands, provides you with the knowledge and practical skills necessary to efficiently work with file content and conversion in a Linux environment. It explores essential commands such as tail and file to examine and analyze file content. It also covers the convert command for file format conversion and introduces tools such as dos2unix to convert MS-DOS files to the Unix format and unix2dos to convert Unix files to the MS-DOS format. Additionally, the chapter discusses the recode command, offering you a comprehensive toolkit to manage and convert file content effectively.

Chapter 8, Linux SWAP Commands, provides you with the essential knowledge and practical skills required to efficiently manage SWAP memory in a Linux environment. It focuses on critical SWAP commands such as swapon and free, enabling you to effectively manage and optimize SWAP memory to enhance system performance.

Chapter 9, Linux Monitoring and Debugging Commands, equips you with an extensive toolkit to effectively monitor, troubleshoot, and debug Linux systems. Delving into an array of critical commands, including top, ps, pstree, strace, watch, smartctl, and uptime for real-time monitoring and system analysis, this chapter ensures that you have the tools at your disposal to maintain a smoothly running Linux environment. It also covers essential commands such as lsof, lsmod, last reboot, last, w, and vmstat to track system processes and resource utilization. You'll explore the kill and pkill commands to terminate processes, further enhancing your proficiency in Linux system management.

Chapter 10, Linux IPTABLES and Network Commands, equips you with a comprehensive toolkit to manage network security and configuration in a Linux environment. This chapter delves into essential iptables rules such as iptables -t ACCEPT and iptables -t DROP, allowing you to control network traffic effectively. It also explores network management commands such as ifconfig, ip, `route`, and `netstat` to configure and monitor network settings. Additionally, the chapter covers `hostname` and `nslookup` to manage system and network identities, along with `host` for domain name resolution, ensuring you have the skills to master network control and security.

Chapter 11, File Transfer, Downloading, and Managing Log Files, provides the tools to efficiently transfer files, download content, and manage log files in a Linux environment. This chapter explores methods to copy files into remote systems using `netcat` and `socat`, providing versatile file transfer solutions. It also covers the use of `wget` and `curl` to download files from the web. Additionally, the chapter delves into the exploration of common log files, enhancing your skills in managing and analyzing system logs for troubleshooting and monitoring.

Chapter 12, Exploring Linux Security, equips you with the knowledge and tools to enhance the security of your Linux system. This chapter delves into topics such as enforcing and permissive modes, enabling or disabling SELinux Boolean values, locking user accounts, and securing SSH. It provides you with a comprehensive understanding of Linux security measures and practical techniques to safeguard your system from potential threats and vulnerabilities.

Chapter 13, Linux in the Cloud, provides an in-depth exploration within the scope of AWS services, with a focus on creating EC2 instances on AWS, guiding you through the process of establishing secure connections using PuTTY and efficiently working within these instances. It equips you with the essential knowledge and skills required to seamlessly launch a Linux environment within the cloud.

To get the most out of this book

Software/hardware covered in the book	OS requirements
VMware	Windows
PuTTY	Windows
`convert` (ImageMagick)	Linux

The `convert` command doesn't come with Linux by default; it's typically part of the `ImageMagick` software suite. To install this, execute the following:

```
sudo yum install ImageMagick
```

The following are essential prerequisites to get the most out of this book:

- **Basic Linux knowledge**: While *Essential Linux Commands* is designed to be accessible to beginners. Having a basic understanding of Linux fundamentals, such as filesystem navigation and command-line usage, can be helpful.

- **Desire to learn**: You should approach the book with a willingness to learn and experiment with the Linux commands presented. The more you practice, the more proficient you'll become.

- **Willing to experiment and explore**: Don't limit yourself to the commands in the book. Experiment with variations, and explore additional Linux commands that are relevant to your specific interests or work.

We also have other code bundles from our rich catalog of books and videos available at `https://github.com/PacktPublishing/`. Check them out!

Conventions used

There are a number of text conventions used throughout this book.

`Code in text`: Indicates code words in text, database table names, folder names, filenames, file extensions, pathnames, dummy URLs, user input, and Twitter handles. Here is an example: "The `useradd` command in Linux is used to create a new user account or update an existing one."

A block of code is set as follows:

```
username:password:lastpasswordchanged:minpasswordage:maxpasswordage:
passwordwarningperiod:inactivityperiod:expirationdate:reservedfield
```

When we wish to draw your attention to a particular part of a code block, the relevant lines or items are set in bold:

```
username:password:lastpasswordchanged:minpasswordage:maxpasswordage:
passwordwarningperiod:inactivityperiod:expirationdate:reservedfield
```

Any command-line input or output is written as follows:

```
sudo "useradd [options] username"
```

Bold: Indicates a new term, an important word, or words that you see on screen. For example, words in menus or dialog boxes appear in the text like this. Here is an example: "Our second step is to select the **x86_64** option for all architectures."

> **Tips or important notes**
> Appear like this.

Get in touch

Feedback from our readers is always welcome.

General feedback: If you have questions about any aspect of this book, mention the book title in the subject of your message and email us at customercare@packtpub.com.

Errata: Although we have taken every care to ensure the accuracy of our content, mistakes do happen. If you have found a mistake in this book, we would be grateful if you would report this to us. Please visit www.packtpub.com/support/errata, select your book, click on the **Errata Submission Form** link, and enter the details.

Piracy: If you come across any illegal copies of our works in any form on the internet, we would be grateful if you would provide us with the location address or website name. Please contact us at copyright@packt.com with a link to the material.

If you are interested in becoming an author: If there is a topic that you have expertise in and you are interested in either writing or contributing to a book, please visit authors.packtpub.com.

Share your thoughts

Once you've read *Essential Linux Commands*, we'd love to hear your thoughts! Scan the QR code below to go straight to the Amazon review page for this book and share your feedback.

https://packt.link/r/1803239034

Your review is important to us and the tech community and will help us make sure we're delivering excellent quality content.

Download a free PDF copy of this book

Thanks for purchasing this book!

Do you like to read on the go but are unable to carry your print books everywhere?

Is your eBook purchase not compatible with the device of your choice?

Don't worry, now with every Packt book you get a DRM-free PDF version of that book at no cost.

Read anywhere, any place, on any device. Search, copy, and paste code from your favorite technical books directly into your application.

The perks don't stop there, you can get exclusive access to discounts, newsletters, and great free content in your inbox daily

Follow these simple steps to get the benefits:

1. Scan the QR code or visit the link below

https://packt.link/free-ebook/9781803239033

2. Submit your proof of purchase

3. That's it! We'll send your free PDF and other benefits to your email directly

Part 1:
Server Installations and Management Commands

In this part, we dive into fundamental system administration tasks for Linux systems, including setup, maintenance, and the crucial role of package management in software installation. You'll gain proficiency in file structure navigation, user and group management, and file compression and archiving. Each chapter equips you with distinct commands, essential knowledge, and practical skills for effective server installations and management in a Linux environment.

This section contains the following chapters:

- *Chapter 1, Getting a CentOS Server Up and Running*
- *Chapter 2, Linux User and Group Commands*
- *Chapter 3, File Compression and Archival Commands*

1

Getting a CentOS Server Up and Running

As a system administrator, one of the most fundamental tasks you may encounter is defining your roles and responsibilities. However, how to do this varies greatly depending on who you ask. Different individuals and companies may have their own unique perspectives on what the title of system administrator entails.

Welcome to the first chapter of this book, where we will be learning about server installations and management commands. Setting up a Linux system and keeping it up to date are the basic tasks that most system administrators perform in their day-to-day work. In this chapter, we will start by setting up a Linux server and then learn about the purpose of package management and how it provides an easy way to install software on Linux hosts. We will then explore commands that allow us to view the Linux file structure, add users and groups, and archive files.

By the end of this chapter, you will have a solid foundation of how to set up and manage Linux servers. We will begin by learning how to download the CentOS server installation file, set up a hypervisor, and install packages. We will also explore commands that allow you to view system, kernel, hardware, and processor information. With the skills you learn in this chapter, you will be able to set up and manage Linux servers with confidence.

In this chapter, we are going to cover the following main topics:

- Downloading the operating system (OS) installation file
- Downloading and setting up a hypervisor
- Package installation commands
- Information commands

Downloading the OS installation file

In this section, we will cover the process of downloading the Linux server operating system, including which Linux distributions are recommended and the requirements that need to be met.

When it comes to choosing a Linux distribution for your server, there are many options to choose from. Some popular choices include Ubuntu, Debian, and Red Hat. However, one of the most popular and stable choices for enterprise and web server environments is the **Community Enterprise Operating System (CentOS)**.

CentOS is a free and open source Linux distribution based on **Red Hat Enterprise Linux (RHEL)**. It is known for its stability and reliability, making it a popular choice for enterprise and web server environments. It is also widely used in the hosting industry, education, research, and for personal use. It is compatible with the Red Hat ecosystem, meaning that users can leverage their existing knowledge, skills, and tools of RHEL. The distribution is maintained by a large community of developers and users who work together to provide updates and security patches, making it a secure and stable choice. Additionally, it is designed to be fully compatible with the upstream vendor, Red Hat, and it provides an almost identical environment. This means that users can use the same set of commands and packages as in Red Hat Linux, and they can also access the Red Hat customer portal and support. As we'll be making use of CentOS throughout this book, we'll be downloading the installation image from the official website (`https://www.centos.org/`). The website offers both DVD and minimal ISO images, which can be used to install the server. Make sure to download the correct version for your architecture (32-bit or 64-bit).

When it comes to downloading the installation image for CentOS 8, there are two options available:

- `CentOS-Stream-8-x86_64-20220104-boot.iso`
- `CentOS-Stream-8-x86_64-20220104-dvd1.iso`

The `CentOS-Stream-8-x86_64-20220104-boot.iso` file is a minimal image used for booting the system and performing a network installation. It is designed to be used with a network-based installation process and contains only the packages required to start the installation process. Additional files will be downloaded during the installation.

The `CentOS-Stream-8-x86_64-20220104-dvd1.iso` file is the DVD image containing all the packages included in the distribution. It can be used for a local installation (also known as an **offline installation**, as there is no need to download files during the installation), and it contains a complete set of packages.

It's important to note that, depending on your system requirements and the intended use of the server, one of these images may be more suitable than the other. The minimal image is recommended for servers with limited resources, while the DVD image is recommended for servers with more resources and a wider range of needs. The following are the system requirements for setting up our own server:

- **Processor**: A 64-bit processor is required

- **Memory**: A minimum of 2GB of RAM is recommended, but 8 GB or more is recommended for servers with a high workload

- **Disk space**: A minimum of 20 GB of storage space is recommended, but the more storage space, the better

- **Network connectivity**: A network connection is required for downloading the installation image and performing updates

- **Graphics card**: A graphics card is not necessary for a server, but if you're planning on using the server for graphical applications, a graphics card is recommended

- **Operating system**: A 64-bit version of Windows, macOS, or Linux is required for running a hypervisor

Now that we know our system requirements, our first step is to open a web browser and go to `www.google.com`:

1. In the search bar, type `download CentOS ISO` and press *Enter*. This will bring up the official website for CentOS, which is `https://www.centos.org/` (see *Figure 1.1*).

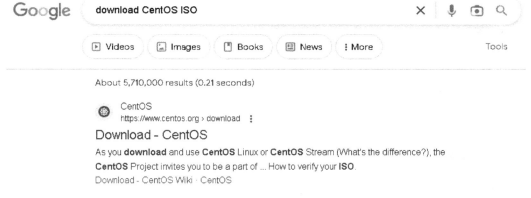

Figure 1.1 – Google search

2. Our second step is to select the **x86_64** option for all architectures:

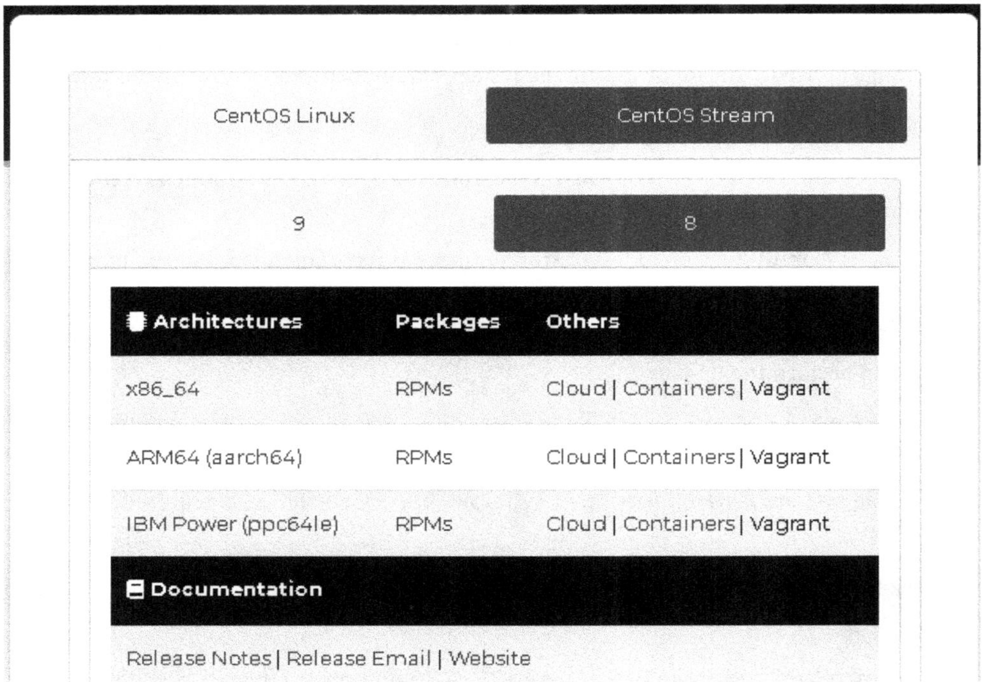

Figure 1.2 – x86_64 architectures

3. Next, we select the available link for our region. As we can see from the figure, mine is `http://mirror.web4africa.ng/centos/8-stream/isos/x86_64/`:

In order to conserve the limited bandwidth available, ISO images are not downloadable from mirror.centos.org

The following mirrors in your region should have the ISO images available:

http://mirror.web4africa.ng/centos/8-stream/isos/x86_64/

Other mirrors further away:

http://mirror.ufs.ac.za/centos/8-stream/isos/x86_64/
http://www.ftp.saix.net/linux/distributions/centos/8-stream/isos/x86_64/
http://mirror.ictglobe.com/centos/8-stream/isos/x86_64/
http://centos.mirror.liquidtelecom.com/8-stream/isos/x86_64/

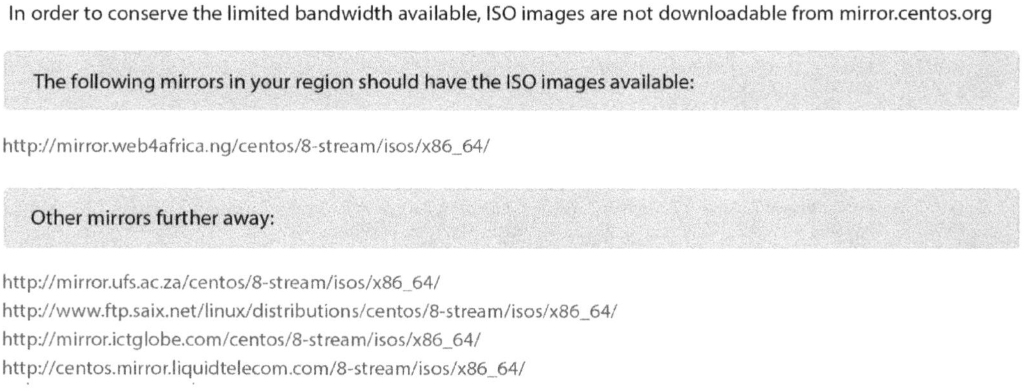

Figure 1.3 – Selection by region

From the index **/centos/8-stream/isos/x86_64/**, we'll need to download the `CentOS-Stream-8-x86_64-20221222-dvd1.iso` DVD version. As we have read previously, the DVD image contains all the packages that are included in the distribution, which means that it can be used to perform a local installation.

Index of /centos/8-stream/isos/x86_64/

```
../
CHECKSUM                                       12-Jan-2023 16:50            704
CHECKSUM.asc                                   12-Jan-2023 17:13           1564
CentOS-Stream-8-x86_64-20221027-boot.iso       27-Oct-2022 15:34      908066816
CentOS-Stream-8-x86_64-20221027-boot.iso.manifest   27-Oct-2022 15:44      635
CentOS-Stream-8-x86_64-20221027-dvd1.iso       27-Oct-2022 16:13    11559501824
CentOS-Stream-8-x86_64-20221027-dvd1.iso.manifest   27-Oct-2022 16:13   539552
CentOS-Stream-8-x86_64-20221222-boot.iso       22-Dec-2022 18:51      941621248
CentOS-Stream-8-x86_64-20221222-boot.iso.manifest   22-Dec-2022 19:01      635
CentOS-Stream-8-x86_64-20221222-dvd1.iso       22-Dec-2022 19:29    11729371136
CentOS-Stream-8-x86_64-20221222-dvd1.iso.manifest   22-Dec-2022 19:29   535836
CentOS-Stream-8-x86_64-20230112-boot.iso       12-Jan-2023 15:34      940572672
CentOS-Stream-8-x86_64-20230112-boot.iso.manifest   12-Jan-2023 15:44      635
CentOS-Stream-8-x86_64-20230112-dvd1.iso       12-Jan-2023 16:14    11735662592
CentOS-Stream-8-x86_64-20230112-dvd1.iso.manifest   12-Jan-2023 16:14   535854
CentOS-Stream-8-x86_64-latest-boot.iso         12-Jan-2023 15:34      940572672
CentOS-Stream-8-x86_64-latest-boot.iso.manifest   12-Jan-2023 15:44      635
CentOS-Stream-8-x86_64-latest-dvd1.iso         12-Jan-2023 16:14    11735662592
CentOS-Stream-8-x86_64-latest-dvd1.iso.manifest   12-Jan-2023 16:14   535854
```

Figure 1.4 – DVD download page

After downloading the image, we'll need to download a hypervisor.

Downloading and setting up a hypervisor

In this section, we will cover the process of downloading and setting up a hypervisor. A hypervisor is software that allows you to create and run virtual machines on a physical host. This is essential knowledge for a system administrator, as it allows for more flexibility and resource management. There are several hypervisors available, such as VMware, VirtualBox, and Hyper-V. In this book, we will be using VMware as an example.

Figure 1.5 – VMWare (Workstation 16 Pro)

The steps for downloading and setting up a hypervisor are as follows:

1. The first step is to download the VMware software from the official website:

Figure 1.6 – Downloading VMWare Workstation

2. Make sure to download the correct version for your operating system. Once the download is complete, you will need to install the software on your physical host. This process is straightforward and involves following the prompts during the installation process.

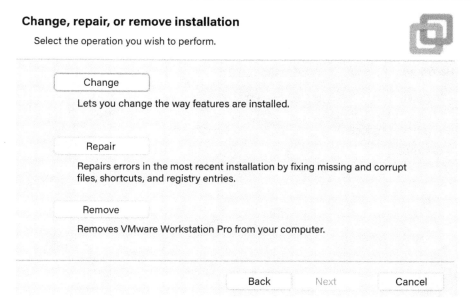

Change, repair, or remove installation

Select the operation you wish to perform.

Change

Lets you change the way features are installed.

Repair

Repairs errors in the most recent installation by fixing missing and corrupt files, shortcuts, and registry entries.

Remove

Removes VMware Workstation Pro from your computer.

Back   Next   Cancel

Figure 1.7 – Setting up

Once the installation is complete, you will need to create a new virtual machine.

3.   We'll utilize the **Custom** configuration wizard. This process involves specifying the amount of memory and storage and the network settings for the virtual machine.

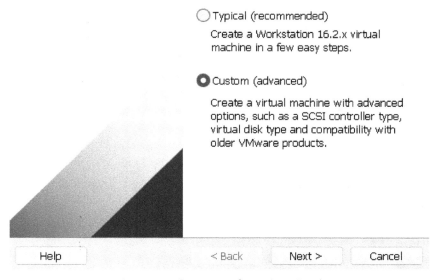

○ Typical (recommended)

Create a Workstation 16.2.x virtual machine in a few easy steps.

● Custom (advanced)

Create a virtual machine with advanced options, such as a SCSI controller type, virtual disk type and compatibility with older VMware products.

Help   < Back   Next >   Cancel

Figure 1.8 – Custom configuration wizard

4.   Configure the **Virtual machine hardware compatibility** settings as follows:

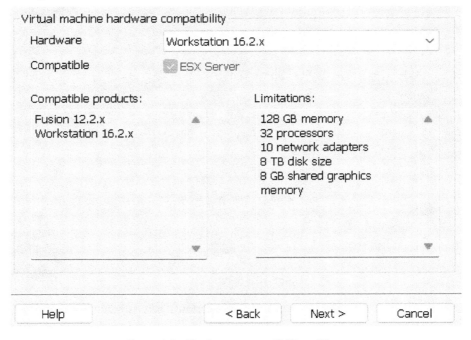

Figure 1.9 – Hardware compatibility settings

5.   Choose the operating system media, then choose the **I will install the operating system later** option for a hands-on setup process:

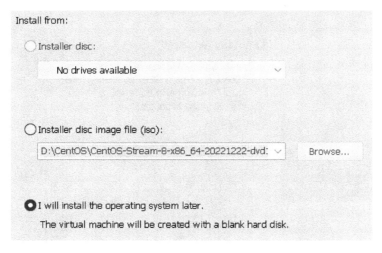

Figure 1.10 – Choosing the operating system media

6. Provide a name for the virtual machine and choose a location.

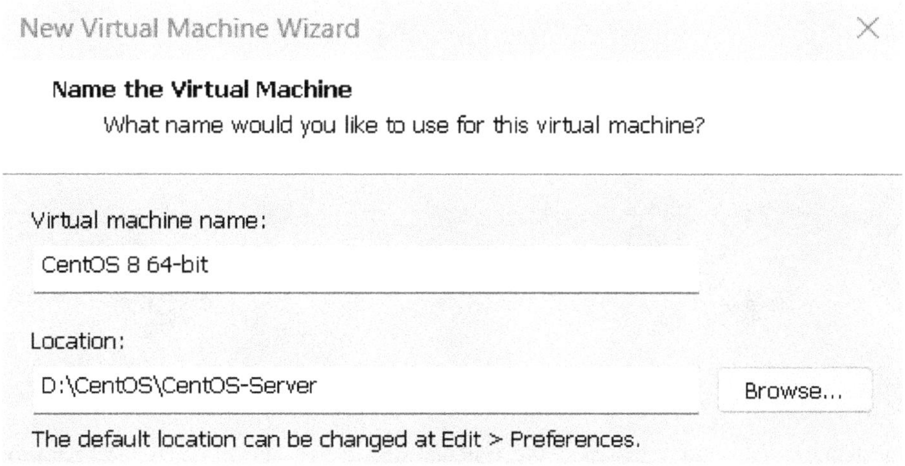

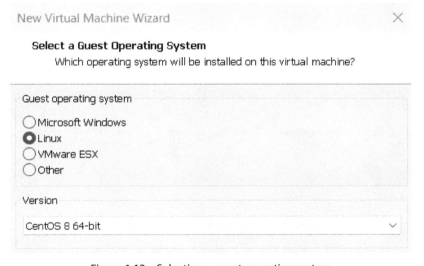

Figure 1.11 – Choosing a virtual machine name

7. Select a guest operating system:

New Virtual Machine Wizard   X

Select a Guest Operating System
Which operating system will be installed on this virtual machine?

Guest operating system

○ Microsoft Windows
◉ Linux
○ VMware ESX
○ Other

Version

CentOS 8 64-bit   ∨

Figure 1.12 – Selecting a guest operating system

8. Allocate processor resources:

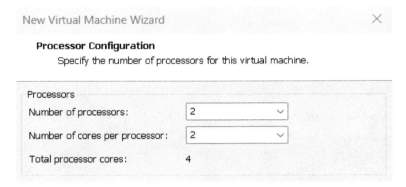

Figure 1.13 – Specifying the number of processors to allocate

9. Allocate memory to the virtual machine. Calculating memory allocation should be approached in the same manner as processor allocation. Ensure that the host system has adequate memory and allocate the remainder to the virtual machine. For this example, we'll be going with 8 GB or more.

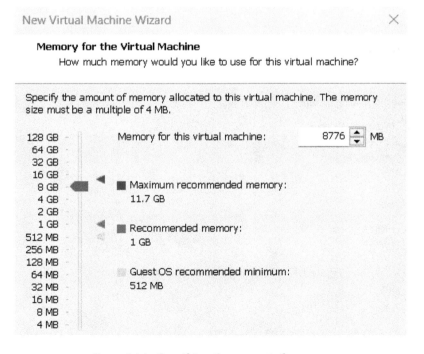

Figure 1.14 – Specifying the amount of memory

10. Configure the network settings. Choose the network configurations that meet your needs, or just select the default NAT Network. Why do this?

Network address translation (**NAT**) in VMware is a networking feature that allows virtual machines to access the internet and other network resources with the use of a host computer's IP address. This feature provides a secure and convenient way to access the internet for virtual machines that do not have their own IP addresses. In NAT mode, the virtual machine's network traffic is transparently translated between the virtual network and the host's physical network, allowing the virtual machine to access network resources as if it were directly connected to the physical network. NAT is often used in virtualization environments for testing and development, where virtual machines need access to the internet for downloading software, updates, and so on but do not require public access.

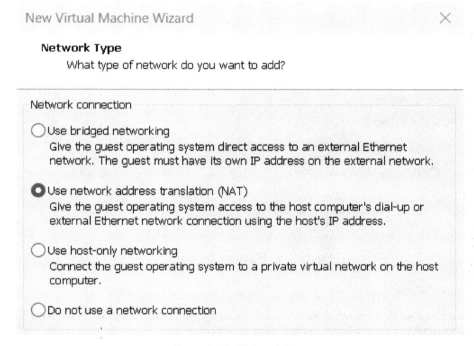

Figure 1.15 – Network type

11. Select the I/O controller type.

The SCSI controller type is the type of controller that is used to control a virtual disk. The following figure contains these options:

- **BusLogic**: This controller type is not available for 64-bit guests. It is an older controller type that is no longer commonly used.

- **LSI Logic** (recommended): This controller type is recommended for most guests. It is a newer controller type that offers better performance and compatibility than the BusLogic controller.

- **LSI Logic SAS**: This controller type is designed for use with **Serial Attached SCSI (SAS)** disks. It offers better performance than the LSI Logic controller, but it is not as widely supported by guest operating systems.

- **Paravirtualized SCSI**: This controller type is a high-performance controller that is designed for use with VMware guest operating systems. It requires that the guest operating system have a special driver installed.

If you are not sure which SCSI controller type to choose, I recommend using the LSI Logic controller. It is a good all-purpose controller that is widely supported by guest operating systems.

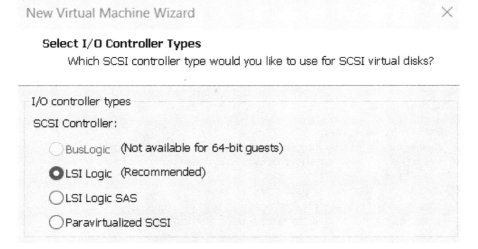

Figure 1.16 – I/O controller types

12. Choose the disk type.

The screenshot that follows shows the different disk type options available in the **New Virtual Machine Wizard** window. The options are as follows:

- **Integrated Drive Electronics** (IDE): This is an older disk type that is not as fast as newer disk types, such as SATA and NVMe. However, it is still supported by most guest operating systems.

- **Small Computer Systems Interface** (SCSI): This is a faster disk type than IDE. It is also more versatile, as it can support multiple disks and devices.

- **Serial ATA** (SATA): This is the most common disk type in use today. It is faster and more reliable than IDE and SCSI.

- **Open non-volatile memory express (ONVMe)**: This is the newest and fastest disk type. It is still under development, but it is becoming increasingly popular in high-performance servers and workstations.

If you are running a guest operating system that supports newer disk types, such as SATA and NVMe, then I recommend choosing one of those disk types. They will offer better performance and reliability.

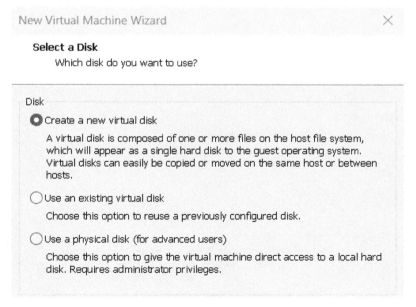

Figure 1.17 – Disk type

13. Select a virtual disk (select the virtual disk if you have one, or create one).

Figure 1.18 – Creating a new virtual disk

14. Specify the disk capacity. The recommended disk space is 20 GB, but we'll be allocating 30 GB of space to ensure sufficient room for your virtual machine. Be sure to tick the **Store virtual disk as a single file** option.

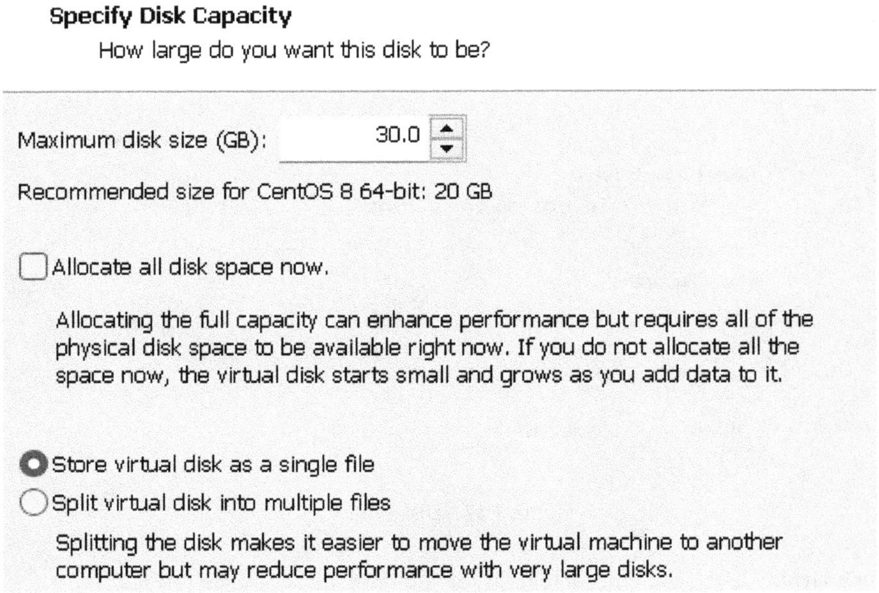

Specify Disk Capacity
How large do you want this disk to be?

Maximum disk size (GB):   30.0

Recommended size for CentOS 8 64-bit: 20 GB

☐ Allocate all disk space now.

Allocating the full capacity can enhance performance but requires all of the physical disk space to be available right now. If you do not allocate all the space now, the virtual disk starts small and grows as you add data to it.

◉ Store virtual disk as a single file
◯ Split virtual disk into multiple files

Splitting the disk makes it easier to move the virtual machine to another computer but may reduce performance with very large disks.

Figure 1.19 – Setting the disk capacity

15. Define the virtual disk file.

New Virtual Machine Wizard   ✕

Specify Disk File
Where would you like to store the disk file?

Disk file
One 30 GB disk file will be created using this file name.

CentOS 8 64-bit.vmdk   Browse...

Figure 1.20 – Specify Disk File

16. Create the virtual machine by selecting **Finish**.

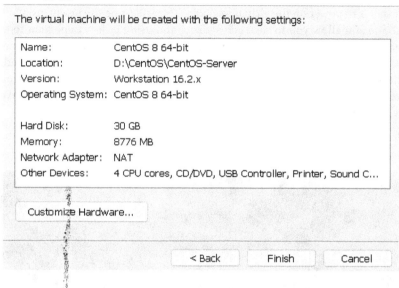

Figure 1.21 – Ready to Create Virtual Machine

17. Next, to initiate the CentOS installation on VMware Workstation, provide the virtual machine with the CentOS ISO image. Once you've done this, click on the **Power on this virtual machine** option. This will create a new virtual machine and configure it according to the specifications you have provided.

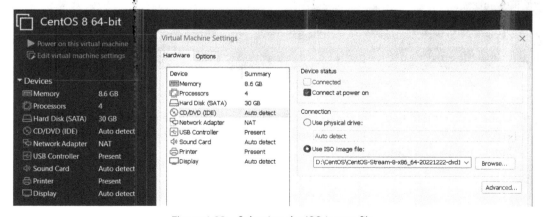

Figure 1.22 – Selecting the ISO image file

After the installation is complete, you will power on the newly created virtual machine, which will boot up and be ready for use. This process will allow you to have a fully functional CentOS installation running within a virtual environment, providing you with the ability to easily test, run, and manage multiple operating systems on a single physical machine.

The next step is to power on the virtual machine. This will bring the newly installed operating system to life and allow you to start configuring and using it. It is important to ensure that the virtual machine is properly configured before proceeding with the power-on process. This includes verifying the network configuration, memory and processor allocation, and disk space availability. Once you have confirmed that all the necessary parameters are set up correctly, you can power on the virtual machine by clicking the **Power On** button in VMware Workstation. This will move us into the next stage of the configuration process.

18. We'll select **Install CentOS Stream 8-Stream** from the list of options. To navigate between the options, use the arrow keys and press the *Enter* key to select the desired one.

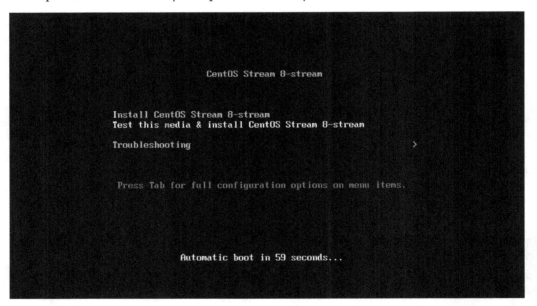

Figure 1.23 – Powering on CentOS 8-Stream

19. Upon successful initiation of the CentOS installation, you will be presented with a welcome screen that gives you the option to choose your preferred language. Simply select your desired language and click **Continue** to proceed.

Figure 1.24 – Choosing your preferred language

20. To move forward with the installation of CentOS, it is important to set up certain parameters such as keyboard layout, language support, time and date settings, software packages to be installed, root password, installation media, and disk partition information. These parameters will ensure a smooth and successful installation.

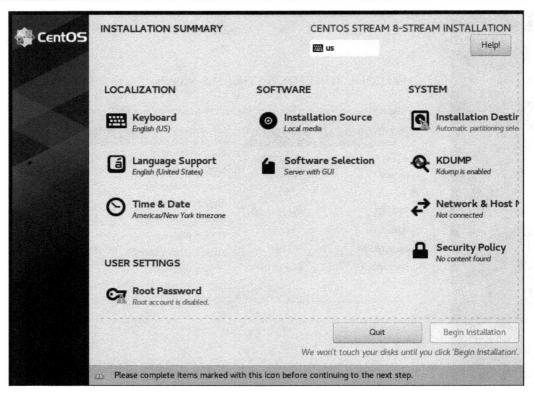

Figure 1.25 – The installation summary

21. The installation wizard in CentOS 8 can automatically detect all the locally accessible network interfaces prior to the installation process. These interfaces will be displayed in the left pane (see *Figure 1.26*), allowing you to easily choose the desired network and configure it as active or inactive based on your specific requirements. This step ensures that the correct network connection is established for the system during the installation process.

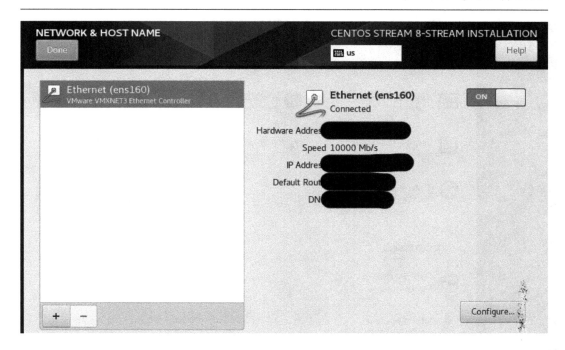

Figure 1.26 – The Network & Host Name page

22. With all the necessary settings configured, it's time to commence the installation process. Click the **Begin Installation** button:

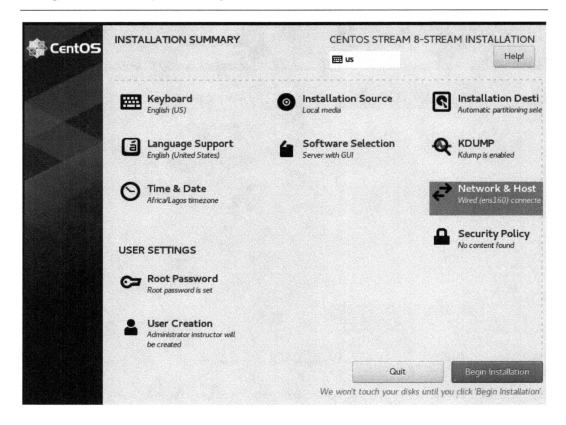

Figure 1.27 – The Begin Installation button

As the installation process begins, the setup wizard will commence the installation of CentOS. The process may take several minutes to complete, depending on the speed of your system and the configuration settings selected. Keep an eye on the progress bar to track the installation's progress.

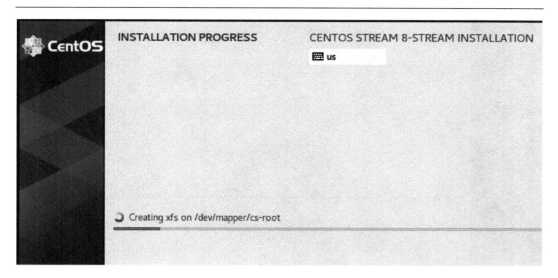

Figure 1.28 – Installation progress

23. After the successful installation of CentOS, it's important to reboot the virtual machine to ensure that all changes made during the installation process take effect. This will help in initializing the newly installed operating system and making it ready to use. To reboot the virtual machine, simply select the **Reboot System** button to restart from the system menu and wait for the machine to complete the reboot process.

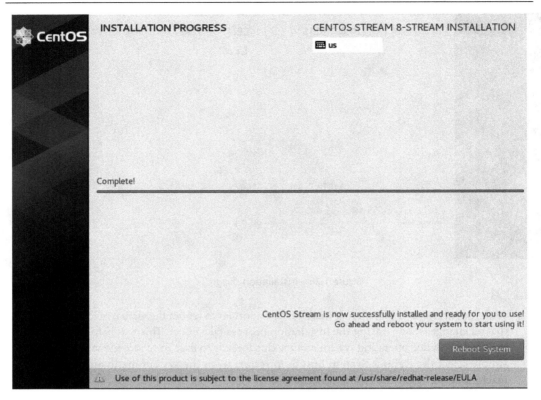

Figure 1.29 – The Reboot System button

24. Upon rebooting the virtual machine, select the first option presented in the GRUB menu for successful boot into the installed CentOS operating system.

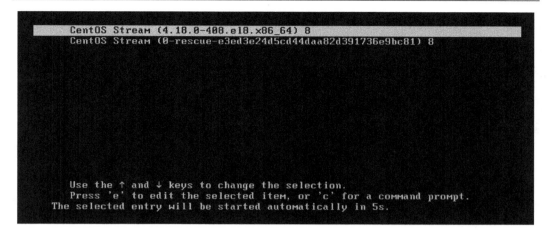

Figure 1.30 – The CentOS 8 GRUB menu

25. One more important step to remember is to read and accept the license information, as it is required to proceed with the boot process.

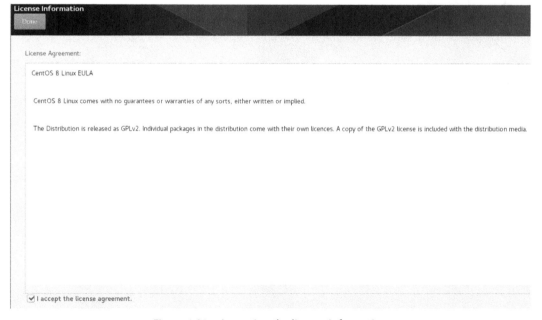

Figure 1.31 – Accepting the license information

26. Upon accepting the license information, the final step in the process is to complete the configuration by clicking the **Finish Configuration** button. This action finalizes the setup and configuration process and enables the system to boot into the newly installed CentOS operating system.

Figure 1.32 – Finishing the configuration

27. With your credentials, log in to your newly installed CentOS Linux system.

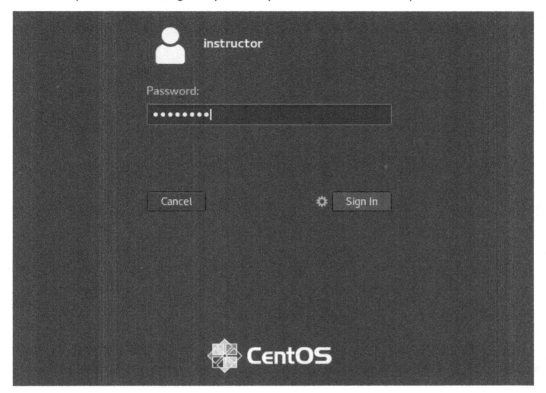

Figure 1.33 – Logging in

28. Upon logging in, select the **Start Using CentOS Linux** option to begin utilizing the full
     functionality of the operating system.

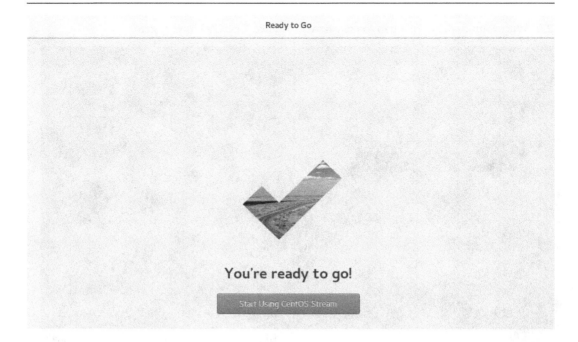

Figure 1.34 – Ready to Go

It is recommended that you log in as the root superuser as soon as possible and run the commands in the next section to ensure your newly installed CentOS Linux system has the latest updates and fixes.

Package installation commands

Package installation commands are used in CentOS to install and manage software packages on the system. The package management system in CentOS is called **Yellowdog Updater Modified** (**YUM**), and it provides a centralized method for managing and installing software packages.

YUM package management system

YUM is the default package manager for CentOS. It makes it easy to manage software packages by resolving dependencies and downloading required packages. With YUM, users can install new packages, update existing packages, and remove packages as needed. YUM provides a command line interface that allows users to manage packages from the terminal, as well as a graphical user interface for users who prefer a visual approach.

Common package installation commands

The most common commands used with YUM include yum install to install a new package, yum update to update an existing package, and yum remove to remove a package. Additionally, yum list can be used to list all available packages, and yum search can be used to search for packages. It is important to remember that when using YUM to manage packages, it is necessary to have an active internet connection and to run the commands as root or with administrative privileges.

The following commands are the starting point of the *100 Linux Commands Every System Administrator Should Know* journey:

- yum upgrade: The yum upgrade command is used in CentOS Linux to upgrade all installed packages to their latest available version. The command updates the system with the latest packages, bug fixes, and security patches, ensuring the system remains secure and stable. The yum upgrade command is executed in the terminal and it is executed with administrative privileges, usually as the root user. By running the command, the system will upgrade all installed packages and resolve any dependencies or conflicts that might arise during the upgrade process.

```
[root@localhost instructor]# yum upgrade
CentOS Stream 8 - AppStream
                                            143 kB/s |  28 MB     03:16
CentOS Stream 8 - BaseOS                59% [========================-         ] 237 kB/s |  16 MB
00:47 ETCentOS Stream 8 - BaseOS            60% [========================-      ] 234 kB/s |  16 MB
00:CentOS Stream 8 - BaseOS             61% [======================           ] 220 kB/s |  17 MB     00:49
ETCentOS Stream 8 - BaseOS              61% [======================-          ] 221 kB/s |  17 MB     00:48 E
CentOS Stream 8 - BaseOS                                                        226 kB/s |  27 MB     02:03
CentOS Stream 8 - Extras                                                         21 kB/s |  18 kB     00:00
CentOS Stream 8 - Extras common packages                                        7.9 kB/s | 5.2 kB     00:00
Last metadata expiration check: 0:00:01 ago on Fri 03 Feb 2023 09:20:17 PM WAT.
Dependencies resolved.
```

Figure 1.35 – Upgrading the server

- yum update: This package management tool is used in CentOS and other Linux distributions to upgrade and update system software packages. It downloads the latest package updates from a repository and installs them on the system, ensuring that your system has the most up-to-date security patches and bug fixes. Running yum update on a regular basis is an important part of system maintenance, as it helps keep your system secure and running smoothly.

```
[root@localhost instructor]# yum update
Last metadata expiration check: 1:00:24 ago on Fri 03 Feb 2023 09:21:12 PM WAT.
Dependencies resolved.
Nothing to do.
Complete!
```

Figure 1.36 – Updating the server

- reboot: This command is used to restart a computer running on a Unix-based operating system such as Linux. It is used to apply changes made to the system or to refresh the system after completing a process. The command can be executed by a user with root or superuser privileges. Upon executing the command, the system initiates a reboot sequence and all running processes are terminated. Then, the system is restarted. The reboot command is often used after completing a system update or upgrade to ensure the changes are applied.

```
[root@localhost instructor]# reboot
```

Figure 1.37 – Rebooting the server

Information commands

CentOS provides system administrators with a range of commands for obtaining information about various aspects of the system, including hardware, software, networks, and users. These commands are essential tools for monitoring and troubleshooting the system and its components, providing insight into the current status, configuration, and performance of the system. With the ability to obtain accurate and up-to-date information about the system, system administrators can quickly identify and resolve issues, ensuring optimal performance and the stability of the system. These commands provide information about the system's hostname, disk usage, processes, CPU, and network interfaces, respectively, making them valuable tools for system administrators who need to diagnose and resolve system issues.

Here are a few commonly used information commands in CentOS:

- uname: The uname command is used to display information about the operating system and the system's hostname. This command can also display the type of hardware, the version of the operating system, and the release number of the kernel.

```
[instructor@localhost ~]$ uname
Linux
```

Figure 1.38 – Displaying the operating system

The uname command comes with different flags that can be executed; for example, the -a parameter displays the whole information, including the system name, network node hostname, kernel release, version, and machine hardware name, as we can see in the following terminal:

```
[instructor@localhost ~]$ uname -a
Linux localhost.localdomain 4.18.0-448.el8.x86_64 #1 SMP Wed Jan 18 15:02:46 UTC 2023 x86_64 x86_64 x86_64 GNU/Linux
```

Figure 1.39 – Displaying all system information

- lsb_release: The lsb_release command is used to display information about the **Linux Standard Base (LSB)** version, distributor ID, and release number. The LSB is a standard that defines the Linux operating system and ensures compatibility among different Linux distributions.

```
[instructor@localhost ~]$ lsb_release
LSB Version:     :core-4.1-amd64:core-4.1-noarch
```

Figure 1.40 – Displaying the Linux Standard Base version

To execute additional flags, we'll make use of a flag commonly used by administrators to display the distributor indicator.

```
[instructor@localhost ~]$ lsb_release --id
Distributor ID: CentOSStream
```

Figure 1.41 – Displaying Distributor Indicator

- hostnamectl: The hostnamectl command is used to display and modify the system hostname and to view various system settings such as the operating system architecture, boot mode, and system time zone. This command is useful for changing the hostname or viewing system settings without having to log in to the system as a root user.

```
[instructor@localhost ~]$ hostnamectl
      Static hostname: localhost.localdomain
            Icon name: computer-vm
              Chassis: vm
           Machine ID: e3ed3e24d5cd44daa82d391736e9bc81
              Boot ID: 64d5cf5d7d7b4db9ab3e3eaa57894b74
       Virtualization: vmware
     Operating System: CentOS Stream 8
          CPE OS Name: cpe:/o:centos:centos:8
               Kernel: Linux 4.18.0-448.el8.x86_64
         Architecture: x86-64
[instructor@localhost ~]$
```

Figure 1.42 – Displaying the system settings and architecture

Let us execute hostnamectl with another flag, set-hostname. This flag is used to set the system hostname to a specified value. For example, you might execute hostnamectl set-hostname myhost:

```
[instructor@localhost ~]$ hostnamectl set-hostname Instructor
[instructor@localhost ~]$ hostname
Instructor
[instructor@localhost ~]$
```

Figure 1.43 – Setting a system hostname

The preceding useful information commands that we covered in this section will help you gather information about your system. Throughout this chapter, we emphasized the importance of proper server setup and installations, including regular software upgrades and updates, to ensure that your system runs smoothly and remains secure. By following the steps outlined in this chapter, you will be well on your way to setting up a reliable and secure server for your personal use, as well as building a foundation to further learn about Linux system administration.

Summary

In our first chapter, we focused on the steps involved in downloading and setting up a server. We began by discussing the process of downloading the server's operating system, which is a crucial step in the setup process. We then delved into the topic of downloading and setting up a hypervisor, which is a virtualization platform that enables the creation of virtual machines. The hypervisor provides an isolated environment for each virtual machine, which allows multiple virtual machines to run on the same physical server.

Moving on, we discussed the importance of package installation commands in the server setup process. These commands allow system administrators to install, upgrade, and remove packages from the server, which are essential for the server to function properly. We also provided an overview of some common package installation commands such as yum.

Finally, in the fourth section, we highlighted the role of informational commands in the server setup process. These commands provide important information about the system, including information about the operating system and the hardware. We covered three common information commands in CentOS, including uname, lsb_release, and hostnamectl, and described their uses and benefits. These information commands are useful for monitoring and troubleshooting the server and ensuring that it is functioning optimally.

In our next chapter, we dive into Linux users and groups management. Essential for system security, stability, and resource allocation, this chapter covers key commands and tools for system administrators to manage users and groups.

2

Linux User and Group Commands

As important as it is to choose the right distribution of Linux, it's equally important to understand the key components of Linux system administration, including Linux user and group management. The Linux operating system allows administrators to create multiple users and assign different permissions and group policies, ensuring system security, stability, and resource allocation. In this chapter, we will dive into Linux user and group management and focus on the key commands and tools used by Linux system administrators to manage users and groups.

The history of Linux user and group commands dates back to the early days of the Unix operating system, where user and group management was a key aspect of system security and resource allocation. With the growth of the open source movement, Linux adopted these concepts and expanded upon them, allowing for granular control over user and group permissions, user authentication and access control, and more. Today, Linux user and group commands form a critical component of any Linux system, providing system administrators with the tools they need to manage users, assign permissions, and ensure secure access to sensitive resources and data.

In this chapter we are going to cover the following main topics:

- useradd, userdel, and usermod
- Files, directories, and permission commands
- groupdel, groupmod, groupadd, and grpck
- pwck, chage, and passwd commands
- find, locate, and whereis commands

useradd, userdel, and usermod

In a Linux system, it is important to manage users and groups to ensure security and access control. The useradd, userdel, and usermod commands are fundamental tools for creating, deleting, and modifying users on a Linux system. These commands allow administrators to create user accounts, assign permissions, and limit access to resources. Understanding how to use these commands is essential for managing users on a Linux system. Whether you are setting up a single-user system or an enterprise-level environment, the useradd, userdel, and usermod commands are indispensable tools for Linux administrators. We will explore these commands in detail, including their usage, options, and examples, to give you a comprehensive understanding of user management on a Linux system.

These tools—useradd, userdel, and usermod—are part of the Shadow Password Suite, which is commonly used on Linux systems to manage user accounts. It is essential to understand how to use these tools properly to ensure the security and stability of a Linux system. While these tools are primarily used on Linux systems, they can also be used on other Unix-like systems.

We will cover their usage in detail, including the options and syntax for each command. We will also discuss best practices for managing user accounts on a Linux system, such as creating a standard user account and using sudo for administrative tasks. Now, let's dive into these commands in the following subsections.

useradd

The useradd command in Linux is used to create a new user account or update an existing one. It is a powerful tool that can be used to manage user accounts in a variety of ways, from assigning a home directory and shell to setting the user's password and expiration date. When creating a new user account, useradd requires several pieces of information to be provided, such as the username, the **user ID (UID)**, and the **group ID (GID)**. The UID is a unique number assigned to the user, while the GID is the primary group that the user belongs to. These values are used by the system to identify and manage user accounts. In addition to the required information, there are several optional flags that can be used with useradd to customize the user account. For example, the -m flag can be used to create a home directory for the user, while the -s flag specifies the default shell for the user. The -c flag can be used to add a comment or description to the user account, which can be helpful in identifying the purpose of the account. Once the user account has been created, it can be modified using the usermod command. This command is used to modify the user's account information, such as their password or expiration date. It can also be used to add or remove the user from groups, change the user's default shell, and much more. The basic syntax of the useradd command is as follows (note that you will need sudo access to successfully run the command):

```
sudo "useradd [options] username"
```

The following figure shows more details on the usage and options for the `useradd` command:

```
[instructor@Instructor ~]$ useradd
Usage: useradd [options] LOGIN
       useradd -D
       useradd -D [options]

Options:
  -b, --base-dir BASE_DIR       base directory for the home directory of the
                                new account
  -c, --comment COMMENT         GECOS field of the new account
  -d, --home-dir HOME_DIR       home directory of the new account
  -D, --defaults                print or change default useradd configuration
  -e, --expiredate EXPIRE_DATE  expiration date of the new account
  -f, --inactive INACTIVE       password inactivity period of the new account
  -g, --gid GROUP               name or ID of the primary group of the new
                                account
  -G, --groups GROUPS           list of supplementary groups of the new
                                account
  -h, --help                    display this help message and exit
  -k, --skel SKEL_DIR           use this alternative skeleton directory
  -K, --key KEY=VALUE           override /etc/login.defs defaults
  -l, --no-log-init             do not add the user to the lastlog and
                                faillog databases
  -m, --create-home             create the user's home directory
  -M, --no-create-home          do not create the user's home directory
  -N, --no-user-group           do not create a group with the same name as
                                the user
  -o, --non-unique              allow to create users with duplicate
                                (non-unique) UID
  -p, --password PASSWORD       encrypted password of the new account
  -r, --system                  create a system account
  -R, --root CHROOT_DIR         directory to chroot into
  -P, --prefix PREFIX_DIR       prefix directory where are located the /etc/* files
  -s, --shell SHELL             login shell of the new account
  -u, --uid UID                 user ID of the new account
  -U, --user-group              create a group with the same name as the user
  -Z, --selinux-user SEUSER     use a specific SEUSER for the SELinux user mapping
```

Figure 2.1 – useradd usage and options

To create a new user account named `tester1` and a corresponding home directory, as well as displaying the UID, use the following command:

```
[instructor@Instructor ~]$ sudo useradd -m tester1
[sudo] password for instructor:
[instructor@Instructor ~]$ id tester1
uid=1001(tester1) gid=1001(tester1) groups=1001(tester1)
[instructor@Instructor ~]$ 
```

Figure 2.2 – Creating a user and a home directory for the user

The `-m` option tells the system to create the home directory, which is where the user will store their files and settings. The purpose of creating a home directory for a new user is to ensure that they have their own space on the system to work in and allow them to store files and customize their environment without affecting other users. Additionally, it provides a place for the user to store configuration files and other settings that are specific to their account.

We also introduced another command, id, in the process of creating a new user.

The id command from the preceding example is a Linux/Unix command that is used to display the UID and GID of our tester1 user account. When used with a specific username as an argument, such as id username, the id instructor command will display output similar to the following if the instructor user exists on the system:

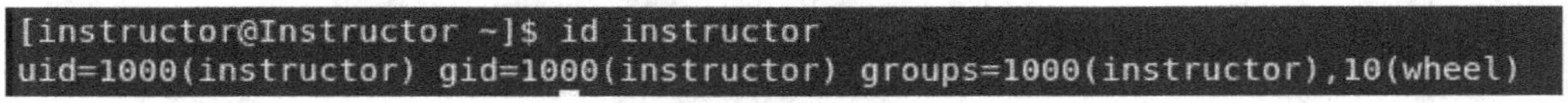

```
[instructor@Instructor ~]$ id instructor
uid=1000(instructor) gid=1000(instructor) groups=1000(instructor),10(wheel)
```

Figure 2.3 – Displaying the ID

We can also check the existence of this user in the /etc/passwd file:

```
instructor:x:1000:1000:instructor:/home/instructor:/bin/bash
tester1:x:1001:1001::/home/tester1:/bin/bash
```

The following screenshot shows the result:

```
instructor:x:1000:1000:instructor:/home/instructor:/bin/bash
tester1:x:1001:1001::/home/tester1:/bin/bash
[instructor@Instructor ~]$
```

Figure 2.4 – Evidence of the existence of the users

The following are the details of the user information in the preceding figure:

- tester1: Username
- 1001: UID
- 1001: GID
- /home/tester1: User's home directory
- /bin/bash: Login shell
- :: Separator
- ::: A password-less user account
- x: The stored password in the /etc/shadow file

userdel

userdel is a Linux command used to delete a user account and its associated files and directories. It's important to note that when a user account is deleted using userdel, all the files and directories under the user's home directory are also deleted. Therefore, userdel should be used with caution to avoid the accidental deletion of important files. The command requires root privileges, and the syntax is userdel [options] username. The most commonly used option is -r, which removes the home directory and mail spool of the deleted user. When deleting a user with userdel, it's important to make sure that the user account is no longer needed. It's also important to consider the impact that deleting the user account will have on any applications or services that rely on the user account. This is especially true if the user account is used for system administration or runs any critical services. In such cases, it's important to create a backup or a copy of the user's files and directories before deleting the account.

Another consideration when using userdel is that it only deletes the user account from the system's user database. Any processes that were started by the user before the account was deleted will continue to run until they are finished or manually stopped. It's also possible that some system files or configuration files might still reference the deleted user, which could cause issues in the future.

The following screenshot shows the usage and options of the userdel command:

```
[instructor@Instructor ~]$ userdel
Usage: userdel [options] LOGIN

Options:
  -f, --force                       force some actions that would fail otherwise
                                    e.g. removal of user still logged in
                                    or files, even if not owned by the user
  -h, --help                        display this help message and exit
  -r, --remove                      remove home directory and mail spool
  -R, --root CHROOT_DIR             directory to chroot into
  -P, --prefix PREFIX_DIR           prefix directory where are located the /etc/* files
  -Z, --selinux-user                remove any SELinux user mapping for the user

[instructor@Instructor ~]$
```

Figure 2.5 – userdel usage and options

To delete the tester2 user, you would run the following command:

```
[instructor@Instructor ~]$ sudo userdel tester2
[sudo] password for instructor:
```

Figure 2.6 – Deleting the user account

As we observe the deletion of the tester2 entry from the /etc/passwd file, we can also confirm whether the tester2 user's home directory is still accessible:

```
[root@Instructor instructor]# cd /home/tester2/
[root@Instructor tester2]# pwd
/home/tester2
[root@Instructor tester2]#
```

Figure 2.7 – Switching to the user's home directory

When you run the `userdel` command, it removes the user's entry in the `/etc/passwd` file and the user's group, but it does not remove the user's home directory, `/home/tester2`. To remove a user and their home directory simultaneously, execute the `userdel` command followed by the `-r` option. Attempting to switch to the deleted user's home directory will not be successful, as it has been removed. This can be verified by the following example:

```
[root@Instructor tester2]# userdel -r tester2
[root@Instructor tester2]# su tester2
su: user tester2 does not exist
[root@Instructor tester2]# cd /home/tester2
bash: cd: /home/tester2: No such file or directory
[root@Instructor tester2]#
```

Figure 2.8 – Deleting the user and the home directory

Here are the steps we took:

1. Deleted the user and the home directory using the `-r` flag
2. Verified whether we could do a switch to the user for confirmation
3. Checked whether we could switch to that user's home directory

Overall, `userdel` is a powerful command that should be used with caution. It's important to ensure that the user account being deleted is no longer needed and that all necessary backups and precautions have been taken to avoid data loss or system issues.

usermod

The `usermod` command is a powerful Linux administration tool that allows system administrators to modify user account information. This includes changes to the user's home directory, login shell, UID, GID, and other account properties. Additionally, `usermod` can be used to add or remove user groups, set password-aging policies, and more. This tool helps system administrators to manage user accounts on a Linux system effectively.

To use `usermod`, the command is followed by options that specify the changes to be made. For example, to add a user to a specific group, the `-aG` option is used, followed by the group name. Similarly, to change the user's home directory, the `-d` option is used, followed by the new directory path. When making changes to a user's account, it is important to consider the impact that the changes will have on the system and other users.

`usermod` also has a useful feature that allows for the modification of multiple user accounts at once using a script or a list of usernames. This feature saves time and effort when making changes to a large number of user accounts. However, it is important to use `usermod` with caution, as improper use of the command can result in unintended consequences or even system damage. We'll take a look at execution examples using `usermod`:

- **Adding a user to a group**: Let's say you want to add a user named `tester1` to the `developers` group and verify that the user has been added to the group. You can use the following command:

```
[instructor@Instructor ~]$ sudo usermod -aG developers tester1
[instructor@Instructor ~]$ groups tester1
tester1 : tester1 developers
[instructor@Instructor ~]$
```

Figure 2.9 – Adding a user to a group

- **Changing the home directory of a user**: Suppose you want to change the home directory of a user named `tester1` to `/home/tester1_new`. You can use the following command:

```
[instructor@Instructor ~]$ sudo usermod -d /home/tester1_new1 tester1
[instructor@Instructor ~]$ grep tester1 /etc/passwd
tester1:x:1001:1001::/home/tester1_new1:/bin/bash
[instructor@Instructor ~]$
```

Figure 2.10 – Changing the user's home directory

- **Lock/unlock a user account**: If you want to lock/unlock the account of a user named `tester1`, you can use the following command:

```
[instructor@Instructor ~]$ sudo usermod -L tester1
[instructor@Instructor ~]$ sudo grep ^tester1 /etc/shadow
tester1:!!:19409:0:99999:7:::
```

Figure 2.11 – Locking a user

The exclamation mark indicates that the `tester1` account is locked. If the account is not locked, the second field will contain the password hash for the user's password.

Now let's unlock the `tester1` user:

```
[instructor@Instructor ~]$ sudo usermod -p 12345 tester1
[instructor@Instructor ~]$ sudo usermod -U tester1
[instructor@Instructor ~]$ sudo grep ^tester1 /etc/shadow
tester1:12345:19441:0:99999:7:::
[instructor@Instructor ~]$ sudo grep ^tester1 /etc/passwd
tester1:x:1001:1001::/home/tester1_new1:/bin/bash
```

Figure 2.12 – Unlocking a user

- **Changing the UID and GID of a user**: Let's say you want to change the UID of a user named `tester1` to `1001` and the GID to `1002`. You can use the following command:

```
[instructor@Instructor ~]$ sudo usermod -u 1001 -g 1002 tester1
[sudo] password for instructor:
[instructor@Instructor ~]$ id tester1
uid=1001(tester1) gid=1002(developers) groups=1002(developers)
[instructor@Instructor ~]$ █
```

Figure 2.13 – Changing a user's UID and GID

This will change the UID of the user tester1 to 1001 and the GID to 1002.

Files, directories, and permission commands

Files and directories are organized in a hierarchical structure, with the root directory as the top-most level. Each file and directory has a set of permissions that determine who can read, write, or execute it. The file permissions are divided into three categories—user, group, and others:

- **user**: This refers to the owner of the file

- **group**: This refers to a group of users assigned to the file (e.g., developers)

- **others**: This refers to anyone else who is not the owner or part of the assigned group

Let's take a look at the hierarchical structure:

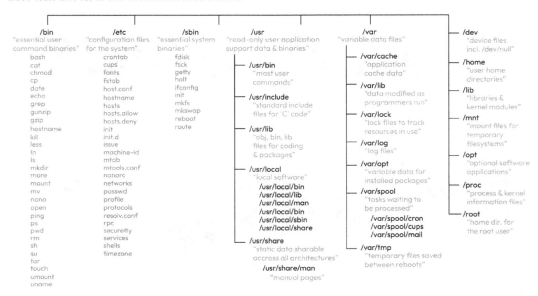

Figure 2.14 – Linux files and directory hierarchical structure

To manage file and directory permissions in Linux, there are several command line tools available. Some of the commonly used commands include chmod, chown, and chgrp.

chmod

The chmod command is used to change the permissions of a file or directory. To recursively change the permissions of all files and subdirectories within a directory, we can use the -R flag of the chmod command. This flag is essential for applying permissions changes to all contents within a directory.

However, the suggested text after that doesn't seem to directly address the significance of the 700 permission setting.

For example, in the following screenshot, 700 signifies that the owner of the Confidential_files directory has **read, write, and execute** (**RWX**) permissions (7), while the group and others have no permissions (0). This configuration ensures that only the owner can access, modify, or execute files within the directory, providing a high level of security for sensitive information:

```
[instructor@Instructor Documents]$ chmod -R 700 Confidential_files/
[instructor@Instructor Documents]$ ls -l
total 4
drwx------. 2 instructor instructor  6 Mar 26 13:51 Confidential_files
-rw-rw-r--. 1 instructor instructor 77 Mar 26 13:49 sensitive_file.txt
[instructor@Instructor Documents]$
```

Figure 2.15 – Granting the owner RWX permissions

chown

The chown command is used to change the owner and group of a given file or directory. To change the owner and group of a directory, we must pass both arguments separated by the : sign. Just like the chmod command, you can replicate the new settings recursively by adding -R to the command:

```
[instructor@Instructor office-docs]$ sudo chown -R tester1:developers /home/instructor/Documents/office-docs/
[instructor@Instructor office-docs]$ cd ..
[instructor@Instructor Documents]$ ls -la office-docs/
total 0
drwxrwxr-x. 2 tester1    developers 71 Mar 26 14:06 .
drwxr-xr-x. 4 instructor instructor 77 Mar 26 14:00 ..
-rw-rw-r--. 1 tester1    developers  0 Mar 26 14:05 doc-1
-rw-rw-r--. 1 tester1    developers  0 Mar 26 14:06 doc-2
-rw-rw-r--. 1 tester1    developers  0 Mar 26 14:06 doc-3
-rw-rw-r--. 1 tester1    developers  0 Mar 26 14:06 doc-4
-rw-rw-r--. 1 tester1    developers  0 Mar 26 14:06 doc-5
```

Figure 2.16 – Changing the owner and group of a directory

This command changes the owner and group of the directory located at /home/instructor/Documents/office-docs/ along with all its content recursively. The -R option stands for **recursive**.

chgrp

chgrp is used to change the group of a file or directory without touching the owner's permission. To change the group ownership of a directory named project-001 and all of its contents to a group named developers, use the following command:

```
[instructor@Instructor Documents]$ sudo chgrp -R developers project-001/
[sudo] password for instructor:
[instructor@Instructor Documents]$ ls -la project-001/
total 0
drwxrwxr-x. 2 instructor developers 137 Mar 26 14:13 .
drwxr-xr-x. 5 instructor instructor  96 Mar 26 14:13 ..
-rw-rw-r--. 1 instructor developers   0 Mar 26 14:13 doc-1
-rw-rw-r--. 1 instructor developers   0 Mar 26 14:13 doc-10
-rw-rw-r--. 1 instructor developers   0 Mar 26 14:13 doc-2
-rw-rw-r--. 1 instructor developers   0 Mar 26 14:13 doc-3
-rw-rw-r--. 1 instructor developers   0 Mar 26 14:13 doc-4
-rw-rw-r--. 1 instructor developers   0 Mar 26 14:13 doc-5
-rw-rw-r--. 1 instructor developers   0 Mar 26 14:13 doc-6
-rw-rw-r--. 1 instructor developers   0 Mar 26 14:13 doc-7
-rw-rw-r--. 1 instructor developers   0 Mar 26 14:13 doc-8
-rw-rw-r--. 1 instructor developers   0 Mar 26 14:13 doc-9
[instructor@Instructor Documents]$
```

Figure 2.17 – Changing the group ownership of a directory

Security is also an essential aspect of file and directory management in Linux. System administrators must ensure that files and directories are secured and only accessible to authorized users. This can be achieved by implementing access control measures such as using strong passwords and configuring user access permissions appropriately.

groupdel, groupmod, groupadd, and grpck

Group management is an important aspect of Linux system administration. Groups are used to organize users and define their access privileges to files and directories on the system. The four main commands used for group management are groupadd, groupmod, grpck, and groupdel.

groupadd is used to create a new group on the system. To use this command, type groupadd followed by the desired options and the new group name. For example, to create a new group called DevSec-group, the command would be groupadd DevSec-group:

```
[instructor@Instructor ~]$ sudo groupadd DevSec-group
[instructor@Instructor ~]$ cat /etc/group | grep DevSec-group
DevSec-group:x:1003:
[instructor@Instructor ~]$
```

Figure 2.18 – Adding a new group

This command will create a new group with the default settings, including a new GID.

Now that we've created our groups, let's do some modifications such as changing its membership using the groupmod command. This is a command used to modify an existing group on the system. This command can be used to change the group's name, GID, or membership. To modify a group, type groupmod followed by the desired options and the group name. For example, to change the name of the group DevSec-group to DevSec-group-new, the command would be groupmod -n DevSec-group-new DevSec-group:

```
[instructor@Instructor ~]$ cat /etc/group | grep DevSec-group
DevSec-group:x:1003:
[instructor@Instructor ~]$ sudo groupmod -n DevSec-group-new DevSec-group
[sudo] password for instructor:
[instructor@Instructor ~]$ cat /etc/group | grep DevSec-group-new
DevSec-group-new:x:1003:
[instructor@Instructor ~]$
```

Figure 2.19 – Modifying an existing group

Our next command is grpck, which is used to check the integrity of the group files on the system. This command will check the group file (/etc/group) and make sure that all groups listed in the file have valid entries in the password file (/etc/passwd). To use this command, simply type grpck -r /etc/passwd:

```
[instructor@Instructor ~]$ grpck -r /etc/passwd
group root: no user 0
delete member '0'? No
group bin: no user 1
delete member '1'? No
group daemon: no user 2
delete member '2'? No
group adm: no user 4
delete member '4'? No
group lp: no user 7
delete member '7'? No
group sync: no user 0
```

Figure 2.20 – Checking the integrity of the /etc/passwd file

Lastly, the groupdel command is used to delete a group from the system. To use this command, simply type groupdel followed by the group name. For example, to delete a group called DevSec-group-new, the command would be groupdel -f DevSec-group-new.

```
[instructor@Instructor ~]$ cat /etc/group | grep DevSec-group
DevSec-group-new:x:1003:
[instructor@Instructor ~]$ cat /etc/group | grep DevSec-group-new
DevSec-group-new:x:1003:
[instructor@Instructor ~]$ sudo groupdel -f DevSec-group-new
[instructor@Instructor ~]$ cat /etc/group | grep DevSec-group-new
[instructor@Instructor ~]$
```

Figure 2.21 – Deleting a group

This command will remove the group from the system. The -f option is used to force the deletion of the group, along with any users who were assigned to that group.

Overall, group management is a critical aspect of Linux system administration. Proper management of groups can ensure the security and accessibility of files and directories on the system. The four main commands used for group management, groupdel, groupmod, groupadd, and grpck, provide system administrators with the necessary tools to effectively manage groups on a Linux system.

pwck, chage, and passwd commands

The pwck command is a Linux system administration tool that is used to verify the consistency of the passwd, shadow, and group files. The purpose of the command is to ensure that the user accounts and groups listed in these files are valid and to detect any inconsistencies between them. It is useful in maintaining the integrity and security of a Linux system, as it can help to identify and correct errors that may arise due to manual edits of these files. For example, if a user account exists in the passwd file but not in the shadow file, pwck will detect this and prompt the user to fix the inconsistency. Let's take a look at some examples using this tool:

- Verify the consistency of the passwd file with sudo pwck /etc/passwd.

    The following output from the pwck command checks the consistency of the /etc/passwd file on our Linux system:

```
[instructor@Instructor ~]$ sudo pwck /etc/passwd  ◀━━━━
[sudo] password for instructor:
user 'gluster': directory '/run/gluster' does not exist
user 'pipewire': directory '/var/run/pipewire' does not exist
user 'pulse': directory '/var/run/pulse' does not exist
user 'saslauth': directory '/run/saslauthd' does not exist
user 'cockpit-ws': directory '/nonexisting' does not exist
user 'cockpit-wsinstance': directory '/nonexisting' does not exist
user 'clevis': directory '/var/cache/clevis' does not exist
user 'gnome-initial-setup': directory '/run/gnome-initial-setup/' does not exist
user 'tester1': directory '/home/tester1_new1' does not exist
pwck: no changes
```

Figure 2.22 – Checking the consistency of the /etc/passwd file

- Check the consistency of the shadow file:

```
[instructor@Instructor ~]$ sudo pwck /etc/shadow
user 'bin': directory '7' does not exist
user 'daemon': directory '7' does not exist
user 'adm': directory '7' does not exist
user 'lp': directory '7' does not exist
user 'sync': directory '7' does not exist
user 'shutdown': directory '7' does not exist
user 'halt': directory '7' does not exist
user 'mail': directory '7' does not exist
user 'operator': directory '7' does not exist
user 'games': directory '7' does not exist
user 'ftp': directory '7' does not exist
user 'nobody': directory '7' does not exist
user 'rpc': directory '7' does not exist
user 'testerl': directory '7' does not exist
invalid password file entry
delete line 'instructor:$6$hGj28e04fYjh2pRs$f/Bsr2SrDSjifBfAYkv8/Zaapcjmc
g84/::0:99999:7:::'? ^C
```

Figure 2.23 – Checking the consistency of /etc/shadow file

The invalid password file entry message for the instructor user suggests deleting the invalid line for the instructor user account. However, we can keep the instructor user and resolve the error without deleting the invalid line by correcting it to ensure that it is properly formatted.

First, open the /etc/shadow file with the vipw command to edit the /etc/passwd and /etc/shadow files, or their respective shadow versions (/etc/gshadow and /etc/gshadow), with vigr. Locate the line that corresponds to the instructor user or any user you created and correct any syntax errors.

Using vipw and vigr is the recommended and safer approach to editing these critical system files, as these commands are specifically designed for this purpose and set appropriate locks to prevent file corruption.

The line should contain nine fields separated by colons (:). We'll fix this error using our next command. Overall, the purpose of the pwck command is to ensure that the user and group information stored on a Linux system is accurate and consistent:

```
username:password:lastpasswordchanged:minpasswordage:maxpasswordage:
passwordwarningperiod:inactivityperiod:expirationdate:reservedfield
```

The chage command is a Linux system administration tool that is used to change the aging and expiration policy of a user's password. The purpose of the command is to enforce password policies and increase the security of a system by setting limits on the age of a password, the time between password changes, and the maximum number of failed logins attempts before a user is locked out. This helps to ensure that passwords are changed regularly and that users are prompted to create strong and secure passwords. Now, let's use this command to correct our error.

We'll use the `chage -d 2023-12-1 instructor` command to set the date of the last password change for the `instructor` user to December 1st, 2023. The `-d` option in the `chage` command is used to set the date of the last password change. By default, the last password change date is set to the current date, but using the `-d` option allows you (the admin) to set it to a specific date. In this case, the date is set to December 1st, 2023.

`chage -E 2023-12-31 instructor` is used to set the account expiration date for a specific user. The `-E` option is used to specify the expiration date, and the `2023-12-31` argument is the date when the account will expire. The `instructor` parameter at the end of the command is the username of the account that we want to set the expiration date for.

The `chage -l instructor` command shows the password aging information for the user account named `instructor`:

```
[root@Instructor instructor]# chage -d 2023-12-1 instructor
[root@Instructor instructor]# chage -E 2023-12-31 instructor
[root@Instructor instructor]# chage -l instructor
Last password change                                    : Dec 01, 2023
Password expires                                        : never
Password inactive                                       : never
Account expires                                         : Dec 31, 2023
Minimum number of days between password change          : 0
Maximum number of days between password change          : 99999
Number of days of warning before password expires       : 7
```

Figure 2.24 – Using chage

It displays the following information:

- **Last password change date**: This shows the date when the password for the account was last changed
- **Password expiration date**: This shows the date when the current password will expire
- **Password inactive date**: This shows the date when the password will be disabled and the account will no longer be accessible
- **Account expiration date**: This shows the date when the account will expire and be disabled
- **Minimum password age**: This shows the minimum number of days that must pass before the password can be changed
- **Maximum password age**: This shows the maximum number of days that the password can be used before it must be changed
- **Password warning period**: This is the number of days before the password expiration date that a warning is given to the user

`chage` is a very powerful command that's useful for every system administrator who wants to improve the security of their systems by enforcing strong password policies.

The `passwd` command, on the other hand, is used to manage user passwords, allowing users to change their own password, while administrators can use it to change the password of another user. Its purpose is to ensure that user passwords are secure and that the password policies are enforced. The following are some examples:

- Configure password policies.

  The `/etc/security/pwquality.conf` file is used to configure password quality-checking policies. It defines rules and settings that control the complexity and strength of user passwords. This file is used by the **pluggable authentication module (PAM)** system to enforce password policies on the system, such as minimum length, complexity requirements, and reuse prevention. Administrators can edit this file to customize password policy settings to align with their security requirements.

  As the admin with `sudo` privileges, you can locate and edit the `/etc/security/pwquality.conf` file using the Vim editor. Here are the specific requirements for password quality configuration you need to follow:

  - `minlen` = 8 or 16 (for the sake of this example we selected 8)

  - `minclass` = 3

  - `maxrepeat` = 2

  - `minsequence` = 4

  - `maxclassrepeat` = 4

  - `reject_username` = true

```
#
# Minimum acceptable size for the new password (plus one if
# credits are not disabled which is the default). (See pam_cracklib manual.)
# Cannot be set to lower value than 6.
# minlen = 8    ←
#
```

Figure 2.25 – Editing /etc/security/pwquality.conf

Here's a brief summary of the configuration parameters:

- `minlen`: This specifies the minimum length of a password (eight characters)

- `minclass`: This sets the minimum number of character classes required (three classes, e.g., lowercase, uppercase, and digits)

- `maxrepeat`: This limits the maximum number of consecutive identical characters (two consecutive identical characters are allowed)

- `minsequence`: This sets the minimum length of a sequence (four characters, e.g., '1234' or 'abcd')

- maxclassrepeat: This limits the maximum number of consecutive characters from the same character class (four consecutive characters from the same class are allowed)

- reject_username: This ensures that the password does not contain the username

- Change the password of a specific user:

```
[root@Instructor instructor]# passwd tester1
Changing password for user tester1.
New password:
Retype new password:
passwd: all authentication tokens updated successfully.
```

Figure 2.26 – Changing a user's password

- Lock a user's password:

```
[root@Instructor instructor]# passwd -l tester1
Locking password for user tester1.
passwd: Success
[root@Instructor instructor]#
```

Figure 2.27 – Locking a user's password

- Unlock a user's password:

```
[root@Instructor instructor]# passwd -u tester1
Unlocking password for user tester1.
passwd: Success
[root@Instructor instructor]#
```

Figure 2.28 – Unlocking a user's password

Unlocking a user's account with the passwd -u tester1 command is a crucial part of managing user account settings in Linux. In our next topic, we'll explore techniques for discovering and locating files and identifying them within the Linux filesystem.

find, locate, and whereis commands

One of the most common tasks in Linux system administration is finding files. In CentOS 8, there are several commands that you can use to find files based on different criteria. The most commonly used commands for finding files are find, locate, and whereis. Each command has its own syntax and options, making them suitable for different use cases.

The find command is used to search for files and directories based on various criteria such as name, size, type, and modification time. Here's an example of how to use the find command to search for all files with the .txt extension in the current directory and its subdirectories:

```
[instructor@Instructor ~]$ find . -name "*.txt"
././cache/tracker/db-version.txt
././cache/tracker/db-locale.txt
././cache/tracker/parser-version.txt
././cache/tracker/locale-for-miner-apps.txt
././cache/tracker/last-crawl.txt
././cache/tracker/first-index.txt
./Templates/.secret-text.txt
./Documents/sensitive_file.txt
[instructor@Instructor ~]$
```

Figure 2.29 – Finding files with the .txt extension

The first argument of the command is the starting directory for the search. In our example, the dot . character means "current directory," and -name is used to specify the filename pattern to match. The * character is a wildcard that matches any number of characters, and *.txt matches all files that end with .txt.

The locate command, on the other hand, uses a pre-built database to search for files based on name or pattern. The advantage of locate over find is that it's much faster since it searches a pre-built database.

Here's an example of how to use the locate command to find all files with sensitive in their names:

```
[instructor@Instructor ~]$ locate sensitive
/home/instructor/Documents/sensitive_file.txt
/usr/share/gtk-doc/html/gst-plugins-good-plugins-1.0/left-insensitive.png
/usr/share/gtk-doc/html/gst-plugins-good-plugins-1.0/right-insensitive.png
/usr/share/gtk-doc/html/gst-plugins-good-plugins-1.0/up-insensitive.png
/usr/share/themes/Adwaita/gtk-2.0/assets/button-insensitive.png
/usr/share/themes/Adwaita/gtk-2.0/assets/checkbox-checked-insensitive.png
/usr/share/themes/Adwaita/gtk-2.0/assets/checkbox-mixed-insensitive.png
/usr/share/themes/Adwaita/gtk-2.0/assets/checkbox-unchecked-insensitive.png
/usr/share/themes/Adwaita/gtk-2.0/assets/combo-entry-ltr-button-insensitive.png
```

Figure 2.30 – Using the locate command to find all files

Finally, the whereis command is used to locate the binary, source, and manual page files for a given command. Here's an example of how to use the whereis command to find the location of the ls command:

```
[instructor@Instructor ~]$ whereis ls
ls: /usr/bin/ls /usr/share/man/man1/ls.1.gz /usr/share/man/man1p/ls.1p.gz
[instructor@Instructor ~]$
```

Figure 2.31 – Locating binary, source, and manual page files for the ls command

Here's another example using whereis to find the location of the passwd command:

```
[instructor@Instructor ~]$ whereis passwd
passwd: /usr/bin/passwd /etc/passwd /usr/share/man/man1/passwd.1.gz /usr/share/man/
man5/passwd.5.gz
[instructor@Instructor ~]$
```

Figure 2.32 – Locating binary, source, and manual page files for the passwd command

These commands are essential tools for managing and locating files on a Linux system. By mastering these commands, you can easily search for and identify files based on various criteria and improve your productivity as a system administrator.

Summary

In this chapter, we explored Linux user and group management, a crucial aspect of system security, stability, and resource allocation. We began by introducing the concept of user management and explained how to use commands such as useradd, userdel, and usermod to add, remove, and modify users on a Linux system. We also covered how to verify and set password expiration using the pwck, chage, and passwd commands, ensuring that user accounts remain secure.

The second section focused on file permissions and security basics, essential knowledge for any system administrator. We discussed the various file and directory permissions and how to use commands such as chmod and chown to modify them. In the third section, we delved into group management and covered commands such as groupadd, groupmod, groupdel, and grpck. We explained how groups allow for the efficient management of multiple users with similar permissions and access, and we learned how to use these commands to create and modify groups on a Linux system.

Moving on to the fourth section, we discussed the pwck and chage commands, which are used to verify the integrity of user and password files and set password expiration policies, respectively. We also covered the passwd command, which is used to change user passwords. Finally, the fifth section, *find, locate, and whereis commands*, covered how to locate files in directories and print their location using the find, locate, and whereis commands, which are particularly useful for system administrators who need to quickly locate files on a Linux system.

The next chapter delves into the topic of file compression and archiving in Linux. Through this chapter, readers will gain an understanding of how to use various commands such as gzip, tar, zip, and more to compress and decompress files.

3
File Compression and Archival Commands

File compression and archival commands have become an essential part of modern computing. With the ever-increasing amount of data being generated and shared, it has become necessary to use compression techniques to reduce the size of files, making them easier to store, transfer, and share. This process involves using software tools that compress files by removing any unnecessary data from them. The compressed file can then be stored in a smaller amount of space or transmitted over the internet more quickly.

There are several file compression and archival commands available in Linux, including `gunzip` and `gzip`, `tar`, `rar` and `unrar`, `zip` and `unzip`, `bunzip2` and `bzip2`, and many more. Each command has its own unique features, benefits, and limitations, making them suitable for specific use cases. For instance, the `gzip` command is a simple and easy-to-use compression utility that can compress files quickly. On the other hand, `tar` is a popular utility for creating and managing tarballs, which can be used to bundle multiple files into a single archive file. In this chapter, we will explore these commands and more, giving readers an overview of the different compression and archival options available in Linux.

In this chapter, we are going to cover the following main topics:

- gunzip and gzip
- tar, rar, and unrar
- zip and unzip
- bunzip2, bzip2, and more

gunzip and gzip

The gunzip (**GNU Unzip**) and gzip (**GNU Zip**) commands are used for file compression and decompression on Linux systems. The gzip command is used to compress files and create a compressed file with a .gz extension, while the gunzip command is used to decompress these .gz files. These commands are particularly important for system administrators who need to save disk space by compressing files and folders, as well as transfer files over a network using less bandwidth.

In addition to their practical benefits, the gunzip and gzip commands are also important for maintaining system security. Compressed files can be used to hide malicious code, so system administrators must be able to quickly and easily scan compressed files for security threats. The gzip command also includes options for setting file permissions and modifying the timestamp of files, allowing system administrators to maintain granular control over file access and modification.

gunzip is a command-line tool used to decompress files that have been compressed using the gzip utility. The tool is used to extract the compressed data from a .gz file and restore it to its original state. The command is vital for system administrators because it helps to reduce file sizes and save disk space. Additionally, the command can be used to compress and decompress files while transferring them over a network, which reduces the amount of bandwidth used. A scenario-based example should help us understand the basic use of gunzip.

Suppose a system administrator receives a compressed file called largefile.txt.gz from another team member. The file contains important data that they need to access. However, the file is too large to be transferred over email or other messaging platforms in its uncompressed form. To access the data in the file, the administrator will need to decompress it using the gunzip command. Here's how it is done:

1. First, navigate to the directory where the compressed file is located. For example, if the file is located in the /home/instructor/Desktop/administrator/data directory, you can navigate to that directory by running the following command in the terminal:

```
[root@Instructor ~]# cd /home/instructor/Desktop/administrator/data/
[root@Instructor data]# ls -l
total 996
-rw-rw-r--. 1 instructor instructor 1017661 Apr  1 10:15 largefile.txt.gz
[root@Instructor data]# 
```

Figure 3.1 – Navigating to the file location

2. Next, use the `gunzip` command to decompress the file. We'll do this by running the following command in the terminal:

```
[root@Instructor data]# gunzip largefile.txt.gz
[root@Instructor data]# ls -l
total 1024000
-rw-rw-r--. 1 instructor instructor 1048576000 Apr  1 10:15 largefile.txt
[root@Instructor data]#
```

Figure 3.2 – Decompressing the large file using gunzip

This will decompress the file and restore it to its original state, then we can access the data in the file using our preferred text editor or other tool.

`gzip` is a command-line utility that is used to compress and decompress files. It is commonly used in Linux and Unix systems to reduce the size of files for storage or transfer. The `gzip` command works by compressing a file into a smaller size using a compression algorithm. This makes it easier to store or transfer the file, as it takes up less space.

The `gzip` command is an important tool for system administrators, as it allows them to manage large files more efficiently. For example, if a system administrator needs to transfer a large file over the internet, they can use the `gzip` command to compress the file before sending it. This will reduce the amount of time it takes to transfer the file and reduce the amount of bandwidth required. Let's take a look at the following two examples:

*   A system administrator wants to compress a log file named `app.log` that is located in the `/var/log` directory. The administrator can use the following command to compress the file:

```
[root@Instructor log]# gzip /var/log/app.log && ls -la
total 7000
drwxr-xr-x. 19 root     root        4096 Apr  4 17:39 .
drwxr-xr-x. 22 root     root        4096 Feb  3 20:50 ..
drwxr-xr-x.  2 root     root        4096 Feb  3 20:37 anaconda
-rw-r--r--.  1 root     root     1017655 Apr  1 10:52 app.log.gz
drwx------.  2 root     root          23 Feb  3 20:50 audit
```

Figure 3.3 – Compressing a log file using gzip

This will create a compressed file named `app.log.gz` in the same `/var/log/` directory:

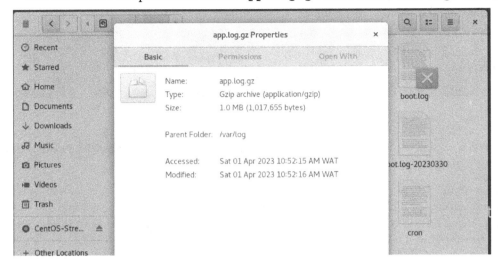

Figure 3.4 – Compressed app.log.gz file from 1 GB to 1.0 MB

- A system administrator wants to compress a directory named `backup` located in the `/home/instructor` directory. This directory compression process is often referred to as creating a "tarball," which is a common method for bundling and compressing multiple files or directories into a single archive file. The administrator can use the following command to compress the `backup` directory:

```
[instructor@Instructor ~]$ tar -czvf backup.tar.gz backup/
backup/
backup/site.html
[instructor@Instructor ~]$ ls -l backup
backup/          backup.tar.gz
```

Figure 3.5 – Compressing a directory called backup.tar.gz

This will create a compressed file named `backup.tar.gz` in the same directory. The `tar` command will also be introduced for our next topic. The `czvf` option supplied in the preceding command is used to create a compressed archive in `gzip` format.

The options are as follows:

- Create an archive
- Compress the archive using `gzip`
- Display progress information
- Specify the name of the archive file

tar, rar, and unrar

The `tar`, `rar`, and `unrar` commands are essential tools for system administrators, providing them with the ability to compress and archive files for more efficient storage and transfer. With these commands, administrators can bundle up multiple files and directories into a single archive file, which can then be compressed to save even more space. These archive files can then be transferred between systems, backed up to remote storage, or stored for future use.

The `tar` command is particularly useful for creating archive files, as it allows administrators to specify a range of options for compression and file organization. The `rar` and `unrar` commands, on the other hand, are proprietary tools developed by RARLAB for creating and extracting RAR archive files. These commands are widely used in the Windows environment but can also be used on Linux systems with the proper installation.

Overall, the `tar`, `rar`, and `unrar` commands have greatly simplified the process of managing and organizing files for system administrators. With their ability to bundle up files into archive files and compress them for efficient storage and transfer, these commands have made it much easier to manage large amounts of data across multiple systems.

`tar`, short for **tape archive**, is a command-line tool used in Linux and other Unix-based operating systems for creating, manipulating, and extracting archive files. It is an essential tool for system administrators, developers, and other users who frequently work with large amounts of data. The `tar` command allows users to bundle multiple files and directories into a single file using the following syntax:

```
tar [options] [archive-file] [file or directory to be archived]
```

This archive file can then be easily compressed, transferred, and backed up.

This tool is important because it simplifies the process of creating and managing backups, as well as allowing users to easily share files with others.

One common use case for `tar` is for creating backups of important files and directories on a system. For example, a system administrator may use the `tar` command to create a backup of critical configuration files and directories before making any major changes to the system. In this scenario, the `tar` command can be used to bundle all of the necessary files and directories into a single archive file, which can then be stored on a separate backup device or transferred to a remote location for safekeeping. Another use case for `tar` is for distributing software packages. Developers can use `tar` to bundle all of the necessary files and directories for a software package into a single archive file, which can then be easily distributed to end users.

A system administrator may need to transfer a large file or directory to another server over the network. In this case, the `tar` command can be used to bundle the necessary files and directories into a single archive file, which can then be compressed and transferred over the network using tools such as **secure copy (SCP)** or **remote sync (RSYNC)**. For example, a system administrator may use the following command to create a TAR archive of a directory named `webBackups` and compress it using the `gzip` compression algorithm:

```
[instructor@Instructor Desktop]$ tar -cvzf webBackups.tar.gz webBackups/
webBackups/
webBackups/admin-site.html
[instructor@Instructor Desktop]$ ls -l
total 996
drwxrwxr-x. 3 instructor instructor      18 Apr  1 10:26 administrator
drwxrwxr-x. 2 instructor instructor      29 Apr  5 18:24 webBackups
-rw-rw-r--. 1 instructor instructor 1017791 Apr  5 18:27 webBackups.tar.gz
```

Figure 3.6 – Creating a TAR archive of a directory

`rar` is a proprietary file-archiving utility used to compress and decompress files on Linux systems. The tool was developed by Eugene Roshal and is used to create compressed files with the `.rar` extension. It's a popular file compression format that allows users to compress large files into smaller archives for easier storage, transfer, and distribution. `rar` supports features such as password protection, error recovery, and archive spanning, making it a versatile and efficient tool for managing large sets of files.

System administrators can use `rar` to compress large files or sets of files, reducing their size and freeing up disk space. This can help improve system performance and reduce the amount of storage required for backups and file transfers. Additionally, RAR archives can be protected with a password to provide an extra layer of security to sensitive files. System administrators can also use `rar` to split large files into multiple smaller files, which can be useful for transferring files over the internet or storing them on portable media such as USB drives.

Scenario 1

A system administrator needs to transfer a large backup file to another server over the internet. The file is too large to transfer in its current format, so the administrator decides to compress it using `rar`. The administrator uses the `rar a backup.rar backup_folder` command to create an archive of the `backup` folder:

```
[instructor@Instructor Documents]$ rar a backup.rar backup_folder

RAR 6.02   Copyright (c) 1993-2021 Alexander Roshal    11 Jun 2021
Trial version              Type 'rar -?' for help

Evaluation copy. Please register.

Creating archive backup.rar

Adding     backup_folder                                        OK
Done
[instructor@Instructor Documents]$ ls -l backup_folder backup.rar
-rw-rw-r--. 1 instructor instructor 77 Apr  5 18:44 backup.rar

backup_folder:
total 0
```

Figure 3.7 – Creating an archive of the backup folder

The resulting RAR archive is smaller than the original backup folder and can be easily transferred over the internet.

zip and unzip

zip and unzip are file compression and archiving commands widely used by system administrators. zip is used to compress and archive files, while unzip is used to extract and uncompress files from ZIP archives. zip and unzip are important commands because they allow system administrators to efficiently manage large files and directories, reduce storage space usage, and speed up file transfers. The commands are easy to use and support various compression and archive formats, making them versatile tools for system administration tasks.

zip is used to compress and archive files into a single file for easier backup, storage, and transfer. The compressed .zip file takes up less storage space, reducing the need for additional storage devices. System administrators can use the zip command to compress and archive files, directories, and even entire filesystems. Let's look at some scenario-based examples next.

A system administrator needs to create a backup of a web server directory on a Linux machine. The directory contains several files and subdirectories, and the administrator decides to use zip to compress and archive the directory into a single file for easier backup and storage. The administrator uses the zip -r backup.zip web_server command to create a ZIP archive of the web server directory, including all subdirectories and files. The resulting ZIP archive can be stored on a portable hard drive or transferred over the network to another server for safekeeping:

```
[instructor@Instructor Desktop]$ zip -r backup.zip web_server
  adding: web_server/ (stored 0%)
  adding: web_server/login.html (deflated 100%)
[instructor@Instructor Desktop]$ ls -l
total 1984
drwxrwxr-x. 3 instructor instructor      18 Apr  1 10:26 administrator
-rw-rw-r--. 1 instructor instructor 1017971 Apr 11 18:03 backup.zip
drwxrwxr-x. 2 instructor instructor      24 Apr 11 18:02 web_server
[instructor@Instructor Desktop]$
```

Figure 3.8 – Creating a backup of a web server directory

In this example, the administrator compresses the web_server directory into a ZIP archive called backup.zip using the -r flag to include all subdirectories and files recursively. Later, when the administrator needs to restore the directory, they use the unzip command with the -d flag to extract the archive to a new directory called restored_web_server.

unzip can also be used to list the contents of a ZIP archive, test the integrity of the archive, and extract specific files from the archive. It is also used to extract and uncompress files from ZIP archives, allowing system administrators to retrieve and use files contained in the archive. Here is an example of using unzip:

```
[instructor@Instructor Desktop]$ unzip backup.zip -d restored_web_server
Archive:  backup.zip
   creating: restored_web_server/web_server/
   inflating: restored_web_server/web_server/login.html
[instructor@Instructor Desktop]$
```

Figure 3.9 – Using the unzip "-d" flag to extract the archive to a new directory

The unzip backup.zip -d restored_web_server command is used to extract the contents of a ZIP archive named backup.zip into a directory named restored_web_server.

To determine the directory size, you can use the du -H restored_web_server/ command, which calculates the disk usage of files and directories, as shown in the following screenshot:

```
[instructor@Instructor Desktop]$ du -H restored_web_server/
1024000  restored_web_server/web_server
1024000  restored_web_server/
[instructor@Instructor Desktop]$
```

Figure 3.10 – The restored_web_server command

The -d flag specifies the destination directory for the extracted files. In this case, the destination directory is restored_web_server. The contents of the ZIP archive will be extracted into this directory, preserving the directory structure of the original archive. In our next topic, we will explore how to use the tar command to compress files using the bzip2 and bunzip formats. We will also touch on other archiving commands that system administrators commonly use in their daily tasks.

bunzip2, bzip2, and more

bzip2 and bunzip2 are two commands that are used for file compression and decompression on Unix-based systems. The bzip2 command is used to compress a file, while the bunzip2 command is used to decompress a file that has been compressed using bzip2. These commands are commonly used by system administrators to save disk space and to transfer large files between systems.

bzip2 is a powerful compression tool that compresses files using the Burrows-Wheeler block sorting text compression algorithm, followed by Huffman coding. This algorithm allows bzip2 to achieve a high level of compression while maintaining a relatively fast decompression time. This makes bzip2 ideal for compressing large files, such as backups, databases, and software distributions. When a file is compressed using bzip2, it is typically given a .bz2 extension. Here are a couple of examples to demonstrate this.

Scenario 1

A system administrator wants to compress a large log file and save disk space on the server. The administrator decides to use bzip2 to compress the file. The administrator navigates to the directory where the log file is located and enters the bzip2 -k -v syslog.log command to compress the log file using bzip2:

```
[root@Instructor instructor]# cd /var/log/
[root@Instructor log]# bzip2 -k -v syslog.log
  syslog.log: 1392531.208:1,  0.000 bits/byte, 100.00% saved, 1048576000 in, 753 out.
[root@Instructor log]#
```

Figure 3.11 – Using bzip2 to compress a large log file

Then, we verify the compressed syslog.log file:

```
[root@Instructor log]# ls -l syslog.log.bz2
-rw-r--r--. 1 root root 753 Apr 12 17:39 syslog.log.bz2
[root@Instructor log]#
```

Figure 3.12 – Verifying the compressed log file

The -k option keeps the original file and creates a compressed version, while the -v option displays the progress of the compression process. The compressed file is now much smaller than the original and can be safely deleted to free up disk space.

Scenario 2

A system administrator needs to back up a large directory containing multiple files and subdirectories. The administrator decides to use bzip2 to compress the directory and its contents into a single file. The administrator enters the tar -cvf - directory_to_backup | bzip2 -9 -c > backup.tar.bz2 command to create a TAR archive of the directory, compress it using bzip2 with the highest compression level (-9), and redirect the output to a backup file:

```
[root@Instructor Desktop]# tar -cvf - /home/instructor/Desktop/administrator/ | bzip2 -9 -c > backup.tar.
bz2
tar: Removing leading '/' from member names
/home/instructor/Desktop/administrator/
/home/instructor/Desktop/administrator/data/
/home/instructor/Desktop/administrator/data/largefile.txt
[root@Instructor Desktop]# ls
administrator  backup.tar.bz2  backup.zip  restored_web_server  web_server
[root@Instructor Desktop]#
```

Figure 3.13 – Compressing a directory with a subdirectory

Let's dive into the chained commands.

The `tar -cvf - /home/instructor/Desktop/administrator` command is used to create a TAR archive of the `/home/instructor/Desktop/administrator` directory; this was the first command we introduced in this chapter. The `-c` option specifies that a new archive is being created, the `-v` option enables verbose mode to display the progress of the archiving process, and the `-f` option specifies the output file. The hyphen after the `-f` option indicates that the output should be sent to **standard output (stdout)** instead of a file on disk.

The `|` (pipe) symbol is used to redirect the output of the `tar` command to the input of the `bzip2` command; then, we have the `bzip2 -9 -c` command, which is used to compress the TAR archive created by the `tar` command using the `bzip2` algorithm. The `-9` option specifies the highest compression level, while the `-c` option sends the output to stdout. Finally, `> backup.tar.bz2` redirects the compressed output to a file named `backup.tar.bz2`.

Here's a brief explanation of the common compression levels in `bzip2`:

- `-1` (fastest): This level provides the fastest compression but generates larger compressed files. It's suitable for situations where speed is more critical than file size reduction.

- `-9` (maximum compression—our choice in *Figure 3.13*): This level offers the highest compression, resulting in smaller compressed files. However, it is slower than lower levels. It's useful when saving disk space is a top priority and you don't mind waiting for the compression process to finish.

- `-2` to `-8` (intermediate levels): These levels offer a trade-off between compression speed and resulting file size. As you move from `-2` to `-8`, the compression becomes better (smaller file size) but slower compared to lower levels. Choose an intermediate level based on your specific requirements for speed and file size reduction.

The resulting backup file is much smaller than the original directory and can be easily transferred or stored for safekeeping.

The `bunzip2` command is used to decompress files that have been compressed using `bzip2`. When a compressed file is decompressed using `bunzip2`, the original file is restored with the same name and directory path as the compressed file, but without the `.bz2` extension. The `bunzip2` command is also able to decompress files that have been compressed using the `gzip` command.

System administrators can make use of `bzip2` and `bunzip2` in a variety of ways. One common use case is to compress and decompress large log files on a web server. By compressing log files using `bzip2`, system administrators can save disk space and transfer the logs to another system for analysis. Another use case is to compress and transfer database backups between servers. By compressing backups using `bzip2`, system administrators can reduce transfer times and conserve network bandwidth. Let's delve into an example to further clarify this.

Scenario 1

A system administrator needs to extract and decompress a large compressed file that has been split into multiple parts. The compressed file has a `.bz2` extension and was created using the `bzip2` command. To extract and decompress the file, the administrator can use the `bunzip2` command followed by the filename. If the compressed file has been split into multiple parts, the administrator can use the `cat` command to concatenate the files and then pipe the output to the `bunzip2` command. The following is an example command that the administrator can use:

```
[root@Instructor log]# cat syslog.log.bz2 | bunzip2 -c > decompressed_file
[root@Instructor log]# ls -l decompressed_file
-rw-r--r--. 1 root root 1048576000 Apr 12 18:56 decompressed_file
[root@Instructor log]#
```

Figure 3.14 – Using bunzip2 to decompress a compressed file

The `cat syslog.log.bz2` command reads the contents of the `syslog.log.bz2` compressed file and passes it as input to the `bunzip2 -c` command. The `-c` option specifies that the output of the command should be sent to stdout (that is, the terminal) instead of a file.

The `bunzip2 -c` command decompresses the input file using the `bzip2` compression algorithm and sends the uncompressed data to stdout. Finally, the output is redirected to a file named `decompressed_file` using the `>` operator.

Let us explore additional archiving commands that can be utilized, such as `7zip` and `xz`.

7-Zip is a popular open source file archiver that can handle various compression formats such as ZIP, GZIP, TAR, and its own 7z format. It is widely used by system administrators for compressing and extracting files and directories. The tool features a high compression ratio that helps in reducing the file size significantly. The compression format used by 7-Zip is also known to be secure, making it a suitable option for archiving confidential data. It can also create self-extracting archives that allow users to extract compressed files without having to install any additional software. We'll delve into a scenario and explain.

Scenario 1

A system administrator needs to create a compressed archive of a large directory containing confidential information. The administrator uses the `7z a -t7z -p -mhe=on archive.7z directory_to_compress` command to create a password-protected and encrypted 7z archive of the directory. The `-mhe=on` option enables encryption of filenames to ensure the confidentiality of the data:

```
[root@Instructor Desktop]# 7z a -t7z -p -mhe=on archive.7z administrator/

7-Zip [64] 16.02 : Copyright (c) 1999-2016 Igor Pavlov : 2016-05-21
p7zip Version 16.02 (locale=en_US.UTF-8,Utf16=on,HugeFiles=on,64 bits,4
n Vega Mobile Gfx   (810F81),ASM,AES-NI)

Scanning the drive:
2 folders, 1 file, 1048576000 bytes (1000 MiB)

Creating archive: archive.7z

Items to compress: 3


Enter password (will not be echoed):
Verify password (will not be echoed) :

Files read from disk: 1
Archive size: 154280 bytes (151 KiB)
Everything is Ok
```

Figure 3.15 – 7-Zip prompting the user to enter a password

The -p option is used to specify a password for the compressed archive. Since no password is provided after the -p option, 7z will prompt the user to enter a password. The resulting 7z archive can be easily transferred and stored on another server or external drive, and only authorized personnel with the password can extract the data.

XZ is a command-line tool used for data compression and decompression. It is based on the **Lempel-Ziv-Markov-chain algorithm** (**LZMA**), which is known for its high compression ratio and low memory usage. XZ is used for creating compressed archives of large files and directories, particularly in Linux systems. It is also used for compressing the Linux kernel during installation. XZ provides a significant reduction in file size while maintaining the integrity of the original file. Additionally, XZ can be used for compressing and decompressing files on the fly, which is useful in some scenarios.

Scenario 2

A system administrator needs to compress and archive a large log file generated by a web server. The administrator uses the xz -z -k -9 logfile.log command to compress the file with a maximum compression level (-9) and keep the original file (-k). The resulting compressed file is significantly smaller than the original file, making it easier to store and transfer. The administrator can use the xz -d logfile.log.xz command to decompress the file for analysis or further processing.

The following command is used for compressing the log file:

```
[root@Instructor log]# xz -z -k -9 syslog.log
[root@Instructor log]# ls -l syslog.log
syslog.log      syslog.log.xz
```

Figure 3.16 – Compressing the syslog file

Here, the xz command is used to compress the syslog.log file with the maximum compression level of 9 (-9) and keep the original file (-k). The resulting compressed file will have a .xz extension.

The following command is used for decompressing the compressed log file:

```
[root@Instructor log]# xz -d syslog.log.xz
[root@Instructor log]# ls -l syslog.log
-rw-r--r--. 1 root root 1048576000 Apr 13 18:43 syslog.log
[root@Instructor log]#
```

Figure 3.17 – Decompressing the syslog file

To decompress the syslog file, we use the same xz command to decompress the syslog.log.xz compressed file. The resulting file will have the original name, logfile.log.

In conclusion, Linux systems have several powerful tools for compressing and decompressing files, including bunzip2, bzip2, 7z, and xz. These tools are especially useful for archiving large files and directories, as well as for transferring files between systems or over networks. With the ability to password-protect and encrypt data in some of these commands, administrators can ensure the security and confidentiality of their files. By using these commands, system administrators can more efficiently manage their files and storage, and optimize their computing resources. For example, 7z can compress large databases, bzip2 can archive files, and xz can compress log files. Whether the administrator needs to compress, transfer, or decompress files, these tools provide reliable and efficient solutions.

Summary

This chapter covered file compression and archival commands, which are important for efficient file management and transferring files over networks. It also covered several powerful tools, including gunzip, gzip, tar, rar, unrar, zip, unzip, bunzip2, bzip2, 7z, and xz, which enable system administrators to compress and decompress files efficiently, archive large files and directories, and transfer files over networks or between systems. These commands offer various compression levels and encryption options to ensure the security and confidentiality of data. They are particularly useful for managing large databases, backing up important files, and transferring files over the internet. By using these commands, system administrators can efficiently manage their files and storage, making the most of their computing resources.

Overall, this chapter provided a comprehensive guide to file compression and archiving commands in Linux, which are essential for effective file management and storage optimization. By mastering these commands, system administrators can efficiently manage their files and storage, ensuring the security and confidentiality of their data.

As we move to *Part 2*, the next chapter will focus on format and disk space commands, which are essential for system administrators to manage disk space and filesystems. Through this chapter, readers will learn various commands such as mkfs, fdisk, du, df, and more to format disks, partition hard drives, check disk usage, and manage filesystems. By learning these commands, system administrators can effectively manage disk space and optimize storage performance.

Part 2:
Frequently Used
Commands – Part 1

In this part, we explore the essential commands frequently used by system administrators in the **command line interface (CLI)**. We cover their practicality and execution and provide hands-on experience to ensure a proper understanding.

This section contains the following chapters:

- *Chapter 4, Format and Disk Space Commands*
- *Chapter 5, Linux Permissions Commands*
- *Chapter 6, Filesystem Mount and Manipulation Commands*

4

Format and Disk Space Commands

As we progress in our comprehensive series on frequently used commands for system administrators, the **command-line interface (CLI)** is an essential tool for getting many tasks done. The CLI offers a streamlined and efficient way to perform various tasks, from managing files and directories to monitoring system performance and troubleshooting issues. In this section, we will delve into frequently used commands and explore their usefulness, execution, and best practices for effective system administration. By mastering these commands, system administrators can work more efficiently and effectively, making the most of their computing resources.

As a system administrator, managing storage and filesystems is an essential part of ensuring the smooth operation of a system. The ability to format, partition, and manage disk space is critical for managing files, backing up important data, and maintaining system stability. In this chapter, we will explore the various commands used for formatting and disk space management, including `fdisk`, `lsblk`, `df`, `du`, and more.

We will begin by discussing the history and evolution of disk formatting and partitioning, from the early days of magnetic tapes to modern **solid-state drives (SSDs)**. We will then delve into the steps involved in creating a partition and explore various commands for disk space management. Additionally, we will cover the use of package managers to display package space and explore various formatting commands such as `mkfs`, `mke2fs`, `fdformat`, and others. By the end of this chapter, you will have a comprehensive understanding of formatting and disk space commands, enabling you to effectively manage storage and filesystems. It's important to note that formatting a disk results in deleting all data on that disk, so you should exercise caution when using these commands.

In this chapter, we are going to cover the following main topics:

- The history and evolution of disk formatting and partitioning in Linux
- Steps to create a partition

- fdisk, lsblk, df, and du

- Displaying (dpkg and rpm) package space

- mkfs, mke2fs, and fdformat, and more

The history and evolution of disk formatting and partitioning in Linux

The history of disk formatting and partitioning in Unix/Linux dates back to the early days of computing when disk storage was a scarce resource. Disk partitioning was essential in organizing disk space into smaller, manageable sections. It allowed system administrators to allocate disk space more efficiently and reduced the risk of data loss in the event of a disk failure. In the early days of Unix, disk partitioning was done using the `fdisk` command, which allowed the user to create, delete, and modify disk partitions. With the introduction of Linux, the partitioning tool was updated to use the more advanced **GUID Partition Table** (**GPT**) format, which provided support for larger disks and more partitions.

Over time, disk formatting and partitioning in Unix/Linux have become more sophisticated, with new commands and utilities being added to improve the process. For instance, the `mke2fs` command, which is used to create an `ext2` or `ext3` filesystem, was introduced in Linux version 1.2. This command created a more efficient filesystem, which reduced the risk of data loss and made disk management more manageable. The introduction of the `mke2fs` command was a significant milestone in the evolution of disk formatting and partitioning in Unix/Linux as it allowed administrators to create more reliable filesystems and manage disk space more efficiently. The advent of cloud computing and virtualization has also had a significant impact on disk formatting and partitioning in Unix/Linux. Cloud computing has enabled the use of virtual disks, which can be partitioned and formatted using the same tools as physical disks. In virtualized environments, administrators can easily create, modify, and resize virtual disks, making it easier to manage storage space. Additionally, cloud storage providers have developed their own disk formatting and partitioning tools, such as Amazon **Elastic Block Store** (**EBS**), which allows users to create and attach virtual disks to their instances. These tools have made it easier for administrators to manage disk space in the cloud and ensure that their data is stored securely.

There are three types of partitions:

- **Primary partition**: A primary partition is a basic partition that can be used to boot an operating system. In a hard disk, you can create up to four primary partitions. If you want to create more partitions, you can create an extended partition, which is a special partition that can contain multiple logical partitions.

- **Logical partition**: A logical partition is a partition that is created within an extended partition. You can create multiple logical partitions within an extended partition, which can be useful when you want to create multiple partitions but you have already created four primary partitions.

- **Extended partition**: An extended partition is a special partition that is used to create multiple logical partitions. An extended partition can only be created if there are no more than four primary partitions on the hard disk. Once an extended partition has been created, you can create multiple logical partitions within it.

These partition types are used to organize and manage data on a hard disk. By creating multiple partitions, you can separate different types of data and manage them more effectively. For example, you could create a separate partition for the operating system, one for user data, and one for backup files. This can make it easier to manage your data and protect it in the event of a failure or data loss. The different types of partitions offer flexibility in how you organize your data on a hard disk, depending on your needs and the limitations of the hard disk.

Steps to create a partition

Partitioning is the process of dividing a physical hard drive into multiple logical storage units. In Linux, the process of creating a partition involves defining the size and location of a new partition on a physical hard drive, and then formatting it with a filesystem such as ext4, XFS, or btrfs. Creating partitions is essential for managing disk space effectively and efficiently. With partitioning, system administrators can organize and allocate space on a hard drive to various functions such as the operating system, application files, user data, and swap space.

The process of creating partitions in Linux involves several steps. The first step is to identify the physical hard drive that needs to be partitioned, using the fdisk command or other disk management tools such as lsblk, df, and du. Next, the system administrator must decide on the size and location of the new partition and use the fdisk command to create it. The new partition must then be formatted with a filesystem using the mkfs command. Finally, the system administrator must mount the new partition to make it accessible to the operating system and its applications.

Partitioning is important for several reasons. Firstly, it allows system administrators to manage disk space efficiently by organizing data into logical units. With partitioning, it becomes easier to back up and restore data, as well as to allocate space for specific applications or functions. Secondly, partitioning can improve system performance by reducing disk fragmentation and optimizing access times. Additionally, partitioning can improve security by isolating sensitive data on separate partitions and protecting it from unauthorized access. Remember that partitioning is a critical tool for system administrators to manage disk space, optimize system performance, and enhance security.

The demonstration will be easy as we only require a drive connected to the Linux machine, and we can begin partitioning by launching the Terminal. The commands we'll be making use of for this partitioning are lsblk and fdisk. The lsblk command will list the available devices so that we can select the correct one to format, and fdisk command will effectively format the selected device. Let's get started with the demonstration:

1. To verify the available devices, execute the lsblk command:

```
[root@Instructor instructor]# lsblk
NAME          MAJ:MIN RM   SIZE RO TYPE MOUNTPOINT
sda             8:0    0    30G  0 disk
├─sda1          8:1    0     1G  0 part /boot
└─sda2          8:2    0    29G  0 part
  ├─cs-root   253:0    0    26G  0 lvm  /
  └─cs-swap   253:1    0     3G  0 lvm  [SWAP]
sdb             8:16   1  58.6G  0 disk
└─sdb1          8:17   1  58.6G  0 part
sr0            11:0    1  10.9G  0 rom  /run/media/instructor/Ce
```

Figure 4.1 – Verifying disk space

As we can see, we have listed the available devices and their respective disk spaces, but our main target is the connected drive on /dev/sdb. Note that /dev represents the device directory in Linux, where hardware devices are represented as files. In this case, /dev/sdb is the second SCSI disk drive on the system. Notice that it already has a partition (sdb1). We will delete that partition, verify it again, and then create our own partition. Let's proceed with the next steps.

2. Next, execute the fdisk command to open its utility for the /dev/sdb drive. Please ensure you have sudo access to run this command. Once you have opened the utility, you can create a new partition, but first, let's delete the previous one:

```
[root@Instructor instructor]# fdisk -l /dev/sdb
Disk /dev/sdb: 58.6 GiB, 62914560000 bytes, 122880000 sectors
Units: sectors of 1 * 512 = 512 bytes
Sector size (logical/physical): 512 bytes / 512 bytes
I/O size (minimum/optimal): 512 bytes / 512 bytes
Disklabel type: dos
Disk identifier: 0x01937f69

Device     Boot Start       End    Sectors  Size Id Type
/dev/sdb1  *     2048 122879999 122877952 58.6G  7 HPFS/NTFS/exFAT
[root@Instructor instructor]# fdisk /dev/sdb

Welcome to fdisk (util-linux 2.32.1).
Changes will remain in memory only, until you decide to write them.
Be careful before using the write command.


Command (m for help): p
Disk /dev/sdb: 58.6 GiB, 62914560000 bytes, 122880000 sectors
Units: sectors of 1 * 512 = 512 bytes
Sector size (logical/physical): 512 bytes / 512 bytes
I/O size (minimum/optimal): 512 bytes / 512 bytes
Disklabel type: dos
Disk identifier: 0x01937f69

Device     Boot Start       End    Sectors  Size Id Type
/dev/sdb1  *     2048 122879999 122877952 58.6G  7 HPFS/NTFS/exFAT
```

Figure 4.2 – Viewing the fdisk utility for the /dev/sdb drive

Here, we used the p command, which stands for print, to display information about the existing partition we had previously identified using the lsblk command. Now, we need to delete that partition so that we can create a new one according to our needs.

3. To delete the sdb1 partition, use the d command, which stands for delete, to remove the sdb1 partition:

```
Command (m for help): d
Selected partition 1
Partition 1 has been deleted.

Command (m for help): w
The partition table has been altered.
Calling ioctl() to re-read partition table.
Syncing disks.
```

Figure 4.3 – Deleting and saving changes made

4. After that, we can make use of the lsblk command to check whether the partition was really deleted. As we can see, the deleted partition (sdb1) is not listed anymore, proving that the deletion succeeded:

```
[root@Instructor instructor]# lsblk
NAME          MAJ:MIN RM  SIZE RO TYPE MOUNTPOINT
sda             8:0    0   30G  0 disk
├─sda1          8:1    0    1G  0 part /boot
└─sda2          8:2    0   29G  0 part
  ├─cs-root 253:0    0   26G  0 lvm  /
  └─cs-swap 253:1    0    3G  0 lvm  [SWAP]
sdb            8:16    1 58.6G  0 disk
sr0           11:0    1 10.9G  0 rom  /run/media/ins
```

Figure 4.4 – Verifying that the partition was deleted

Once we have confirmed this, we can proceed with creating our own partition.

5. Now, call the fdisk utility for the /dev/sdb drive, and type p to print the current partition table. This will help you understand how the disk is currently partitioned. Next, type n to create a new partition. The n command in the fdisk tool is used to create a new partition on the selected disk. When the command is entered, we are prompted to select the type of partition we wish to create. In this case, we are presented with two partition types – primary and extended:

```
[root@Instructor instructor]# fdisk /dev/sdb

Welcome to fdisk (util-linux 2.32.1).
Changes will remain in memory only, until you decide to write them.
Be careful before using the write command.


Command (m for help): p
Disk /dev/sdb: 58.6 GiB, 62914560000 bytes, 122880000 sectors
Units: sectors of 1 * 512 = 512 bytes
Sector size (logical/physical): 512 bytes / 512 bytes
I/O size (minimum/optimal): 512 bytes / 512 bytes
Disklabel type: dos
Disk identifier: 0x01937f69

Command (m for help): n
Partition type
   p   primary (0 primary, 0 extended, 4 free)
   e   extended (container for logical partitions)
```

Figure 4.5 – Creating a new partition

6. Next, we selected p for the primary partition type. Then, we were prompted to select the number of partitions, and we left it as the default value by pressing *Enter*. For the first sector, we also pressed *Enter*. The same went for the last sector. Finally, we confirmed that we wanted to remove the signature by typing yes and then used the w command to save all the changes that we made:

```
Partition type
   p   primary (0 primary, 0 extended, 4 free)
   e   extended (container for logical partitions)
Select (default p): p
Partition number (1-4, default 1):
First sector (2048-122879999, default 2048):
Last sector, +sectors or +size{K,M,G,T,P} (2048-122879999, default 122879999):

Created a new partition 1 of type 'Linux' and of size 58.6 GiB.
Partition #1 contains a exfat signature.

Do you want to remove the signature? [Y]es/[N]o: Yes

The signature will be removed by a write command.

Command (m for help): w
The partition table has been altered.
Calling ioctl() to re-read partition table.
Syncing disks.
```

Figure 4.6 – Choosing the primary partition and saving changes

7. Verify its creation by calling `fdisk -l /dev/sdb` and `lsblk`:

```
[root@Instructor instructor]# fdisk -l /dev/sdb
Disk /dev/sdb: 58.6 GiB, 62914560000 bytes, 122880000 sectors
Units: sectors of 1 * 512 = 512 bytes
Sector size (logical/physical): 512 bytes / 512 bytes
I/O size (minimum/optimal): 512 bytes / 512 bytes
Disklabel type: dos
Disk identifier: 0x01937f69

Device     Boot Start        End    Sectors  Size Id Type
/dev/sdb1       2048 122879999 122877952 58.6G 83 Linux
[root@Instructor instructor]# lsblk
NAME           MAJ:MIN RM  SIZE RO TYPE MOUNTPOINT
sda              8:0    0   30G  0 disk
├─sda1           8:1    0    1G  0 part /boot
└─sda2           8:2    0   29G  0 part
  ├─cs-root   253:0    0   26G  0 lvm  /
  └─cs-swap   253:1    0    3G  0 lvm  [SWAP]
sdb              8:16   1 58.6G  0 disk
└─sdb1           8:17   1 58.6G  0 part
sr0             11:0    1 10.9G  0 rom  /run/media/instructor/Cent
[root@Instructor instructor]#
```

Figure 4.7 – Verifying the new partition (sdb1)

Congratulations! You have successfully created a partition.

fdisk, lsblk, df, and du

Among the utilities used in Linux systems to manage filesystems, there's `fdisk`, `lsblk`, `df`, and `du`. Each of these utilities performs a specific function in disk management, and their proper use is essential to ensure the efficient functioning of the system.

We introduced `fdisk`, a command-line utility that's used to partition disks, previously. It allows us to create and modify partition tables, enabling administrators to organize storage space as required. Partitioning is essential for efficiently utilizing storage space, improving system performance, and simplifying the management of the filesystem. `fdisk` can create different types of partitions, including primary, logical, and extended partitions. Additionally, it can be used to change the partition size, delete partitions, and modify partition types. Without `fdisk`, managing and organizing the filesystem would be complex, cumbersome, and prone to errors. We can call this command by simply typing `fdisk -l` to list the partition:

```
[root@Instructor instructor]# fdisk -l
Disk /dev/sda: 30 GiB, 32212254720 bytes, 62914560 sectors
Units: sectors of 1 * 512 = 512 bytes
Sector size (logical/physical): 512 bytes / 512 bytes
I/O size (minimum/optimal): 512 bytes / 512 bytes
Disklabel type: dos
Disk identifier: 0x193772f7

Device     Boot    Start       End  Sectors Size Id Type
/dev/sda1  *        2048   2099199  2097152   1G 83 Linux
/dev/sda2        2099200  62914559 60815360  29G 8e Linux LVM


Disk /dev/mapper/cs-root: 26 GiB, 27913093120 bytes, 54517760 sectors
Units: sectors of 1 * 512 = 512 bytes
Sector size (logical/physical): 512 bytes / 512 bytes
I/O size (minimum/optimal): 512 bytes / 512 bytes


Disk /dev/mapper/cs-swap: 3 GiB, 3221225472 bytes, 6291456 sectors
Units: sectors of 1 * 512 = 512 bytes
Sector size (logical/physical): 512 bytes / 512 bytes
I/O size (minimum/optimal): 512 bytes / 512 bytes
```

Figure 4.8 – List partition with fdisk

lsblk is another command-line utility that's used in Linux systems to list all the available block devices, including hard drives, USB devices, and CD-ROM drives. This utility is useful in identifying the storage devices attached to the system, and the details of each block device. The output of lsblk provides critical information about the block devices, such as the device name, the size, the filesystem type, and the mount point. An example of this can be seen here:

```
[root@Instructor instructor]# lsblk
NAME         MAJ:MIN RM  SIZE RO TYPE MOUNTPOINT
sda            8:0    0   30G  0 disk
├─sda1         8:1    0    1G  0 part /boot
└─sda2         8:2    0   29G  0 part
  ├─cs-root  253:0    0   26G  0 lvm  /
  └─cs-swap  253:1    0    3G  0 lvm  [SWAP]
sr0           11:0    1 10.9G  0 rom  /run/media/instructor/CentOS-Stream-8-x86_64-dvd
[root@Instructor instructor]#
```

Figure 4.9 – Output of block devices

This information is crucial in making decisions on how to allocate storage space and organize the filesystem efficiently. lsblk is essential in disk management as it helps system administrators identify the storage devices attached to the system, troubleshoot device connectivity issues, and make informed decisions regarding partitioning and disk organization.

The df (**Disk Free**) utility is a command-line tool that displays the disk space used and available in filesystems on Linux systems. This tool is important in monitoring filesystem usage, identifying storage space consumption patterns, and making decisions on how to allocate storage space efficiently. Let's try and display the disk space usage for a specific filesystem, such as the root filesystem:

```
[root@Instructor instructor]# df -h /
Filesystem          Size  Used Avail Use% Mounted on
/dev/mapper/cs-root  26G   14G   13G  51% /
```

Figure 4.10 – Displaying disk usage with df

With df, administrators can identify filesystems that are running low on disk space, which can cause system performance issues or data loss:

```
[root@Instructor dlaw-site]# df -h /var/www/html/dlaw-site/index.html
Filesystem            Size  Used Avail Use% Mounted on
/dev/mapper/cs-root    26G   26G  504K 100% /
[root@Instructor dlaw-site]#
```

Figure 4.11 – Monitoring disk usage

In this example, the administrator is monitoring the disk space usage on the filesystem where the website files are stored, which is mounted on /var/www/html. The df command is used with the -h option to display the output in a human-readable format, making it easier to understand the disk space usage. The output shows the total size of the filesystem, the amount of space used, the available space, the percentage of space used, and the mount point. The administrator can use this information to identify the directories that are consuming the most space and optimize them for better performance. Additionally, the administrator can use this information to plan for future disk space needs. The df utility provides a detailed report on the filesystem usage, including the filesystem type, the total size, the used space, the available space, and the percentage of the disk space used. With this information, administrators can optimize disk usage, increase performance, and avoid system crashes.

The du utility is another essential command-line tool that's used in Linux systems to determine the amount of space used by specific directories and files. With du, administrators can identify files or directories that are consuming too much space and decide whether to delete, archive, or move them to another filesystem. The du utility also displays the amount of space used by each subdirectory, enabling administrators to pinpoint storage hogs quickly. The du utility's importance in disk management cannot be overstated as it helps system administrators optimize disk usage, identify space-hogging files, and troubleshoot space consumption issues.

Checking the disk space usage of a directory

In this example, we will use the du command to check the disk space usage of a directory.

The steps are as follows:

1. Navigate to the directory whose disk space usage you want to check.
2. Type the following command:

```
[instructor@Instructor html]$ cd dlaw-site/
[instructor@Instructor dlaw-site]$ du -sh
13G     .
[instructor@Instructor dlaw-site]$
```

Figure 4.12 – Using du to check disk usage

We have used the du -sh command to check the disk space usage of the directory. The output shows that the directory is using 13 GB of disk space.

Finding large files in a directory

In this example, we will use the du command to find large files in a directory.

The steps are as follows:

1. Navigate to the directory whose large files you want to find.
2. Type the following command:

```
[instructor@Instructor dlaw-site]$ ls -la
total 13571076
drwxr-xr-x. 2 apache apache           24 May  8 21:15 .
drwxr-xr-x. 4 root   root             46 May  8 21:12 ..
-rw-r--r--. 1 root   root   13896777728 May  8 21:17 index.html
[instructor@Instructor dlaw-site]$ du -a | sort -rn | head -n 10
13571076        ./index.html
13571076        .
[instructor@Instructor dlaw-site]$ █
```

Figure 4.13 – Using du to find large files

Utilize the du -a | sort -rn | head -n 10 command to identify the 10 largest files in the directory. The resulting output provides the size of each file in bytes, along with its corresponding file path. Let's apply this command to a different folder and observe the results:

```
15571348        .
13571076        ./www/html/dlaw-site/index.html
13571076        ./www/html/dlaw-site
13571076        ./www/html
13571076        ./www
1094324 ./log
1024000 ./log/decompressed_file
509140  ./cache
396780  ./lib
390764  ./lib/rpm
```

Figure 4.14 – Viewing the file size with du

Utilities such as fdisk, lsblk, df, and du are essential in managing and organizing disk space in Linux systems. fdisk is used in partitioning disks, lsblk is used in identifying the storage devices attached to the system, df is used in monitoring filesystem usage, and du is used in determining the amount of space used by specific directories and files. Proper use of these utilities is crucial in optimizing disk usage, increasing system performance, and avoiding data loss.

Displaying (dpkg and rpm) package space

Package management systems such as dpkg and rpm are used to install, remove, and manage software packages in Linux and Unix operating systems. The dpkg tool is used in Debian-based systems such as Ubuntu and the rpm tool is used in Red Hat-based systems such as CentOS. These tools not only provide an easy way to manage software packages but also offer valuable information about disk space usage by the installed packages. One important use of the dpkg and rpm tools is to display the package space, which refers to the amount of disk space used by the installed packages. By using these tools, administrators can identify the packages that are consuming the most disk space and make decisions on whether to remove or keep them. This is particularly useful in systems with limited disk space, where optimizing the use of disk space is critical to avoid system crashes, performance issues, or data loss.

In addition, the dpkg and rpm tools provide information about the package dependencies, which are other packages that are required by the installed package to function properly. This information is useful in identifying the packages that can be safely removed without affecting the system's stability or functionality. By removing unnecessary packages, administrators can free up disk space, reduce system complexity, and improve system performance. The dpkg and rpm tools also offer an easy way to upgrade or install packages with their dependencies automatically resolved. With these tools, administrators can easily install security patches, updates, and new software packages without worrying about the dependencies. This reduces the time and effort required to manage packages and ensures that the system is up to date with the latest software versions. We are currently using CentOS 8, meaning rpm (**Red Hat Package Manager**) will be our number one example.

Installing a package

The following example demonstrates how to utilize rpm to install packages on CentOS 8:

```
[root@Instructor Downloads]# rpm -i ftp-0.17-78.el8.x86_64.rpm
        package ftp-0.17-78.el8.x86_64 is already installed
[root@Instructor Downloads]#
```

Figure 4.15 – Using rpm to install a package

This command installs the specified package using RPM. It searches for the package file in the current directory, or you can specify a path to the package file. This command is useful for installing new software on a Linux system, whether it is a single package or a set of packages.

Querying the details of a package

The rpm command can be used to query the details of a package installed on the system. For example, to query the details of the ftp package, use the following command:

```
[root@Instructor Downloads]# rpm -qi ftp
Name         : ftp
Version      : 0.17
Release      : 78.el8
Architecture: x86_64
Install Date: Tue 09 May 2023 09:06:45 PM WAT
Group        : Applications/Internet
Size         : 114803
License      : BSD with advertising
Signature    : RSA/SHA256, Mon 01 Jul 2019 10:37:38 PM WAT, Key ID 05b555b38483c65d
Source RPM   : ftp-0.17-78.el8.src.rpm
Build Date   : Tue 14 May 2019 12:44:19 AM WAT
Build Host   : x86-02.mbox.centos.org
Relocations  : (not relocatable)
Packager     : CentOS Buildsys <bugs@centos.org>
Vendor       : CentOS
URL          : ftp://ftp.linux.org.uk/pub/linux/Networking/netkit
Summary      : The standard UNIX FTP (File Transfer Protocol) client
Description  :
The ftp package provides the standard UNIX command-line FTP (File
Transfer Protocol) client.  FTP is a widely used protocol for
transferring files over the Internet and for archiving files.
```

Figure 4.16 – Querying the details of a package that's been installed

The dpkg and rpm tools are essential for managing software packages and optimizing the use of disk space in Linux and Unix systems. By providing valuable information about package space, dependencies, and upgrade options, these tools enable administrators to make informed decisions and ensure the stability, security, and performance of the system.

mkfs, mke2fs, fdformat, and more

Disk formatting is the process of preparing a storage device such as a hard drive, SSD, or USB flash drive for data storage. Formatting creates a filesystem on the storage device, which allows the operating system to organize and manage files on the device. In Linux, several disk formatting tool commands can be used to format storage devices. These tools include mkfs, mke2fs, fdformat, and more.

mkfs is a command that's used to create a filesystem on a storage device. This command can be used to create a variety of filesystems, including ext2, ext3, ext4, XFS, btrfs, and more. The mkfs command is important in preparing storage devices for use in Linux systems. For example, when a new hard drive is added to a Linux server, it must be formatted before it can be used for data storage. Let's examine a straightforward approach to utilize this tool on CentOS 8:

```
[root@Instructor instructor]# mkfs.ext4 /dev/sdb1
mke2fs 1.45.6 (20-Mar-2020)
Creating filesystem with 15359744 4k blocks and 3842048 inodes
Filesystem UUID: 8f037efb-bd35-4dbd-8680-85e926a75a86
Superblock backups stored on blocks:
        32768, 98304, 163840, 229376, 294912, 819200, 884736, 1605632, 2654208,
        4096000, 7962624, 11239424

Allocating group tables: done
Writing inode tables: done
Creating journal (65536 blocks): done
Writing superblocks and filesystem accounting information: done
```

Figure 4.17 – Formatting a partition using mkfs.ext4

This will format the /dev/sdb1 partition with the ext4 filesystem. The newly formatted partition can then be mounted and used for data storage.

mke2fs is a variant of the mkfs command that is specifically designed to create ext2, ext3, and ext4 filesystems. The mke2fs command is important in creating and managing Linux filesystems. With this command, administrators can specify the size of the filesystem, the block size, and other parameters to optimize the filesystem for specific use cases. For example, a filesystem created with the mke2fs command can be optimized for high-performance workloads or used with large files, as shown in the following example:

```
[root@Instructor instructor]# mke2fs -t ext3 /dev/sdb1
mke2fs 1.45.6 (20-Mar-2020)
Creating filesystem with 15359744 4k blocks and 3842048 inodes
Filesystem UUID: 9dea5946-6494-4593-af0b-5acd62f8fe62
Superblock backups stored on blocks:
        32768, 98304, 163840, 229376, 294912, 819200, 884736, 1605632, 2654208,
        4096000, 7962624, 11239424

Allocating group tables: done
Writing inode tables: 37/469
```

Figure 4.18 – Creating an ext3 filesystem

Here, the command creates an ext3 filesystem on the /dev/sdb1 partition. The -t ext3 option specifies the filesystem type as ext3.

The fdformat command is primarily used for low-level formatting of floppy disks, which are legacy storage media. It writes a new disk geometry and sector layout to the floppy disk, preparing it for use. However, this command is not intended for formatting modern storage devices such as pen drives or USB flash drives.

For formatting pen drives or USB flash drives in Linux, mkfs (make filesystem) commands are typically used, such as mkfs.fat for creating a FAT filesystem or mkfs.ext4 for creating an ext4 filesystem, as shown in the previous examples. These commands are specifically designed for formatting different types of storage devices, including pen drives, USB flash drives, and hard drives.

The mkswap command is used to create a swap area on a Linux system. A swap area is a dedicated space on a hard drive that the system can use as virtual memory when it runs out of physical memory. The mkswap command initializes a disk partition or a file as a swap area and assigns it a unique identifier.

Let's delve into comprehensive examples to demonstrate the practical utilization of these commands:

1. Check the available disk partitions:

```
[root@Instructor instructor]# lsblk
NAME          MAJ:MIN RM   SIZE RO TYPE MOUNTPOINT
sda             8:0    0    30G  0 disk
├─sda1          8:1    0     1G  0 part /boot
└─sda2          8:2    0    29G  0 part
  ├─cs-root   253:0    0    26G  0 lvm  /
  └─cs-swap   253:1    0     3G  0 lvm  [SWAP]
sdb             8:16   1  58.6G  0 disk
└─sdb1          8:17   1  58.6G  0 part
sr0            11:0    1  10.9G  0 rom  /run/media/in
[root@Instructor instructor]#
```

Figure 4.19 – Viewing the available disk partitions

2. Identify the desired partition for swap, such as /dev/sdb1, and then proceed to execute the sudo mkswap /dev/sdb1 command. This command formats the partition as swap, resulting in the following output:

```
[root@Instructor instructor]# sudo mkswap /dev/sdb1
Setting up swapspace version 1, size = 58.6 GiB (62913507328 bytes)
no label, UUID=603fd2d8-894b-4778-af9f-81d984aae45c
[root@Instructor instructor]# sudo swapon /dev/sdb1
[root@Instructor instructor]# lsblk
NAME          MAJ:MIN RM   SIZE RO TYPE MOUNTPOINT
sda             8:0    0    30G  0 disk
├─sda1          8:1    0     1G  0 part /boot
└─sda2          8:2    0    29G  0 part
  ├─cs-root   253:0    0    26G  0 lvm  /
  └─cs-swap   253:1    0     3G  0 lvm  [SWAP]
sdb             8:16   1  58.6G  0 disk
└─sdb1          8:17   1  58.6G  0 part [SWAP]
```

Figure 4.20 – Using mkswap to format the partition as swap

The gdisk command is a variant of the fdisk command and is used to partition hard drives on Linux systems. gdisk is primarily designed for GPT, which is a newer partitioning scheme that has replaced the older **Master Boot Record (MBR)** partitioning scheme on many modern systems. The gdisk command is a powerful tool that allows you to create, modify, and delete partitions on GPT disks.

3. In this scenario, the system administrator is using the gdisk command to create a new partition on the /dev/sdb disk. The administrator enters the gdisk /dev/sdb command to launch the gdisk utility for the specified disk.

4. Once inside the gdisk utility, the administrator uses the n command to create a new partition. The utility prompts for the partition number, first sector, and last sector. The administrator can choose the default values or specify custom values based on their requirements:

```
[root@Instructor instructor]# gdisk /dev/sdb
GPT fdisk (gdisk) version 1.0.3

Warning: Partition table header claims that the size of partition table
entries is 0 bytes, but this program  supports only 128-byte entries.
Adjusting accordingly, but partition table may be garbage.
Warning: Partition table header claims that the size of partition table
entries is 0 bytes, but this program  supports only 128-byte entries.
Adjusting accordingly, but partition table may be garbage.
Partition table scan:
  MBR: MBR only
  BSD: not present
  APM: not present
  GPT: not present


*********************************************************************
Found invalid GPT and valid MBR; converting MBR to GPT format
in memory. THIS OPERATION IS POTENTIALLY DESTRUCTIVE! Exit by
typing 'q' if you don't want to convert your MBR partitions
to GPT format!
*********************************************************************


Command (? for help): n
```

Figure 4.21 – Using gdisk to create a new partition

5. In this example, the administrator sets the partition type to Linux swap by entering a hex code of 8300. After confirming the changes, the administrator uses the w command to write the changes to the disk and exit the gdisk utility:

```
Partition number (1-128, default 1):
First sector (34-122879966, default = 2048) or {+-}size{KMGTP}:
Last sector (2048-122879966, default = 122879966) or {+-}size{KMGTP}:
Current type is 'Linux filesystem'
Hex code or GUID (L to show codes, Enter = 8300): 8300
Changed type of partition to 'Linux filesystem'

Command (? for help): w

Final checks complete. About to write GPT data. THIS WILL OVERWRITE EXISTING
PARTITIONS!!

Do you want to proceed? (Y/N): Y
OK; writing new GUID partition table (GPT) to /dev/sdb.
Warning: The kernel is still using the old partition table.
The new table will be used at the next reboot or after you
run partprobe(8) or kpartx(8)
The operation has completed successfully.
[root@Instructor instructor]#
```

Figure 4.22 – The partition was created

The `parted` command is a partition editor that allows you to create, delete, resize, and move partitions on a hard drive. Parted supports both MBR and GPT partitioning schemes and can work with multiple filesystem types. It is a powerful tool for managing disk partitions and is commonly used in server environments.

Let's explore a practical scenario of using the `parted` command:

1. In this scenario, the system administrator is using the `parted` command to create a new partition on the `/dev/sdb` disk. The administrator enters the `parted /dev/sdb` command to launch the parted utility for the specified disk.

2. Once inside the parted utility, the administrator uses the `mklabel gpt` command to create a new GPT partition table on the disk. This ensures compatibility with modern systems and larger disk sizes.

3. Next, the administrator uses the `mkpart primary ext4 0% 100%` command to create a new primary partition that spans the entire disk. The partition is formatted with the `ext4` filesystem.

4. After creating the partition, the administrator can use the `print` command to verify the partition layout and details. This helps ensure that the partition was created correctly.

5. Finally, the administrator uses the `quit` command to exit the parted utility:

```
[root@Instructor instructor]# parted /dev/sdb
GNU Parted 3.2
Using /dev/sdb
Welcome to GNU Parted! Type 'help' to view a list of commands.
(parted) mklabel gpt
Warning: Partition(s) on /dev/sdb are being used.
Ignore/Cancel? Ignore
Warning: The existing disk label on /dev/sdb will be destroyed and
continue?
Yes/No? Yes
Error: Partition(s) 1 on /dev/sdb have been written, but we have b
because it/they are in use.  As a result, the old partition(s) wil
further changes.
Ignore/Cancel? Ignore
(parted) mkpart primary ext4 0% 100%
(parted) print
Model: Flash Disk 3.0 (scsi)
Disk /dev/sdb: 62.9GB
Sector size (logical/physical): 512B/512B
Partition Table: gpt
Disk Flags:

Number  Start    End     Size    File system  Name     Flags
 1      1049kB   62.9GB  62.9GB  ext4         primary

(parted) quit
Information: You may need to update /etc/fstab.
```

Figure 4.23 – Using parted to create a partition table

By using the `parted` command in this scenario, the system administrator can easily create and manage partitions on the specified disk, allowing for effective disk management and utilization.

The `dd` command is a low-level tool that's used for copying and converting data between files, disks, and partitions. The `dd` command is commonly used for creating bootable USB drives, backing up and restoring disk images, and cloning disks. It can also be used to write zeros to a hard drive, which is useful for securely wiping sensitive data.

Let's explore a practical example scenario for the `dd` command:

1. In this scenario, the system administrator is using the `dd` command to copy the contents of a source file to a USB device represented by `/dev/sdb`.

2. The administrator starts by executing the `dd` command. The `if` option is used to specify the input file, followed by the path to the source file (`/home/instructor/backup.tar.gz` in this example):

```
[root@Instructor instructor]# dd if=/home/instructor/backup.tar.gz of=/dev/sdb bs=4M
0+1 records in
0+1 records out
1017778 bytes (1.0 MB, 994 KiB) copied, 0.0358375 s, 28.4 MB/s
[root@Instructor instructor]#
```

Figure 4.24 – Using the dd command to copy on the USB device

3. Next, the of option is used to specify the output file, which is the USB device represented by /dev/sdb. This means that the contents of the source file will be written to the USB device.

4. The bs option is used to specify the block size for data transfer. In this example, bs=4M indicates a block size of 4 megabytes.

5. By executing this command, the system administrator can effectively copy the contents of the source file to the USB device. This can be useful for tasks such as creating bootable USB drives, transferring large files, or creating disk images.

6. It's important to exercise caution when using the dd command with block devices such as /dev/sdb as any data on the destination device will be overwritten. As an administrator, you should double-check and ensure they are targeting the correct device to avoid accidental data loss.

In conclusion, disk formatting tool commands are an essential part of managing storage devices in Linux systems. These commands allow administrators to prepare storage devices for use, optimize filesystems for specific use cases, and ensure that devices are reliable and performant. Understanding the purpose and use of these commands is important for any Linux administrator who works with storage devices.

Summary

This chapter explored the steps of creating a partition, a fundamental process in disk management. We provided a detailed walk-through of utilizing tools such as fdisk, lsblk, df, and du to create, modify, and analyze partitions on storage devices. These tools play a crucial role in partition management, allowing system administrators to allocate disk space efficiently, monitor disk usage, and make informed decisions for optimal storage utilization. Additionally, this chapter delved into the topic of displaying package space using commands such as dpkg and rpm. These commands enable system administrators to obtain information about installed packages, including their sizes and disk space consumption. By leveraging dpkg and rpm, administrators can keep track of package installations, identify space-intensive packages, and manage package dependencies to ensure efficient disk utilization.

Furthermore, this chapter covered the usage of mkfs, mke2fs, and fdformat, among other disk formatting tools. These commands provide administrators with the ability to format disks and partitions with various filesystems, facilitating data organization and compatibility. Proper disk formatting is crucial for optimal performance and storage utilization. System administrators can utilize these tools to prepare disks for specific purposes, create filesystems for data storage, or format removable media.

In summary, this chapter served as a comprehensive guide to effective file management and storage optimization in Linux. By incorporating the steps of creating a partition, utilizing tools such as `fdisk`, `lsblk`, `df`, and `du`, displaying package space with `dpkg` and `rpm`, and employing disk formatting commands such as `mkfs`, `mke2fs`, and `fdformat`, system administrators can efficiently manage their files and storage resources. This enables them to enhance storage utilization, ensure data integrity, and maintain an organized and optimized system environment.

In the next chapter, we will thoroughly explore and discuss important commands such as `chmod`, `chown`, `chgrp`, `umask`, and `sudo`. These commands play a critical role in granting and managing file permissions, modifying ownership and group settings, setting default file permissions, and executing commands with administrative privileges.

5
Linux Permissions Commands

Linux permissions commands are a fundamental aspect of Linux system administration, providing a powerful mechanism to control access to files and directories. These commands, including chmod, chown, and more, play a crucial role in maintaining security, protecting sensitive data, and managing user privileges. They allow Linux system administrators to define who can read, write, and execute files, as well as specify access permissions for different users and groups. The importance of Linux permissions commands lies in their ability to enforce the principle of least privilege, ensuring that users and processes have only the necessary permissions to perform their intended tasks. By assigning appropriate permissions, system administrators can safeguard critical files and prevent unauthorized access, minimizing the risk of data breaches and unauthorized modifications. Additionally, these commands enable administrators to allocate privileges based on user roles, maintaining a well-defined security model within the system.

The purpose of Linux permissions commands is twofold: security and organization. From a security perspective, they allow administrators to restrict access to sensitive files, directories, and system resources. By granting or revoking permissions, administrators can limit the exposure of critical data and prevent malicious activities. On an organizational front, these commands facilitate the management of files and directories, ensuring that they are properly categorized, protected, and accessible to the intended users. Linux permissions commands are widely used by Linux system administrators due to their versatility and effectiveness in maintaining system security and managing user access. They provide granular control over permissions, allowing administrators to set different access levels for owners, groups, and other users. Furthermore, these commands can be applied recursively, allowing for efficient management of permissions across directories and subdirectories. With the use of symbolic and absolute modes, administrators can easily modify permissions based on specific requirements.

Linux permissions commands are essential for managing file and directory access permissions. System administrators can use these commands to enforce security measures, control user access, and safeguard sensitive data. By the end of this chapter, you will have a comprehensive understanding of Linux permissions commands, enabling you to effectively manage file and directory permissions.

In this chapter, we will cover the following main topics:

- Why permission commands?
- Types of permissions
- chmod
- chown
- Utilizing absolute paths in commands
- chgrp
- umask
- sudo

Why permission commands?

By utilizing permission commands, administrators can enforce the principle of least privilege, granting users only the necessary permissions required to perform their tasks. This practice reduces the risk of unauthorized access or accidental modifications to critical files, minimizing the potential for data breaches and system compromises. With proper permissions in place, organizations can maintain control over their sensitive information and prevent unauthorized disclosure or alteration. Moreover, permission commands enable administrators to implement security policies that align with industry best practices and compliance regulations. For example, by restricting access to configuration files or system directories, administrators can protect system files from unauthorized modifications, ensuring system stability and preventing malicious activities. Additionally, by assigning appropriate ownership and group permissions, administrators can facilitate collaboration among authorized users while maintaining data privacy and segregation.

However, despite their importance, lapses in the proper configuration and management of Linux permissions can lead to security vulnerabilities. Misconfigurations, such as granting excessive permissions or neglecting to revoke access rights when no longer needed, can expose sensitive data to unauthorized individuals or increase the risk of insider threats. Administrators must regularly review and audit permission settings to identify and rectify any inconsistencies or misalignments with organizational security policies.

Furthermore, the complexity of managing permissions in large-scale environments can pose challenges. Ensuring the appropriate permissions for numerous files and directories across multiple users and groups can be time-consuming and prone to human errors. It is crucial for administrators to implement proper access control frameworks, utilize automation tools, follow standardized procedures to mitigate the risk of misconfigurations, and maintain a secure environment. Permission commands serve as a fundamental pillar of securing organizational and administrative files. They provide the means to enforce access control, maintain data confidentiality, and mitigate security risks. However, it is essential for administrators to diligently configure, monitor, and manage permissions to avoid lapses and ensure the ongoing integrity and security of their systems and data.

Types of permissions

In Linux, three types of permissions can be assigned to files and directories: **read** (r), **write** (w), and **execute** (x). These permissions define the level of access and control users have over files and directories. Let's explore each type of permission and understand their meanings and implications:

- Read (r) permission:

  - The read permission allows a user to view and read the contents of a file or list the contents of a directory

  - For directories, the read permission enables the user to see the names of files and subdirectories within the directory

  It's important to note that having read permission allows users to open and view the contents of a file. However, they cannot modify or delete it unless they possess additional permissions.

- Write (w) permission:

  - The write permission allows a user to modify or delete a file's content or create new files within a directory

  - For directories, the write permission enables users to add, delete, and rename files and subdirectories within the directory

- Execute (x) permission:

  - The execute permission allows a user to execute or run a file if it is a program or script

  For directories, the execute permission enables users to access and enter the directory, allowing them to navigate through its contents. Unlike the read permission, the execute permission specifically grants the ability to traverse or navigate the directory structure and access its subdirectories. With the execute permission, users can execute programs, scripts, and commands within the directory, provided they have the necessary read permission to view the file's content. This means they can run executable files within the directory, but listing its contents with commands such as `ls` might not be allowed without read permission.

Permissions are assigned separately for three different entities: *the file owner (also known as "user"), the group associated with the file*, and *all other users (others)* who are not the owner or part of the group. These permissions can be set individually or combined into a three-digit numeric representation (for example, 755) to represent the permissions for the owner, group, and others.

When a user attempts to access a file or directory, Linux follows a specific order to check permissions:

- **User ownership** (**owner**): Initially, Linux checks whether the accessing user is the owner of the file. If the user is the owner, the system evaluates the permissions configured for the owner.

- **Group ownership** (**group**): If the accessing user is not the owner, Linux proceeds to examine whether the user belongs to the group associated with the file. If the user is part of the group, the system considers the permissions specified for the group.

- **Others**: If neither of the previous two conditions applies, Linux assesses the permissions granted to "others," which encompasses all users not falling into the owner or group categories.

This sequential approach to permission checking allows Linux to determine access rights with precision. It ensures that file access and actions (such as read, write, and execute) are granted or denied based on the user's relationship with the file's owner and group, facilitating robust access control.

Let's delve into the various tools employed for granting permissions, beginning with the widely utilized command known as chmod.

chmod

Short for **change mode**, chmod is a command in Linux and Unix-like operating systems that allows users to modify the permissions of files and directories. It plays a fundamental role in controlling access to files and ensuring data security. The importance of chmod lies in its ability to define who can read, write, and execute files, thus determining the level of interaction and control that different users have over the system resources.

One of the primary reasons why chmod is essential is that it can enforce security measures within an organization. By setting appropriate file permissions, system administrators can restrict unauthorized access to sensitive data and prevent unauthorized modifications. For example, critical system configuration files or confidential documents may require strict read-only permissions to ensure that only authorized personnel can view and access them. chmod empowers administrators to establish granular access controls, allowing them to strike a balance between accessibility and security. Another crucial use of chmod is in managing user access privileges. Different users or groups may have different levels of permissions based on their roles and responsibilities. chmod enables administrators to assign specific permissions to individuals or groups, ensuring that each user has the appropriate level of access required to perform their tasks. This level of control helps maintain data integrity and prevents accidental or intentional damage to files by unauthorized users. By using chmod, administrators can ensure that only trusted individuals or groups have the necessary permissions to modify critical files or execute certain programs.

Furthermore, chmod serves a vital purpose in the administrative aspect of file management. It allows administrators to organize and control file permissions efficiently, making it easier to manage access rights across a complex directory structure. By using chmod in conjunction with other tools such as chown (**change owner**), administrators can effectively assign ownership and permissions to files and directories, streamlining the administrative tasks associated with user management. This capability is particularly crucial in large organizations with multiple users and diverse filesystems, where efficient management of permissions is paramount to maintaining order and security. Let's explore and observe several scenarios that illustrate how to utilize this command effectively.

Scenario 1: Granting read and write permissions to a file:

1. Identify the file for which you want to grant read and write permissions.

2. Use the chmod command with the appropriate options to set the desired permissions:

```
[instructor@Instructor ~]$ filename="Management.txt"
[instructor@Instructor ~]$ chmod +rw "$filename"
[instructor@Instructor ~]$ ls -l Management.txt
-rw-rw-r--. 1 instructor instructor 1048576000 May 21 14:04 Management.txt
[instructor@Instructor ~]$
```

Figure 5.1 – Granting permission to files

This command grants read and write permissions to the Management.txt file, allowing users to both read from and write to the file.

Scenario 2: Revoking execute permission for a group:

1. Determine the file or directory from which you want to remove execute permission for a specific group.

2. Use the chmod command with the appropriate options to revoke the execute permission:

    *   g-w: This option removes the write permission for the group that the file belongs to.

    *   g-x: This option removes the execute permission for the group that the file belongs to. This means that the members of the group can no longer execute the file, even if they have read and write access to it:

```
[instructor@Instructor ~]$ filename="ChgMod.sh"
[instructor@Instructor ~]$ ls -l ChgMod.sh
-rw-rwxr--. 1 instructor instructor 1048576000 May 21 14:10 ChgMod.sh
[instructor@Instructor ~]$ chmod g-w "$filename"
[instructor@Instructor ~]$ ls -l ChgMod.sh
-rw-r-xr--. 1 instructor instructor 1048576000 May 21 14:10 ChgMod.sh
[instructor@Instructor ~]$ chmod g-x "$filename"
[instructor@Instructor ~]$ ls -l ChgMod.sh
-rw-r--r--. 1 instructor instructor 1048576000 May 21 14:10 ChgMod.sh
```

Figure 5.2 – Revoking execute permission

This command removes the execute permission for the group from the ChgMod.sh file, ensuring that group members cannot execute the script.

Scenario 3: Setting specific permissions using numeric mode:

1. Determine the file or directory for which you want to set specific permissions.

2. Calculate the numeric value for the desired permissions – for example, read (4), write (2), and execute (1):

```
user_permission=6 # read and write permission for the owner
group_permission=4 # read permission for the group
other_permission=4 # read permission for others
```

In Linux, file and directory permissions are often represented as a three-digit numeric code, where each digit corresponds to a specific permission type. The three digits represent permissions for the owner, the group, and others, in that order. Each digit is a combination of values that signify read, write, and execute permissions, as follows:

- 4: This digit represents read permission. It allows the user (or entity) to view the contents of a file or list the files in a directory.

- 2: This digit represents write permission. It grants the user the ability to modify or delete the file's contents or create new files within a directory.

- 1: This digit signifies execute permission. It enables the user to run executable files and scripts or traverse (enter) directories.

To create the three-digit numeric permission code, you can combine these values based on the desired permissions for the owner, group, and others. Here's an example:

- 6: This code means that the owner has read and write permissions (4 + 2), but no execute permission

- 7: In this code, the owner has read, write, and execute permissions (4 + 2 + 1)

- 4: This code represents read-only permissions for the group, with no write or execute permissions

- 5: Here, the group has read and execute permissions (4 + 1), but no write permission

- 0: This code indicates no permissions for a particular entity (owner, group, or others)

By understanding the meaning of each digit in the permission code, you can precisely control who can read, write, and execute files and directories, ensuring the security and integrity of your system.

3. Use the chmod command with the appropriate numeric mode to set the permissions:

```
[instructor@Instructor ~]$ filename="Approvals.txt"
[instructor@Instructor ~]$ user_permission=6
[instructor@Instructor ~]$ group_permission=4
[instructor@Instructor ~]$ other_permission=4
[instructor@Instructor ~]$ chmod "$user_permission$group_permission$other_permission" "$filename"
[instructor@Instructor ~]$ ls -l Approvals.txt
-rw-r--r--. 1 instructor instructor 1048576000 May 21 14:27 Approvals.txt
[instructor@Instructor ~]$
```

Figure 5.3 – Numeric permissions modes

This command sets the permissions of the Approvals.txt file to read and write for the owner, read for the group, and read for others.

Scenario 4: Applying recursive permissions to a directory and its subdirectories:

1. Identify the directory for which you want to apply permissions recursively.

2. Use the chmod command with the appropriate options to apply the desired permissions recursively:

```
[instructor@Instructor Desktop]$ ls -l ConfigFile/
total 0
drwxrwxr-x. 2 instructor instructor 29 Sep 30 23:26 admin-pass
drwxrwxr-x. 2 instructor instructor 24 Sep 30 23:26 changes
drwxrwxr-x. 2 instructor instructor 26 Sep 30 23:26 configurations
drwxrwxr-x. 2 instructor instructor  6 Sep 30 23:24 Others
drwxrwxr-x. 2 instructor instructor  6 Sep 30 23:25 rules
[instructor@Instructor Desktop]$ directoryname="ConfigFile"
[instructor@Instructor Desktop]$ chmod -R 755 "ConfigFile"
[instructor@Instructor Desktop]$ ls -la ConfigFile/
total 0
drwxr-xr-x. 7 instructor instructor  88 Sep 30 23:27 .
drwxr-xr-x. 7 instructor instructor 140 Sep 30 23:27 ..
drwxr-xr-x. 2 instructor instructor  29 Sep 30 23:26 admin-pass
drwxr-xr-x. 2 instructor instructor  24 Sep 30 23:26 changes
drwxr-xr-x. 2 instructor instructor  26 Sep 30 23:26 configurations
drwxr-xr-x. 2 instructor instructor   6 Sep 30 23:24 Others
drwxr-xr-x. 2 instructor instructor   6 Sep 30 23:25 rules
```

Figure 5.4 – Applying recursive permissions to a directory

This command applies the permissions of 755 (read, write, and execute for the owner, and read and execute for the group and others) to the ConfigFile directory and all its subdirectories.

chmod is a powerful command that plays a vital role in controlling file and directory permissions in Linux and Unix-like systems. Its importance lies in its ability to enforce security measures, manage user access privileges, and streamline administrative tasks. By utilizing chmod effectively, system administrators can ensure the confidentiality, integrity, and availability of data within an organization while maintaining a structured and secure filesystem.

chown

Short for **change owner**, the chown command is a powerful tool in Linux and Unix-based operating systems that's used to change the ownership of files and directories. However, it's important to note that in many cases, you need superuser privileges (often obtained via the sudo command) to execute chown. This command allows system administrators to assign new ownership to files, determining both the user and group that have control over them.

chown plays a crucial role in managing file permissions, enforcing security measures, and organizing administrative files. One of its key purposes is to ensure proper access control and security within a Linux system.

By specifying the correct user and group ownership for files and directories, system administrators can maintain security and control over who can access, modify, or delete specific resources. This is particularly important in multi-user and multi-group environments where precise control over file access is essential for system integrity and data protection.

By changing the ownership of files and directories, administrators can restrict access to sensitive information and prevent unauthorized users from modifying or accessing critical files. This is particularly important in multi-user environments and organizations where data confidentiality is paramount. chown enables administrators to assign ownership to specific users and groups, ensuring that only authorized individuals have the necessary privileges.

Furthermore, chown is essential for system administration tasks and file management. It allows administrators to transfer ownership of files when users are added or removed from the system. When a user account is deleted, for example, it is crucial to assign ownership of their files to another user or a system account to ensure continuity and prevent data loss. chown also facilitates efficient collaboration within teams by enabling the transfer of file ownership between group members, allowing them to work on shared projects or documents.

In addition to its security and administrative benefits, chown is a fundamental tool for organizing and maintaining filesystems. It enables administrators to categorize files and directories by assigning ownership to specific users or groups based on their role or purpose. This helps streamline file management, simplifies permission management, and ensures files are properly organized and accessible to the right individuals. chown plays a vital role in maintaining a well-structured and efficient filesystem, enhancing productivity and ease of use for both administrators and users.

The chown command allows for various types of ownership changes, enabling administrators to modify the ownership of files and directories based on different criteria. Here are the types of ownership changes that are commonly used in Linux permissions:

- **Changing user ownership**: The chown command can be used to change the user ownership of a file or directory. By specifying a new user as the owner, administrators can transfer ownership to a different user account.

- **Changing group ownership**: Along with changing user ownership, chown also supports changing the group ownership of a file or directory. Administrators can assign a new group to a file, allowing members of that group to access and modify the file.

- **Changing user and group ownership**: chown also provides the flexibility to change both user and group ownership simultaneously. This allows administrators to completely modify the ownership of a file or directory, assigning both a new user and a new group.

- **Changing ownership recursively**: In cases where directories contain multiple files and subdirectories, administrators may need to change ownership recursively. The -R option in the chown command enables recursive ownership change, ensuring that ownership is modified for all files and directories within the specified directory.

- **Preserving file context**: On systems that implement **mandatory access control** (**MAC**) mechanisms, such as SELinux, it's important to preserve the file context (a special security label used by MAC systems to focus on the security properties of the file) while changing ownership. The -h option in the chown command ensures that the file context remains unchanged.

Let's explore different scenarios that illustrate how to utilize this command effectively:

- Changing ownership of a directory and its contents:

```
[instructor@Instructor ~]$ ls -l backup
total 1024000
-rw-rw-r--. 1 instructor instructor 1048576000 Apr  4 18:02 site.html
[instructor@Instructor ~]$ sudo chown -R tester1:instructor backup
[sudo] password for instructor:
[instructor@Instructor ~]$ ls -l backup
total 1024000
-rw-rw-r--. 1 tester1 instructor 1048576000 Apr  4 18:02 site.html
[instructor@Instructor ~]$ 
```

Figure 5.5 – Changing ownership of a directory

In this scenario, we pass the ownership of the backup directory and all its contents to the tester1 user, including files and subdirectories. The group ownership is also changed to instructor. This is useful when transferring ownership of a project to a new team lead or when organizing files under a specific user and group.

- Restoring ownership of system files:

```
[instructor@Instructor ~]$ sudo chown -R root:root backup
[instructor@Instructor ~]$ ls -la backup
total 1024004
drwxrwxr-x. 2 root       root              23 Apr  4 18:13 .
drwx------. 18 instructor instructor      4096 May 25 17:41 ..
-rw-rw-r--. 1 root       root       1048576000 Apr  4 18:02 site.html
[instructor@Instructor ~]$ 
```

Figure 5.6 – Restoring ownership of a file

This command recursively changes the ownership of all files and directories under the `backup` directory back to the `root` user and `root` group. This is important for maintaining the integrity and security of system configuration files, ensuring that only the `root` user has the necessary privileges to modify them.

- Assigning ownership to a specific user in a shared directory:

```
[instructor@Instructor ~]$ sudo chown -R instructor:tester1 projects/backup/
[instructor@Instructor ~]$ ls -la projects/
total 4
drwxrwxr-x.  3 instructor instructor   20 May 25 18:11 .
drwx------. 18 instructor instructor 4096 May 25 18:11 ..
drwxrwxr-x.  2 instructor tester1      23 Apr  4 18:13 backup
[instructor@Instructor ~]$
```

Figure 5.7 – Assigning ownership to a specific user in a shared directory

Here, the ownership of the `project/backup/` directory is changed to the `instructor` user and the `tester1` group. This is useful in scenarios where multiple users need access to a shared directory, but specific ownership is required for certain files or folders within that directory.

By customizing the user and group names and applying the appropriate options, you can effectively manage ownership and permissions in various situations.

Finally, `chown` is a crucial command for system administrators. Its ability to change file ownership allows for proper access control, enhances security, facilitates administrative tasks, and contributes to a well-organized filesystem. By leveraging `chown` effectively, administrators can ensure data confidentiality, maintain system integrity, and promote efficient collaboration among users and groups.

Utilizing absolute paths in commands

Utilizing absolute paths in commands is a crucial aspect of working with the Linux operating system. An absolute path refers to the complete and exact location of a file or directory in the filesystem hierarchy. It starts from the `root` directory (`/`) and includes all the necessary directories to specify the location precisely. The primary reason for using absolute paths in commands is to provide an unambiguous and reliable way to refer to files or directories. By using an absolute path, you eliminate any dependency on the current working directory. This ensures that the command will consistently target the intended file or directory, regardless of your current location in the filesystem. Absolute paths eliminate confusion and prevent potential errors that may occur when relying on relative paths.

The importance of utilizing absolute paths becomes evident in scenarios where scripts or commands need to be executed from different directories or by different users. Absolute paths guarantee that the same file or directory is accessed, regardless of the executing environment. This is especially crucial when dealing with system administration tasks, automation scripts, or shared environments where multiple users interact with the same filesystem. The use of absolute paths is widespread in various Linux operations. It is especially vital when executing commands that require precise file or directory targeting, such as file manipulation, data backups, system configuration, or application deployment.

Absolute paths are commonly used in commands such as file copying, moving, deletion, permissions modification, and program execution. By utilizing absolute paths, you can ensure the accuracy and predictability of these operations, minimizing the risk of unintended consequences or errors. To better understand what we're talking about, we'll be focusing on scenario-based examples that demonstrate the use of the absolute command in different situations:

- **Copying a file to a specific directory**: Suppose you have a file named document.txt located in your home directory, and you want to copy it to the /var/www/html directory. You can use the following absolute command:

```
[instructor@Instructor Desktop]$ ls -l document.txt
-rw-rw-r--. 1 instructor instructor 1048576000 May 25 18:34 document.txt
[instructor@Instructor Desktop]$ sudo cp /home/instructor/Desktop/document.txt /var/www/html/
[sudo] password for instructor:
[instructor@Instructor Desktop]$ ls -l /var/www/html/
total 1024000
-rw-r--r--. 1 root root 1048576000 May 25 18:36 document.txt
[instructor@Instructor Desktop]$
```

Figure 5.8 – Copying a file to a specific directory

- **Moving a directory to another location**: Assume you have a directory named document. txt in the current working directory, and you want to move it to the /home/instructor/ Documents directory. You can accomplish this using the following absolute command:

```
[instructor@Instructor html]$ sudo mv document.txt /home/instructor/Documents/
[instructor@Instructor html]$ ls -l /home/instructor/Documents/
total 1024004
drwxrwxr-x. 2 instructor instructor          6 Apr  5 18:44 backup_folder
drwx------. 2 instructor instructor          6 Mar 26 13:51 Confidential files
-rw-r--r--. 1 root       root       1048576000 May 25 18:36 document.txt
```

Figure 5.9 – Moving a directory to another location

- **Accessing a file in a different directory**: Assume you have a script located in the /usr/local/ bin directory, and it needs to access a configuration file named config.ini located in the /etc directory. You can use the following absolute command to reference the file:

```
#!/bin/bash

# Absolute path to the config file
config_file="/etc/config.ini"
```

Figure 5.10 – Accessing a file in a different directory

These examples demonstrate how absolute commands are used to specify the exact location of files and directories, regardless of the current working directory. By providing the complete path, you ensure precise file operations and avoid any ambiguity in file references.

In conclusion, absolute commands enable accurate and reliable referencing of files and directories using their complete paths from the `root` directory. It is important for maintaining consistency, facilitating system administration tasks, enabling precise file access and manipulation in scripts and programs, and ensuring the portability of scripts across different environments. By understanding and leveraging the power of absolute paths, system administrators can effectively navigate the filesystem and perform tasks with confidence and precision.

chgrp

The `chgrp` command in Linux is used to change the group ownership of files and directories. It stands for **change group** and allows administrators to modify the group ownership of a file or directory to a specific group. The primary purpose of `chgrp` is to ensure proper access control and facilitate group-based permissions management in a Linux system. One of the key reasons for using `chgrp` is to align file or directory ownership with a specific group. This is particularly important in multi-user environments where different groups of users require varying levels of access to files and directories. By changing the group ownership using `chgrp`, administrators can ensure that files are accessible to the appropriate group and restrict access to others, enhancing the security and integrity of sensitive data.

The importance of `chgrp` lies in its role in managing file permissions effectively. It works hand in hand with other permission-related commands, such as `chmod`, to define access rights and maintain proper ownership. By using `chgrp`, administrators can assign ownership to a specific group, allowing members of that group to collaborate on files and directories while maintaining control over access privileges. The use of `chgrp` is widespread in various scenarios.

Both `chown` and `chgrp` are used to modify ownership attributes of files and directories in Linux. However, they serve different purposes:

- `chown` is used to change both the owner and group owner of a file or directory. It allows you to transfer full ownership of a file or directory from one user to another, including the associated group ownership.

- `chgrp`, on the other hand, is specifically used to change the group ownership of a file or directory while keeping the owner intact. It doesn't affect the user owner, only the group owner.

When to use `chown` versus `chgrp` depends on your specific needs. If you want to change both the owner and group owner of a file or directory, use `chown`. If you only need to modify the group ownership while preserving the user owner, then `chgrp` is the appropriate choice.

For example, in a project-based environment, administrators can create different groups for each project and assign the appropriate group ownership to project-related files and directories. This ensures that only members of the relevant project group can access and modify those resources. `chgrp` is also valuable when managing shared directories where multiple users need to collaborate on files as it simplifies the process of granting or revoking group-based permissions.

Let's take a look at some examples:

- Assigning group ownership to a directory.

  Suppose you have a directory named project that needs to be accessed and modified by the tester1 group. You can use the following command:

```
[instructor@Instructor Desktop]$ sudo chgrp tester1 project/
[instructor@Instructor Desktop]$ ls -la project/
total 4
drwxrwxr-x. 2 instructor tester1     6 May 25 19:01 .
```

Figure 5.11 – Assigning group ownership to a directory with chgrp

- Recursive group ownership change.

  You want to change the group ownership of all files and directories within a directory named data to the tester1 group. You can use the following command:

```
[instructor@Instructor Desktop]$ sudo chgrp -R tester1 data/
[instructor@Instructor Desktop]$ ls -l data/
total 0
drwxrwxr-x. 6 instructor tester1 165 May 25 19:15 project
[instructor@Instructor Desktop]$ cd data/
[instructor@Instructor data]$ ls -l project/
total 1152
drwxrwxr-x. 3 instructor tester1      18 Apr  1 10:26 administrator
-rw-r--r--. 1 root       tester1  154280 Apr 13 18:10 archive.7z
-rw-r--r--. 1 root       tester1     946 Apr 12 18:05 backup.tar.bz2
-rw-rw-r--. 1 instructor tester1 1017971 Apr 11 18:03 backup.zip
drwxr-xr-x. 2 instructor tester1       6 May 21 14:51 ConfigFile
drwxrwxr-x. 3 instructor tester1      24 Apr 11 18:11 restored_web_server
-rw-rw-r--. 1 instructor tester1       0 May 25 18:44 script.sh
drwxrwxr-x. 2 instructor tester1      24 Apr 11 18:02 web_server
[instructor@Instructor data]$
```

Figure 5.12 – Using chgrp -R recursively

By using chgrp, administrators can enforce group-based permissions, streamline collaboration among users, and ensure that files and directories are accessible only to authorized individuals or groups. It is crucial for managing group ownership in Linux. It provides a means to align file and directory ownership with specific groups, facilitating proper access control and enhancing security.

umask

The umask command is used to set the default file permissions for newly created files and directories. The term umask stands for **user file-creation mode mask**. It is a permission mask that determines which permission bits are turned off by default when a new file or directory is created. The umask value is subtracted from the maximum permissions (usually represented as 666 for files and 777 for directories) to derive the effective permissions. This change reflects the more accurate terminology for the permissions being modified by the umask value.

The importance of the umask command lies in enhancing security and controlling file permissions in a multi-user environment. By setting the appropriate umask value, system administrators can ensure that new files and directories have the desired permissions. This helps in enforcing security policies, preventing unauthorized access, and maintaining the integrity of sensitive data.

The umask command is particularly useful in scenarios where multiple users share the same system or when creating scripts and applications that generate files dynamically. By defining a specific umask value, system administrators can establish a consistent permission scheme across the system, reducing the risk of accidental exposure of sensitive information.

It's important to note that setting a more restrictive umask can have certain consequences. For example, if a highly restrictive umask is applied system-wide, newly installed libraries and their associated files may not be readable by certain applications, potentially causing compatibility issues. System administrators should carefully consider the impact of umask settings and strike a balance between security and functionality when configuring umask values.

Let's look at some examples:

- Restricting file permissions for newly created files:

```
[instructor@Instructor ConfigFile]$ umask 027
[instructor@Instructor ConfigFile]$ touch systemconfig.txt
[instructor@Instructor ConfigFile]$ ls -l systemconfig.txt
-rw-r-----. 1 instructor instructor 0 May 25 19:37 systemconfig.txt
[instructor@Instructor ConfigFile]$
```

Figure 5.13 – Restricting file permissions for newly created files

In this scenario, the umask command is used to calculate the default permissions for newly created files. The umask value of 027 is applied as follows:

- 0 in the leftmost position represents the user's maximum permission, which remains unchanged

- 2 in the middle position (masking writing permission) subtracts the group's write permission (2), effectively removing it

- 7 in the rightmost position (masking all permissions for others) subtracts all permissions for others (4 for read, 2 for write, and 1 for execute), leaving only read permissions

The touch command is then used to create a new file called systemconfig.txt. Finally, the ls -l command is used to list the file's permissions, which should reflect the permissions specified by the umask value.

- Allowing group members to read and write files within a directory:

```
[instructor@Instructor ConfigFile]$ umask 002
[instructor@Instructor ConfigFile]$ mkdir dir_files
[instructor@Instructor ConfigFile]$ chmod g+s dir_files
```

Figure 5.14 – Allowing group read/write permissions

In this scenario, the umask command sets the default permission mask to 002, allowing group members to have read and write permissions for newly created files within a directory. The mkdir command creates a new directory called dir_files.

Now, let's dive into the significance of the setgid bit. The chmod g+s command is used to set the setgid bit on the directory. This bit serves a specific purpose: it ensures that newly created files within the directory inherit not only the group ownership of the parent directory but also the group permissions.

For example, if a user creates a new file inside dir_files, that file will automatically be assigned the group ownership of dir_files, and it will have the same group permissions as dir_files, even if the user is not a member of that group. This is particularly useful in collaborative environments where multiple users need access to shared directories, ensuring that files within those directories maintain the correct group ownership and permissions.

- Setting restrictive permissions for newly created executable files:

```
[instructor@Instructor ConfigFile]$ umask 077
[instructor@Instructor ConfigFile]$ touch devportal.sh
[instructor@Instructor ConfigFile]$ chmod +x devportal.sh
[instructor@Instructor ConfigFile]$ ls -l devportal.sh
-rwx------. 1 instructor instructor 0 May 25 19:43 devportal.sh
```

Figure 5.15 – Setting restrictive permissions for newly created executable files

In this scenario, the umask command is used to set the default permission mask to 077, which means that newly created files will have no permissions for the group and others. The touch command is used to create a new file called devportal.sh. The chmod +x command is then used to make the file executable. Since the umask value restricts permissions for the group and others, the resulting file will only have executed permissions for the owner.

sudo

The sudo command in Linux stands for **superuser do** and it allows users to run commands with the privileges of another user, usually the superuser or root. It provides a way to perform administrative tasks without logging in as the root user. The sudo command is an essential tool for system administrators as it enhances security, restricts access to critical operations, and promotes the principle of least privilege. The importance of the sudo command lies in its ability to control and limit access to privileged operations. By using sudo, administrators can grant specific users or groups the ability to execute certain commands with elevated privileges, while still keeping a record of their actions.

This helps mitigate the risks associated with unrestricted access to the root account as it provides a controlled and auditable way to perform administrative tasks.

The primary use of the sudo command is to execute commands as the root user or another specified user with elevated privileges. It requires users to authenticate themselves using their credentials, such as a password, before executing the privileged command. This adds an extra layer of security by ensuring that only authorized users can perform administrative actions, reducing the chances of accidental or malicious system modifications. The purpose of sudo is to promote the principle of least privilege, which states that users should only be given the minimum privileges necessary to perform their tasks. By using sudo, administrators can grant temporary administrative privileges to regular users on an as-needed basis, without exposing the system to unnecessary risk. This helps maintain the overall security and stability of the system, as well as prevent unauthorized modifications or misuse of privileged commands.

Let's look at some examples:

- Installing software as a privileged user.

  In this scenario, the sudo command is used to run the yum install (yum stands for **Yellowdog Updater Modified**) command with administrative privileges. By prefixing the command with sudo, the user is prompted to enter their password and, if authorized, the command is executed with elevated privileges. This allows the user to install software or make system-wide changes that require administrative access:

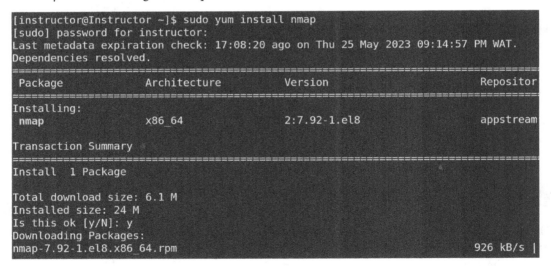

```
[instructor@Instructor ~]$ sudo yum install nmap
[sudo] password for instructor:
Last metadata expiration check: 17:08:20 ago on Thu 25 May 2023 09:14:57 PM WAT.
Dependencies resolved.
================================================================================
 Package          Architecture         Version              Repositor
================================================================================
Installing:
 nmap             x86_64               2:7.92-1.el8         appstream

Transaction Summary
================================================================================
Install  1 Package

Total download size: 6.1 M
Installed size: 24 M
Is this ok [y/N]: y
Downloading Packages:
nmap-7.92-1.el8.x86_64.rpm                                      926 kB/s |
```

Figure 5.16 – Installing software with a privileged user

- Restarting the system and checking services.

In this scenario, the sudo command is employed to restart and verify the status of the sshd system service. By executing the systemctl restart/status command with administrative privileges, users gain the ability to restart and monitor the status of essential services that necessitate root access. This guarantees that any modifications made to the service configuration or updates applied to it are properly implemented and activated:

```
[instructor@Instructor ~]$ sudo systemctl restart sshd
[instructor@Instructor ~]$ sudo systemctl status sshd
● sshd.service - OpenSSH server daemon
   Loaded: loaded (/usr/lib/systemd/system/sshd.service; enabled; ven
   Active: active (running) since Fri 2023-05-26 14:30:16 WAT; 7s ago
     Docs: man:sshd(8)
           man:sshd_config(5)
 Main PID: 15053 (sshd)
    Tasks: 1 (limit: 52372)
   Memory: 1.1M
   CGroup: /system.slice/sshd.service
           └─15053 /usr/sbin/sshd -D -oCiphers=aes256-gcm@openssh.com,

May 26 14:30:16 Instructor systemd[1]: sshd.service: Succeeded.
May 26 14:30:16 Instructor systemd[1]: Stopped OpenSSH server daemon.
May 26 14:30:16 Instructor systemd[1]: Starting OpenSSH server daemon.
```

Figure 5.17 – Using sudo to restart and verify the service's status

In conclusion, Linux permissions commands play a crucial role in managing access to files and directories in Linux systems. These commands allow system administrators to control and enforce permissions, ensuring that only authorized users can read, write, or execute specific files. Understanding the different types of permissions and how to manipulate them is essential for maintaining the security and integrity of the system.

Summary

This chapter delved into the realm of Linux permissions commands, exploring various tools and techniques to manage file and directory access permissions effectively. This chapter began with an introduction to the chmod command, which allows users to modify the permissions of files and directories. Understanding chmod is crucial for enforcing security measures, controlling user access, and safeguarding sensitive data. Through the use of numeric and symbolic representation, administrators can assign specific permissions to users, groups, and others. Next, we explored the chown command, which is used to change the ownership of files and directories. By assigning ownership to specific users and groups, administrators can control access and ensure appropriate responsibility for files and directories. Understanding chown is essential for managing file permissions, facilitating collaboration, and maintaining data integrity. Another important topic that was covered in this chapter was utilizing absolute paths in commands. Absolute paths provide the precise location of a file or directory within the filesystem hierarchy. This knowledge enables administrators to navigate and manipulate files and directories with accuracy and efficiency. Understanding how to work with absolute paths is vital for executing commands, managing permissions, and performing file operations. Additionally, this chapter explored the `chgrp` command, which is used to change the group ownership of files and directories. By assigning files and directories to specific groups, administrators can control access permissions and group-level collaboration. We also covered the `umask` command, which plays a significant role in setting default file permissions for newly created files and directories. By defining the `umask` value, administrators can specify the initial permissions applied to files, ensuring consistency and adherence to security standards. Finally, we delved into the `sudo` command, a powerful tool that grants users the ability to execute commands with elevated privileges. By using `sudo`, administrators can perform administrative tasks that require root access, while maintaining security by limiting the scope of administrative permissions.

In summary, this chapter covered a comprehensive range of Linux permissions commands, including `chown`, `chmod`, `chgrp`, `umask`, and `sudo`. These commands are instrumental in managing group permissions, facilitating collaboration, establishing standardized file permissions, and executing administrative tasks with elevated privileges.

In the next chapter, we will delve into essential tools and techniques that enable system administrators to manage mounted filesystems and perform file manipulation tasks. We will cover four key topics: the `mount` command, the `umount` command, the `fuser` command, and file manipulation using commands such as `cat`, `grep`, and more.

6

Filesystem Mount and Manipulation Commands

The Linux filesystem mount and manipulation commands are a set of essential tools that allow Linux system administrators to manage and manipulate filesystems and storage devices. These commands provide a flexible and efficient way to mount and unmount filesystems, manage disk partitions, and perform various file manipulation tasks. They are widely used in Linux environments due to their versatility, reliability, and ease of use. One of the key reasons why such commands are highly valued by system administrators is their ability to manage filesystems and storage devices. These commands enable administrators to mount different types of filesystems, such as `ext4`, `NTFS`, or `NFS`, making data accessible and usable within the Linux system. They also provide options for managing network filesystems, allowing administrators to connect and access remote filesystems over a network. Another important aspect of these tools is their role in disk partition management. With them, administrators can create, resize, and delete disk partitions, ensuring efficient allocation of disk space and organizing data according to specific requirements. The ability to manipulate partitions is crucial for tasks such as setting up multi-boot systems, creating dedicated storage areas, or managing disk space for virtual machines.

These commands offer an added range of file manipulation capabilities, such as navigating and exploring the filesystem, searching for files, manipulating file permissions and ownership, as well as performing tasks such as copying, moving, and deleting files. This flexibility allows for efficient file management and maintenance operations, ensuring data organization, integrity, and security within the Linux system.

In this chapter, we will explore some of the most important commands in this category. These commands play a vital role in managing filesystems, allowing for the mounting and unmounting of devices, and enabling efficient data access and storage. System administrators heavily rely on these commands to establish connections between devices and the filesystem, exercise control over mounted resources, and carry out various file operations.

In this chapter, we will cover the following main topics:

- Linux mount commands
- The mount command
- The umount command
- The fuser command
- File manipulation using cat, grep, and more

Linux mount commands

Mounting in Linux refers to the process of connecting a filesystem to a specific directory in the directory tree hierarchy, allowing the operating system and its users to access the contents of that filesystem. The mount command plays a crucial role in this process by associating a device or a remote network share with a mount point, which is a directory where the filesystem becomes accessible. By using the mount command, Linux system administrators can dynamically attach various types of filesystems, including local disks, network shares, virtual filesystems, and removable storage devices, to specific mount points in the filesystem hierarchy.

The Linux mount commands are vital tools in Linux for connecting filesystems to specific mount points, allowing administrators to effectively utilize storage resources and provide seamless access to data. Through the mount command, Linux system administrators can configure and manage various filesystem types, set mounting options, and integrate additional storage devices. Mounting is essential for organizing data, facilitating system boot processes, and expanding storage capacity, making it a fundamental aspect of Linux filesystem management.

The mount command

The mount command in Linux is a powerful tool that's used to connect and integrate filesystems into the directory tree structure of the operating system. By using the mount command, administrators can effectively extend the available storage capacity, manage data across different devices, and ensure seamless data access for users. One of the key reasons for the importance of the mount command is its ability to provide flexibility and scalability in storage management. With the mount command, administrators can easily add new storage devices or network shares to the system, making them accessible to users without disrupting the existing filesystem. This allows for efficient allocation and utilization of storage resources, ensuring that data is stored in an organized and accessible manner.

The mount command also plays a crucial role in system boot processes. During boot, the root filesystem, which contains the essential operating system files, is mounted using the mount command. This operation requires superuser (sudo) privileges. Mounting the root filesystem ensures that the system can access and load the necessary files to successfully start up. Without the mount command, the operating system would not be able to locate and access the root filesystem, leading to boot failures and an unusable system.

Let's see a scenario where the mount command is utilized:

- **Mounting NFS shares**: The following screenshot shows the code for mounting NFS shares:

```
kali@kali:~          $ sudo mount 10.10.        :/var /mnt/keno
kali@kali:~       .  $ ls -la /mnt/keno
total 56
drwxr-xr-x 14 root root     4096 Sep  4  2019 .
drwxr-xr-x  3 root root     4096 Sep 18 08:29 ..
drwxr-xr-x  2 root root     4096 Sep  4  2019 backups
drwxr-xr-x  9 root root     4096 Sep  4  2019 cache
drwxrwxrwt  2 root root     4096 Sep  4  2019 crash
drwxr-xr-x 40 root root     4096 Sep  4  2019 lib
drwxrwsr-x  2 root staff    4096 Apr 12  2016 local
lrwxrwxrwx  1 root root        9 Sep  4  2019 lock -> /run/lock
drwxrwxr-x 10 root crontab  4096 Sep  4  2019 log
drwxrwsr-x  2 root mail     4096 Feb 26  2019 mail
drwxr-xr-x  2 root root     4096 Feb 26  2019 opt
lrwxrwxrwx  1 root root        4 Sep  4  2019 run -> /run
drwxr-xr-x  2 root root     4096 Jan 29  2019 snap
drwxr-xr-x  5 root root     4096 Sep  4  2019 spool
```

Figure 6.1 – Mounting NFS shares

We will break down the command for more clarity:

- **The NFS server's IP address**: The command begins with the NFS server's IP address, which is represented by 10.10.XXX.XX. This IP address indicates the network location of the NFS server that hosts the shared directory.

- **Exported share name**: Following the IP address, /var is specified as the exported share name. This refers to the specific directory or filesystem on the NFS server that is being made available for sharing over the network.

- **Mount point**: The command specifies the mount point where the NFS share will be mounted. In this scenario, the mount point is set to /mnt/Keno. This directory serves as the access point on the local system where the NFS share will be integrated.

- Lastly, the ls -la /mnt/Keno command is used to list the contents of the /mnt/Keno directory in a detailed and comprehensive format.

By executing ls -la /mnt/Keno, you will see a detailed listing of all the files and directories present in the /mnt/Keno directory, including hidden files. The output will include information such as the file/directory permissions, ownership, size, modification date, and name.

- **Mounting second storage device and partition**: The following screenshot shows the code for mounting the second storage device and partition:

```
[root@Instructor instructor]# mkdir /mnt/sdb /mnt/sdb1
[root@Instructor instructor]# mount /dev/sdb /mnt/sdb

[root@Instructor instructor]# mount /dev/sdb1 /mnt/sdb1
[root@Instructor instructor]# lsblk
NAME          MAJ:MIN RM  SIZE RO TYPE MOUNTPOINT
sda             8:0    0   30G  0 disk
├─sda1          8:1    0    1G  0 part /boot
└─sda2          8:2    0   29G  0 part
  ├─cs-root   253:0    0   26G  0 lvm  /
  └─cs-swap   253:1    0    3G  0 lvm  [SWAP]
sdb             8:16   1  3.8G  0 disk
└─sdb1          8:17   1  3.8G  0 part /mnt/sdb1
```

Figure 6.2 – Mounting the second storage device and partition 1

Let's break down the command for more clarity:

- This first command creates two directories, /mnt/sdb and /mnt/sdb1, using the mkdir command. The mkdir command is used to make directories in the specified locations. In this case, it creates two directories under the /mnt directory: /mnt/sdb and /mnt/sdb1. These directories will serve as mount points for the corresponding devices.

- The second command attempts to mount the /dev/sdb device to the mount point, /mnt/sdb, using the mount command. The mount command is used to attach a filesystem to the directory hierarchy. In this case, it is trying to mount the /dev/sdb device (which represents the entire disk) to the mount point, /mnt/sdb.

- The third command mounts the /dev/sdb1 device (which represents a specific partition on the disk) to the mount point, /mnt/sdb1, using the mount command. This command successfully mounts the specified partition to the corresponding mount point.

- Finally, the fourth command lists information about all available block devices in a tree-like format. It provides an overview of the block devices present in the system, including their names, sizes, and partition information. Running this command after the previous steps allows you to see the details of the mounted devices (sdb and its partition, sdb1, in this case) and any other connected storage devices.

The mount command without any arguments displays all currently mounted filesystems. To check whether sdb1 is mounted, you can search for its entry in the output. You can do this by using the *Ctrl + F* shortcut, which opens a search pop-up window on your terminal. Type sdb1 in the search field to quickly locate the relevant information. This allows you to easily find out whether sdb1 is mounted and retrieve its associated details. If sdb1 is mounted, you will see its mount point and other relevant information listed:

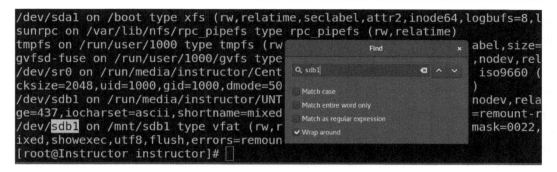

Figure 6.3 – Mounting the second storage device and partition 2

- **Checking the** `/etc/mtab` **file.**

  This displays the content of the `/etc/mtab` file, which contains a list of currently mounted filesystems. Look for a line in the output that corresponds to `sdb1`. The line will include the device path (`/dev/sdb1`), the mount point, and other information:

```
[root@Instructor instructor]# cat /etc/mtab
/dev/sdb1 /run/media/instructor/UNTITLED vfat
charset=ascii,shortname=mixed,showexec,utf8,flu
/dev/sdb1 /mnt/sdb1 vfat rw,relatime,uid=1000,g
exec,utf8,flush,errors=remount-ro 0 0
```

Figure 6.4 – Checking the /etc/mtab file

By checking either the `mount` command output or the `/etc/mtab` file, you can determine whether `sdb1` is currently mounted and find its associated mount point.

The umount command

The `umount` command in Linux is used to unmount or detach a mounted filesystem from the directory tree. It allows system administrators to safely remove mounted devices or network shares, ensuring that all pending read and write operations are completed and any cached data is properly flushed before the filesystem is unmounted. This command is essential for maintaining the integrity of the filesystem and preventing data corruption. One of the primary reasons for using the `umount` command is to safely disconnect storage devices or network shares from the system. When a filesystem is mounted, it establishes a connection between the device or network share and a directory in the filesystem hierarchy. Unmounting the filesystem ensures that any ongoing read or write operations are completed, preventing data loss or corruption. It also releases system resources associated with the mounted filesystem, freeing up memory and improving system performance.

It's important to note that directories mounted with this command are not permanent. They will be unmounted automatically after a system reboot. If you want to make the mount points permanent and have the filesystems mounted automatically at boot, you need to update the /etc/fstab (filesystems table) configuration file with the appropriate entries. This ensures that the mount points are reliable and persist across reboots.

The umount command in Linux is crucial for managing removable media, such as USB drives or external hard disks. Before physically disconnecting the device from the system, it is necessary to unmount it using the umount command. This ensures that all data is written to the device, preventing data loss or filesystem inconsistencies. Additionally, the umount command is used to detach network shares, such as NFS or Samba mounts, allowing users to disconnect from remote filesystems securely.

It's important to note that umount typically requires superuser privileges, so you may need to use sudo to execute it. Executing the umount command is of utmost importance for safely detaching mounted filesystems in Linux. It ensures data integrity, releases system resources, and facilitates the proper removal of storage devices or network shares. By using the umount command, system administrators can effectively manage filesystem connections and maintain the stability and reliability of the overall system.

Let's look at some scenarios where the umount command was utilized:

- **Unmounting a partition**.

  Unmounting a partition ensures that any pending read or write operations are completed, and it allows you to safely disconnect or perform maintenance on the storage device without the risk of data corruption:

```
[root@Instructor instructor]# umount /mnt/sdb1
```

Figure 6.5 – Unmounting a partition

After executing these commands, the system will unmount the specified partition from their respective mount points. You can verify the unmounting by using the mount command or checking the output of the df command to confirm that the devices are no longer listed as being mounted at the specified locations.

- **Unmounting multiple filesystems**:

```
[root@Instructor instructor]# umount /mnt/usb1 /mnt/usb2 /mnt/nfs
```

Figure 6.6 – Unmounting multiple filesystems

This command unmounts multiple filesystems simultaneously. In this example, it unmounts the USB drives mounted at /mnt/usb1 and /mnt/usb2, as well as the NFS share mounted at /mnt/nfs.

The fuser command

The fuser command in Linux is a powerful tool that's used to identify processes that are currently accessing or using specified files, directories, or sockets. It provides information about which processes have active file handles or network connections to a given file or directory. The command is primarily used to investigate and troubleshoot issues related to resource utilization, file locking, and unresponsive processes.

Please note that the fuser command typically requires superuser privileges, so you may need to use sudo to execute it. The importance of the fuser command lies in its ability to help system administrators identify and resolve conflicts related to file access. By running the command with appropriate options and specifying the target file or directory, administrators can obtain a list of **process IDs (PIDs)** that have a file or directory open.

This information can be valuable in scenarios where a file is locked, preventing other processes from accessing or modifying it. By identifying the process responsible for the lock, administrators can take appropriate actions, such as terminating or restarting the process, to release the file lock and restore normal operations.

The significance of the fuser command lies in its role in maintaining the integrity of the filesystem. It ensures that resources tied to a device are properly released before undertaking any maintenance tasks. This is crucial because attempting to unmount or detach a device that is still in use can lead to unexpected errors and data inconsistencies. By identifying which processes are using specific files, directories, or sockets, administrators can address resource contention issues, troubleshoot file access conflicts, and ensure the smooth operation of the system. Furthermore, the fuser command aids in releasing file locks and facilitating safe resource management. It allows administrators to proactively address any potential conflicts or dependencies before making changes to the filesystem. By preventing processes from holding exclusive access to files or directories, the fuser command ensures that other operations can be performed seamlessly. Ultimately, the fuser command enhances system stability, minimizes the risk of data loss, and contributes to the overall efficiency of managing filesystems and storage devices.

Let's explore some scenario-based examples demonstrating the usage of the `fuser` command:

- **Checking for any processes that are currently accessing files or directories**:

```
[root@Instructor instructor]# fuser -v /home/instructor/
                     USER        PID ACCESS COMMAND
/home/instructor:    instructor  11176 ..c.. gdm-wayland-ses
                     instructor  11178 ..c.. dbus-daemon
                     instructor  11181 ..c.. gnome-session-b
                     instructor  11279 ..c.. gnome-shell
                     instructor  11310 ..c.. gvfsd
                     instructor  11328 ..c.. gvfsd-fuse
                     instructor  11339 ..c.. Xwayland
                     instructor  11341 ..c.. at-spi-bus-laun
                     instructor  11346 ..c.. dbus-daemon
                     instructor  11353 ..c.. at-spi2-registr
                     instructor  11356 ..c.. ibus-daemon
                     instructor  11360 ..c.. ibus-dconf
                     instructor  11361 ..c.. ibus-extension-
                     instructor  11365 ..c.. xdg-permission-
                     instructor  11366 ..c.. ibus-x11
                     instructor  11369 ..c.. ibus-portal
                     instructor  11381 ..c.. gnome-shell-cal
                     instructor  11396 ..c.. evolution-sourc
                     instructor  11400 ..c.. gvfs-udisks2-vo
                     instructor  11415 ..c.. gvfs-mtp-volume
                     instructor  11421 ..c.. goa-daemon
                     instructor  11422 ..c.. gvfs-gphoto2-vo
```

Figure 6.7 – Checking for any processes that are currently accessing files or directories

Here's what each part of the command does:

- `fuser` is the actual command that is being executed
- `-v` is an option that stands for **verbose** and provides more detailed information about the processes accessing the directory
- `/home/instructor` is the path to the directory that is being checked

When you run this command, it will display a list of processes, along with their PIDs that are currently using files or directories within the specified directory. The verbose output will include additional details such as the user, the type of access (read, write, or both), and the access time.

- **Checking for processes using a specific file in your current directory**:

```
[root@Instructor Desktop]# fuser .
/home/instructor/Desktop: 12102c
[root@Instructor Desktop]#
```

Figure 6.8 – Checking for processes using a specific file in your current directory

Here's what each part of the command does:

- `fuser` is the actual command that is being executed

- `.` represents the current directory

When you run this command, it will display a list of processes, along with their PIDs that are currently using files or directories within the current directory. This includes any subdirectories and files within the current directory.

The output also shows that the process has a PID of `12102`. This means that the process can be identified by the operating system using this unique identifier and the `c` character in the PID output means that the process has the file open for reading and writing.

The `fuser` command will list the following types of access in the `ACCESS` column:

- `C`: Open for reading and writing

- `R`: Open for reading only

- `W`: Open for writing only

- `U`: Open by a process that is no longer running

- **Determining processes using a network socket**.

  This command checks for processes using the TCP network socket on port `4330`. The `-n` option specifies the network protocol.

```
[root@Instructor Desktop]# fuser -n tcp 4330
4330/tcp:            3930
[root@Instructor Desktop]#
```

Figure 6.9 – Determining processes using a network socket

Here's a breakdown of the command and its components:

- `fuser` is the command itself, which stands for **file user**. It is used to identify processes that are using files or network sockets.

- `-n tcp` is an option that specifies the type of network protocol to search for. In this case, it is set to `tcp`, indicating that we are interested in TCP connections.

- `4330` is the specific TCP port number that we want to check for.

When you run this command, it will provide information about the processes that are currently using TCP port `4330`. It will display the PIDs of the processes, along with additional details, such as the user who owns the process and the command associated with it.

File manipulation using cat, grep, and more

Using commands such as `cat` and `grep` is a fundamental aspect of working with files in Linux and other Unix-like systems. These commands provide powerful and versatile tools for managing and extracting information from files. They are essential for system administrators, developers, and anyone who works with text files regularly. One of the main reasons for the importance of file manipulation commands is their ability to efficiently process and manipulate large amounts of data. Commands such as `cat`, which stands for **concatenate**, allow users to concatenate multiple files or display the contents of a file on the standard output. This can be useful for merging files, redirecting output to other commands or files, and examining the contents of a file without opening it in a text editor. Another essential command is `grep`, which is used for searching and pattern matching within files. `grep` enables users to search for specific text patterns, extract relevant information, and filter out unnecessary data. This is invaluable for analyzing log files, extracting specific lines of code from source files, or searching for specific error messages within a file. Its versatility and efficiency make it an indispensable tool for various tasks, such as data analysis, system troubleshooting, and log file parsing.

In addition to `cat` and `grep`, there are numerous other file manipulation commands available in Linux, each serving a specific purpose. For example, commands such as `sed` and `awk` provide advanced text processing capabilities, allowing users to perform complex operations such as search and replace, pattern-based editing, and field extraction. These commands empower users to automate repetitive tasks, transform data, and manipulate files in a precise and controlled manner. The ability to efficiently manipulate files using these commands enhances productivity, enables effective data analysis, and facilitates automation in various system administration and development tasks. Let's explore how system administrators can leverage these powerful tools in their day-to-day tasks:

- Extracting lines containing a specific pattern using `cat` and `grep`:

```
[root@Instructor instructor]# ls -la output.txt
-rw-r--r--. 1 root root 1083 Jun  8 22:20 output.txt
[root@Instructor instructor]# cat output.txt | grep "pattern"
pattern
pattern
[root@Instructor instructor]#
```

Figure 6.10 – Extracting lines containing a specific pattern using cat and grep

The `cat output.txt | grep "pattern"` command is used to display lines from the `output.txt` file that match the specified pattern. Here, `cat output.txt` is used to display the contents of `output.txt`, and the output is piped (`|`) to the `grep` command. The `grep` command searches for lines containing the specified pattern and displays only those lines. To use `grep`, you can simply run a command such as `grep "search_term" your_file`, where `search_term` is the text or pattern you want to search for, and `your_file` is the file in which you want to perform the search.

- Replacing text in a file using `sed`:

```
[root@Instructor instructor]# sed -i 's/pattern/mad_max/g' output.txt
[root@Instructor instructor]# cat output.txt | grep "mad_max"
mad_max
mad_max
[root@Instructor instructor]#
```

Figure 6.11 – Replacing text in a file using sed

The `sed -i 's/pattern/mad_max/g' output.txt` command is used to replace occurrences of the specified pattern with mad_max in the `output.txt` file and modify the file in place.

Here's a breakdown of the command:

- `sed`: The command for the stream editor, used for text manipulation.

- `-i`: Specifies the "in-place" editing mode, which means the changes will be made directly to the `output.txt` file.

- `'s/pattern/mad_max/g'`: This is the substitution command in the form of `'s/old_text/new_text/g'`. It tells `sed` to search for occurrences of the pattern and replace them with mad_max. The g flag is used to perform the replacement globally on each matching line, not just the first occurrence.

Lastly, the `cat output.txt | grep "mad_max"` command is used to search for lines in the `output.txt` file that contain mad_max.

- Using `awk` to filter lines based on a condition.

This command uses `awk` to filter the lines in the file (`output2.txt`) based on the condition that the first column is greater than 10. Only the lines satisfying the condition are displayed:

```
[root@Instructor instructor]# awk '$1 > 10' output2.txt
    11   untreading
    12   disproperty
    13   fraternities
    14   Muscadet
    15   unhieratically
    16   deltahedron
    17   shut-mouthed
    18   Desiree
    19   Megaloptera
    20   creedbound
```

Figure 6.12 – awk – filtering lines based on a condition

The `awk '$1 > 10' output2.txt` command is used to filter and print lines from a file where the value in the first column is greater than 10. Here's an explanation of each part of the command:

- `awk`: The command-line tool for text processing and pattern scanning in Linux.

- `'$1 > 10'`: The pattern or condition to be matched in the input file. In this case, it checks whether the value in the first column (denoted by `$1`) is greater than 10.

- `output2.txt`: The name of the file from which the command reads the input.

When you run this command, `awk` reads the contents of `output2.txt` and evaluates the given pattern for each line. If the value in the first column of a line is greater than 10, that line is printed to the output.

For example, let's say `file.txt` contains the following lines:

```
5 apple
12 banana
8 orange
15 mango
```

Figure 6.13 – awk example 1

Running the `awk '$1 > 10' file.txt` command will output the following:

```
12 banana

15 mango
```

Figure 6.14 – awk example 2

It filters out the lines where the value in the first column is not greater than 10 and prints only the lines that satisfy the condition.

- Counting the occurrence of a specific word in a file using `cat`, `grep`, and `wc` (**word count**):

```
[root@Instructor instructor]# cat output2.txt | grep -w "disproperty" | wc -l
1
[root@Instructor instructor]# cat output2.txt | grep -w "mad_max" | wc -l
2
[root@Instructor instructor]#
```

Figure 6.15 – Counting the occurrence of a specific word in a file using cat, grep, and wc

This command counts the number of occurrences of the exact word, `disproperty`, in the `output2.txt` file. The output is displayed as a single line count. Here's the breakdown of the command:

- In the first command, `cat output2.txt | grep -w "disproperty" | wc -l`, the `output2.txt` file is passed to the `cat` command, which reads and displays the content of the file. The output is then piped (`|`) to the `grep` command with the `-w` flag, which searches for the exact word, disproperty, in the input. The result is then piped again to the wc -l command, which counts the number of lines (-l). The output of this command is 1, indicating that disproperty appears once in the file.

• In the second command, cat output2.txt | grep -w "mad_max" | wc -l, the same process is followed. The output2.txt file is read by cat, and the output is piped to grep -w "mad_max" to search for the exact word, mad_max. The result is then piped to wc -l to count the number of lines. In this case, the output is 2, indicating that mad_max appears twice in the file.

These examples showcase the versatility and power of the cat, grep, sed, and awk commands in performing various file manipulation tasks, such as filtering lines, replacing text, extracting fields, and counting occurrences.

Overall, file manipulation commands such as cat, grep, sed, and awk play a crucial role in managing and extracting information from files in Linux. They provide powerful and efficient tools for working with text-based data, allowing users to concatenate, search for, filter, and transform files with ease. Their importance lies in their ability to handle large amounts of data, facilitate efficient data analysis, and automate repetitive tasks. By mastering these commands, users gain valuable skills for effectively working with files, enabling them to accomplish tasks more efficiently and improve their overall productivity in a Linux environment.

In conclusion, Linux mount and manipulation commands are vital tools for managing filesystems, mounting and unmounting devices, and manipulating files in Linux. These commands empower system administrators to establish connections between devices and the filesystem, control access to mounted resources, and perform diverse file operations. By skillfully utilizing these commands, system administrators can optimize data access and storage, enforce robust security measures, and uphold the integrity of the filesystem. Overall, Linux mount and manipulation commands are indispensable in ensuring efficient system administration, safeguarding data, and maintaining a secure and well-organized Linux environment.

Summary

This chapter focused on Linux mount and manipulation commands, which are essential tools for managing filesystems, mounting and unmounting devices, and manipulating files in Linux. This chapter began by highlighting the significance of these commands in establishing connections between devices and the filesystem, controlling access to mounted resources, and performing various file operations. The mount command takes center stage as it enables administrators to mount filesystems and devices to specific mount points, ensuring efficient data access and storage. The umount command was introduced as its counterpart, allowing for the safe unmounting of filesystems and detaching storage devices. The fuser command proves invaluable in scenarios where it is necessary to check for active processes accessing files or directories before unmounting or detaching devices, safeguarding against potential data loss or corruption. Additionally, this chapter explored the usage of the cat, `grep`, `sed`, and `awk` commands for file manipulation, including searching for patterns, replacing text, and extracting specific data. These commands provide versatile ways to manipulate and analyze files efficiently. Overall, Linux mount and manipulation commands offer administrators the means to manage filesystems, control access, troubleshoot conflicts, and ensure the integrity and security of the Linux environment.

In the upcoming chapter, which is dedicated to file content and conversion commands, we will delve into a diverse range of potent tools that empower system administrators to effectively handle and modify file content within a Linux environment. This chapter, which is a part of our comprehensive series on frequently used commands, will extensively cover a selection of indispensable commands that are widely employed for seamless file content management and proficient file format conversions.

Part 3: Frequently Used Commands – Part 2

In *Part 3*, we concentrate on commonly used Linux commands for file analysis, conversion, activation, monitoring, troubleshooting, network management, and so on. This section simplifies practical command usage for various tasks.

This section contains the following chapters:

- *Chapter 7, File Content and Conversion*
- *Chapter 8, Linux SWAP*
- *Chapter 9, Monitoring and Debugging*
- *Chapter 10, Linux IPTABLES and Networking*
- *Chapter 11, File Transfer, Downloading, and Log Management*

7

File Content and Conversion Commands

File content and conversion commands play a pivotal role in the daily operations of Linux system administrators. These commands provide a wide array of tools and functionalities for efficiently managing and manipulating file content in a Linux environment. With the ability to access, search, modify, and convert file contents, these commands offer tremendous flexibility and convenience, making them indispensable for administrators. One of the key reasons why file content and conversion commands are extensively used by Linux system administrators is their importance in handling textual data. These commands enable administrators to view and analyze file contents, extract specific information, and perform operations based on patterns or conditions. Whether it's searching for specific keywords, filtering data, or extracting relevant information from log files, these commands streamline the process and allow administrators to efficiently work with large volumes of textual data.

Moreover, file content and conversion commands serve a crucial purpose in managing and manipulating file formats. They provide the capability to convert files between different formats, such as converting between Unix and Windows line endings, character-encoding conversions, and transforming file formats to suit specific requirements. This versatility ensures seamless compatibility and interoperability across different systems and applications, making it easier to exchange data and work with files in various contexts. The extensive usage of file content and conversion commands can also be attributed to their role in automating tasks and enhancing productivity. These commands can be combined with scripting and automation tools to perform complex operations on files, such as batch processing, data extraction, and data transformation. By leveraging the power of scripting and these commands, administrators can create efficient workflows, save time, and ensure consistency in file operations across multiple tasks or systems. These commands are indispensable tools that Linux system administrators highly appreciate for their exceptional capabilities in managing file content, extracting pertinent information, and conducting file format conversions. The significance of these commands stems from their remarkable capacity to handle textual data, efficiently handle various file formats, and streamline tasks through automation, leading to heightened productivity and operational efficiency.

In this chapter, we will explore the fascinating realm of file content and conversion commands, which are highly valued tools for system administrators. These commands play a pivotal role in managing and manipulating file content, extracting relevant information, and performing file format conversions. They offer an array of powerful features that enhance the efficiency and productivity of administrators' tasks. In this chapter, we are going to cover the following main topics:

- The tail and file commands

- The convert command

- Using dos2unix to convert MS-DOS files to Unix

- Using unix2dos to convert Unix files to MS-DOS

- The recode command

The tail and file commands

The `tail` and `file` commands are powerful tools in Linux that play a crucial role in file management and analysis. The `tail` command is used to display the end of a file or continuously monitor file changes in real time. It is particularly useful for monitoring log files, where administrators can view the most recent entries and track system activities. The `tail` command also allows for various options, such as specifying the number of lines to display or continuously updating the output. Its ability to provide real-time insights into file contents makes it an indispensable tool for troubleshooting and system monitoring. On the other hand, the `file` command is used to determine the file type of a given file. It examines the file's contents and provides information about its format, such as whether it is a text file, binary file, or a specific file type such as an image, an audio, or a video file. The `file` command uses a database of file signatures and performs a thorough analysis to accurately identify the file type. This information is valuable in determining how to handle and interpret a file, as different file types may require different processing or manipulation.

The importance of the `tail` and `file` commands lies in their ability to provide critical insights into file contents and characteristics. By using the `tail` command, administrators can quickly access and monitor the latest updates in log files, aiding in debugging and troubleshooting system issues. The `file` command, on the other hand, helps administrators identify unknown or ambiguous file types, ensuring that the appropriate tools and applications are used for further processing or analysis. These commands save time and effort by providing immediate information about files, enabling administrators to make informed decisions and take appropriate actions. Let's examine a few examples:

- **Monitoring a log file in real time**:

    We use the `tail` command to continuously display the last 10 lines of the `syslog.log` file and update the output in real time as new log entries are appended. It helps monitor system events and troubleshoot issues as they occur:

Figure 7.1 – Monitoring a log file in real time

When you run the `tail -f /var/log/syslog.log` command, the cursor will keep blinking because the `tail` command with the `-f` option continuously monitors the specified file for new updates or changes. It follows the file in real time and displays any new content that gets appended to the file. The blinking cursor indicates that the `tail` command is actively monitoring the file and waiting for events to occur. As soon as there are new entries written to the `/var/log/syslog.log` file, they will be displayed in the terminal window, and the cursor will update accordingly.

This functionality is particularly useful for monitoring log files or any other files where real-time updates are important. It allows system administrators to keep track of the latest events or changes without the need to manually refresh the file display. The blinking cursor serves as a visual indicator that the command is actively running and capturing new content as it becomes available.

- **Checking the last 20 lines of a large log file**:

We use the `tail` command to display the last 20 lines of the `messages` log file. By specifying the `-n` option, administrators can customize the number of lines to be shown, which is useful when dealing with large log files:

```
[root@Instructor instructor]# tail -n 20 /var/log/messages
Jun 22 18:49:11 Instructor org.gnome.Shell.desktop[15456]: Window manager warning: W3 ap
ws with a timestamp of 2523641.  Working around...
Jun 22 18:49:20 Instructor org.gnome.Shell.desktop[15456]: libinput error: event3 - Vi
vent processing lagging behind by 13ms, your system is too slow
Jun 22 18:49:23 Instructor org.gnome.Shell.desktop[15456]: libinput error: event3 - Vi
vent processing lagging behind by 13ms, your system is too slow
Jun 22 18:49:39 Instructor org.gnome.Shell.desktop[15456]: libinput error: event3 - Vi
vent processing lagging behind by 14ms, your system is too slow
Jun 22 18:49:41 Instructor org.gnome.Shell.desktop[15456]: libinput error: event3 - Vi
vent processing lagging behind by 12ms, your system is too slow
Jun 22 18:50:01 Instructor systemd[1]: Starting system activity accounting tool...
Jun 22 18:50:01 Instructor systemd[1]: sysstat-collect.service: Succeeded.
Jun 22 18:50:01 Instructor systemd[1]: Started system activity accounting tool.
```

Figure 7.2 – Checking the last 20 lines of a large log file

- **Determining the format or type of a file using the file command**:

We use the `file` command to determine the file type of the `backup.tar.gz` file and provide information about its format. It identifies the file as a `gzip`-compressed file and may display additional details, such as the version:

```
[instructor@Instructor ~]$ file backup.tar.gz  ◄─────
backup.tar.gz: gzip compressed data, last modified: Tue Apr  4 17:17:46 2023, fro
```

Figure 7.3 – Determining the file type of a document

- **Analyzing a binary file**:

  We use the `file` command to analyze the `ftp` binary file and provide information about its format. It identifies the file as a binary file and may provide additional details based on the file's structure and contents:

```
[root@Instructor bin]# ls -l ftp  ◄─────
-rwxr-xr-x. 1 root root 103632 May 14  2019 ftp
[root@Instructor bin]# file ftp
ftp: ELF 64-bit LSB shared object, x86-64, version 1 (SYSV), dynamically linked,
GNU/Linux 3.2.0, BuildID[sha1]=fe93a289ddb32814099d9b6aec32dc566666bc8a, stripped
[root@Instructor bin]#
```

Figure 7.4 – Analyzing a binary file

These examples demonstrate the versatility of the `tail` and `file` commands in various file management and analysis scenarios. Whether it's monitoring log files, inspecting file types, or analyzing binary data, these commands offer powerful capabilities for system administrators. Their ease of use, versatility, and ability to provide crucial insights make the `tail` and `file` commands indispensable in file management and analysis tasks.

The convert command

The `convert` command is a powerful utility used in Linux systems for file conversion and manipulation. It provides a convenient way to convert files between different formats, such as image formats, document formats, and more. The command is highly versatile and supports a wide range of file formats, making it an essential tool for Linux system administrators and users alike. One of the key reasons why the `convert` command is important is its ability to facilitate cross-platform compatibility. It allows files to be converted from one format to another, ensuring that they can be easily accessed and utilized across different systems and applications. For example, it can convert an image file from one format to another, making it compatible with various image-viewing or -editing software. This enhances file interoperability and promotes seamless collaboration. `convert` is commonly used for various purposes, such as resizing images, changing image quality, applying filters or effects, merging or splitting documents, and more. Its use extends beyond basic file format conversion, as it provides additional features for modifying and enhancing files. This versatility makes it a valuable tool in fields such as graphic design, web development, document processing, and multimedia production.

The purpose of the `convert` command is to simplify and automate file conversion tasks. Instead of manually converting files using different software or online tools, the command allows administrators to perform conversions directly from the command line. This saves time and effort, especially when dealing with large batches of files. Moreover, the command can be incorporated into scripts or automated workflows, enabling efficient and consistent file conversion processes. Now that we have discussed the `convert` command in detail, let's put our knowledge into practice by exploring some examples. We will utilize the `convert` command to perform various file conversions:

- **Scenario 1: Converting an image file from PNG to JPEG format**:

  In this scenario, the `convert` command is used to convert a PNG image file to the JPEG format and then save it as a new `output.jpg` file:

```
[instructor@Instructor Downloads]$ file Screenshot\ 2023-06-07\ 211511.png
Screenshot 2023-06-07 211511.png: PNG image data, 853 x 394, 8-bit/color RGBA, non-interlaced
[instructor@Instructor Downloads]$ convert Screenshot\ 2023-06-07\ 211511.png output.jpg  ←
[instructor@Instructor Downloads]$ ls -l output.jpg
-rw-rw-r--. 1 instructor instructor 86573 Jun 23 17:21 output.jpg  ←
[instructor@Instructor Downloads]$ 
```

Figure 7.5 – Converting an image file from PNG to JPEG format (1)

```
[instructor@Instructor Downloads]$ file output.jpg
output.jpg: JPEG image data, JFIF standard 1.01, aspec
, precision 8, 612x792, frames 3
[instructor@Instructor Downloads]$ 
```

Figure 7.6 – Converting an image file from PNG to JPEG format (2)

It can be useful when you need to convert image files to a different format, such as when preparing images for web display or compatibility with certain applications.

Let's break *Figures 7.5* and *7.6* down:

- `file Screenshot\ 2023-06-07\ 211511.png`: This command uses the `file` command to determine the type of the `Screenshot 2023-06-07 211511.png` file. It displays information about the file, such as its format, dimensions, color depth, and interlacing. In this case, it indicates that the file is a PNG image with a resolution of 853 x 394 pixels, using 8-bit RGBA color space, and is non-interlaced.

- `convert Screenshot\ 2023-06-07\ 211511.png output.jpg`: This command utilizes the `convert` command to convert the `Screenshot 2023-06-07 211511.png` file to the JPEG format and save it as `output.jpg`.

The following is a screenshot of the output.jpg file:

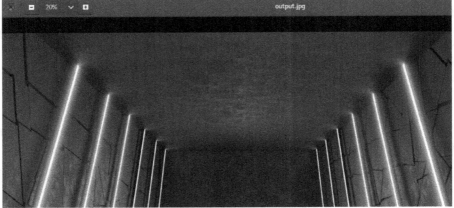

Figure 7.7 – output.jpg

In this case, it performs the conversion from PNG to JPEG, allowing for potential file size reduction or compatibility with applications that only support JPEG images.

- **Scenario 2: Converting a PDF file to a series of JPEG images**:

Using the convert command, you can transform the input.pdf file, which is a PDF document, into a sequence of JPEG images. The resulting images will be named output-1.jpg, output-2.jpg, and so on. This conversion process allows you to extract the content of the PDF and save each page as a separate JPEG image:

```
[instructor@Instructor Downloads]$ file OWASP\ Checklist.pdf  ←
OWASP Checklist.pdf: PDF document, version 1.7
[instructor@Instructor Downloads]$ convert OWASP\ Checklist.pdf output-%d.jpg
[instructor@Instructor Downloads]$ ls -l output*
-rw-rw-r--. 1 instructor instructor 17379 Jun 23 17:37 output-0.jpg
-rw-rw-r--. 1 instructor instructor 15637 Jun 23 17:37 output-1.jpg
-rw-rw-r--. 1 instructor instructor 17153 Jun 23 17:37 output-2.jpg
-rw-rw-r--. 1 instructor instructor 17163 Jun 23 17:37 output-3.jpg
-rw-rw-r--. 1 instructor instructor 16569 Jun 23 17:37 output-4.jpg
```

Figure 7.8 – Converting a PDF file to a series of JPEG images

Each page of the PDF is converted to a separate JPEG image. This can be useful when you want to extract individual pages or convert a PDF into image files for further processing or display.

Let's break *Figure 7.8* down:

- convert OWASP\ Checklist.pdf output-%d.jpg: This command utilizes the convert command to convert the OWASP Checklist.pdf file into a series of JPEG images. The %d character is a placeholder that will be replaced with sequential numbers, creating multiple output files with names such as output-1.jpg, output-2.jpg, and so on. The resulting JPEG images will be saved in the current directory.

- `ls -l output*`: This command uses the `ls` command with the `-l` option to display detailed information about files starting with the name `output`. The asterisk (`*`) acts as a wildcard character, matching any characters that follow `output`. The `-l` option provides a long listing format, showing permissions, owner, group, file size, modification timestamp, and other attributes. This command is used to list the details of the output files created by the previous `convert` command.

This `convert` command presents a versatile and efficient solution for performing file format conversions and manipulations within the Linux environment. With its extensive support for various formats, user-friendly interface, and automation capabilities, the `convert` command becomes an essential tool for efficiently managing and transforming files. Whether the purpose is to achieve cross-platform compatibility, carry out image editing, or facilitate document processing, the `convert` command stands as a dependable means to convert and edit files, simplifying processes and boosting overall productivity.

Using dos2unix to convert MS-DOS files to Unix

`dos2unix` is a powerful tool used to convert text files from the MS-DOS/Windows format to the Unix format. In the MS-DOS format, lines in a text file are terminated by a carriage return followed by a line feed ($\r\n$), while in the Unix format, lines are terminated by a single line feed ($\n$). The `dos2unix` command automatically performs the necessary conversions to ensure compatibility between different platforms. This command is particularly useful when working with text files that need to be processed or executed in a Unix environment. One of the main reasons for using the `dos2unix` command is to ensure seamless file compatibility when transferring or sharing files between MS-DOS/Windows and Unix systems. By converting MS-DOS-formatted files to Unix format, you eliminate any potential issues related to line termination characters. This is crucial when working with scripts, configuration files, or any text-based files that need to be processed by Unix utilities. The `dos2unix` command guarantees that files can be read, edited, and executed correctly in a Unix environment, ensuring consistent and reliable results.

The importance of the `dos2unix` command lies in its ability to facilitate smooth collaboration and interoperability between MS-DOS/Windows and Unix systems. It ensures that files created or modified in MS-DOS can be seamlessly used in a Unix environment, allowing for efficient cross-platform workflows. Additionally, the command is widely used in shell scripting and automation tasks. It allows system administrators to automate the conversion process for multiple files or integrate it into scripts to ensure consistent file format standards. This helps maintain the integrity of files and enhances overall productivity by eliminating manual conversion efforts. We will provide demonstrations and guide you through the following examples:

- **Scenario 1: Converting a single MS-DOS file to Unix format**:

  The `dos2unix` utility is invoked, and it performs the conversion process. The utility detects the file format of `file.txt` as MS-DOS and proceeds to convert it to the Unix format. The conversion involves adjusting the line endings and other formatting elements to comply with the Unix standard:

```
[instructor@Instructor Downloads]$ dos2unix file.txt    ⬅
dos2unix: converting file file.txt to Unix format...
```

Figure 7.9 – Converting a single MS-DOS file to Unix format

In the output of the command, you can see a `dos2unix: converting file file.txt to Unix format...` message. This message indicates that the conversion process is taking place, and the specified file, `file.txt`, is being converted to the Unix format.

- **Scenario 2: Recursively converting all MS-DOS files in a directory and its subdirectories to Unix format**:

  The `find /home/instructor/Downloads/MS-files/ -type f -exec dos2unix {} +` command is used to find and convert multiple files from MS-DOS format to Unix format in a specific directory and its subdirectories:

```
nloads]$ find /home/instructor/Downloads/MS-files/ -type f -exec dos2unix {} +
/home/instructor/Downloads/MS-files/file(1).txt to Unix format...
/home/instructor/Downloads/MS-files/file(2).txt to Unix format...
/home/instructor/Downloads/MS-files/file(3).txt to Unix format...
/home/instructor/Downloads/MS-files/file(4).txt to Unix format...
/home/instructor/Downloads/MS-files/file(5).txt to Unix format...
/home/instructor/Downloads/MS-files/file.txt to Unix format...
```

Figure 7.10 – Recursively converting all MS-DOS files in a directory and its subdirectories to Unix format

Here's how the command works:

- `find`: Initiates the `find` command, which searches for files and directories.

- `/home/instructor/Downloads/MS-files/`: Specifies the starting directory where the search will begin. In this case, it is the `MS-files` directory within the `Downloads` directory.

- `-type f`: Specifies that the search should only consider regular files, excluding directories and other types of files.

- `-exec`: Specifies that the following command should be executed for each file found.

- `dos2unix {} +`: The `dos2unix` command is invoked to convert found files to the Unix format. The `{}` characters serve as a placeholder for each filename found by the `find` command, and the `+` symbol indicates that multiple files can be passed to a single invocation of the `dos2unix` command.

By executing this command, all regular files within the specified directory and its subdirectories will be searched. Once a file is found, the `dos2unix` command will be executed to convert it from the MS-DOS format to the Unix format. The command allows for efficient batch processing of multiple files, reducing the need for individual conversion commands.

`dox2unix` is an essential command designed for converting MS-DOS-formatted text files to the Unix format. Its application guarantees compatibility across various platforms and prevents complications arising from line termination characters. By providing seamless file conversion, it fosters harmonious collaboration and interoperability between MS-DOS/Windows and Unix systems. Moreover, this command holds significance in automation activities and scripting, allowing for streamlined file conversion procedures while upholding file format consistency.

Using unix2dos to convert Unix files to MS-DOS

Now, let's address the *evil twin* known as `unix2dos`. It is a command-line utility used to convert text files from the Unix/Linux format to the MS-DOS/Windows format. `unix2dos` originated in the early days of Unix and was developed to facilitate file compatibility between Unix systems and MS-DOS-based systems. In the Unix format, line endings are represented by a single newline character ($\backslash$n), whereas in the MS-DOS format, line endings are represented by a carriage return followed by a newline character ($\backslash$r$\backslash$n). The importance of the `unix2dos` command lies in its ability to ensure file compatibility and interoperability between Unix and MS-DOS systems. In the early days of computing, Unix and MS-DOS were popular operating systems used on different platforms, and file format differences posed challenges when sharing files across these systems. The `unix2dos` command provided a solution by allowing Unix files to be converted to MS-DOS format, making them readable and usable on MS-DOS-based systems. This conversion process ensures that line endings are correctly interpreted, preserving the integrity of the file content.

The `unix2dos` command is primarily used when transferring text files from Unix/Linux systems to MS-DOS/Windows systems. It is particularly useful when sharing files that contain text-based content, such as code files, configuration files, scripts, or any other text document. By converting Unix files to MS-DOS format using `unix2dos`, users can ensure that the files are compatible and can be properly viewed, edited, and executed on MS-DOS/Windows systems. This command is commonly used in scenarios where collaboration or file exchange is required between Unix and MS-DOS-based environments. For example, let's convert a single file.

This command converts `document.txt` from Unix format to MS-DOS format, but first, let's examine the file:

Figure 7.11 – Converting file.txt from Unix format to MS-DOS format

As we can see from the preceding screenshot, the file we have created, documents.unix, contains content or features that are not readable by MS-DOS-based systems due to their limitations. When attempting to open or read this file on an MS-DOS system, it may encounter errors or display the content incorrectly.

Now, let's convert the file.

The unix2dos --convmode ascii documents.unix command is using the unix2dos utility to convert the file named documents.unix from Unix format to DOS format:

Figure 7.12 – unix2dos converting the documents.unix file to DOS format

When you run this command, a --convmode ascii flag is specified, indicating that the conversion should be performed using **American Standard Code for Information Interchange (ASCII)** character encoding. ASCII encoding is a widely used character encoding scheme that represents text in computers and communication systems. By specifying --convmode ascii, you are instructing unix2dos to convert the file using ASCII encoding.

After running the command, the unix2dos: converting file documents.unix to DOS format... output message indicates that the conversion process is taking place. The original documents.unix file is being converted to the DOS format, which means that the line endings in the file are changed from the Unix newline character (\n) to the DOS format, which consists of a carriage return (\r) followed by a newline character (\n). Once the conversion is completed, the documents.unix file will be in the DOS format, making it compatible with DOS-based systems and applications. This format change ensures that the file will be displayed and processed correctly on DOS or Windows platforms, which expect files to have DOS-style line endings.

The purpose of unix2dos is to facilitate the seamless exchange of text files between Unix and MS-DOS systems by converting the file format to ensure compatibility. It eliminates potential issues caused by incompatible line endings, ensuring that files are correctly interpreted and displayed on MS-DOS/Windows systems. The command achieves this purpose by converting newline characters to carriage return and newline sequences, adhering to the line ending convention of the MS-DOS/Windows platform. This conversion process allows files to be shared, edited, and processed without any loss or distortion of the original content, enabling smooth interoperability between Unix and MS-DOS systems.

The recode command

The `recode` command in Linux is a versatile and powerful tool used for character set conversion and manipulation. Its purpose is to transform the encoding of text files from one character set to another, allowing for seamless compatibility and proper interpretation across different systems and applications. The command supports a wide range of character sets, making it a valuable tool for handling multilingual data and addressing encoding issues that may arise during data exchange. One of the key reasons for the importance of the `recode` command is its ability to ensure consistent and accurate representation of text data. Different systems and applications may use different character sets or encodings, leading to issues such as garbled or incorrectly displayed text. By utilizing `recode`, system administrators can convert text files to a desired character set, eliminating such problems and enabling proper rendering and interpretation of text across various platforms.

The `recode` command finds extensive use in scenarios where character set conversions are required. It enables seamless integration and data exchange between systems that use different encodings, ensuring compatibility and uniformity in text representation. This is particularly valuable in multilingual environments, where text data may contain characters from various languages and character sets. By employing the `recode` command, system administrators can overcome encoding barriers and facilitate smooth communication and collaboration among users working with diverse character sets. By examining the following examples, we can gain insights into the practical applications and benefits of the `recode` command:

- **Example 1: Converting file encoding**:

  Suppose you have a text file encoded in `ISO-8859-1` format and you need to convert it to `UTF-8`. The `recode` command can accomplish this by executing the following command:

```
[root@Instructor instructor]# recode UTF-8..ISO-8859-1 file.txt  ◄──
[root@Instructor instructor]# recode ISO-8859-1..UTF-8 file.txt  ◄──
```

Figure 7.13 – Converting file encoding

Here's a breakdown of the command:

- `recode UTF-8..ISO-8859-1 file.txt`: This command converts the character encoding of `file.txt` from `UTF-8` to `ISO-8859-1`. `UTF-8` is a widely used character encoder that supports a wide range of characters from various languages, while `ISO-8859-1` (also known as **Latin-1**) is a character encoder primarily used for Western European languages. The command performs the conversion by mapping the `UTF-8`-encoded characters to their corresponding `ISO-8859-1` equivalents.

- `recode ISO-8859-1..UTF-8 file.txt`: This command converts the character encoding of `file.txt` from `ISO-8859-1` to `UTF-8`. The command reverses the process of the previous command, mapping the `ISO-8859-1`-encoded characters to their corresponding `UTF-8` representations.

Both commands utilize the `recode` command-line tool, which is commonly used for character encoding conversions in Linux. The purpose of these commands is to facilitate the conversion of text files between different character encodings, allowing them to be correctly interpreted and displayed by systems or applications that expect a specific encoding.

In summary, the `recode` command in Linux is a vital tool for character set conversion and manipulation. Its significance lies in its ability to ensure compatibility, proper rendering, and accurate interpretation of text data across different systems and applications. By employing `recode`, system administrators can address encoding issues, achieve consistency in text representation, and promote seamless data exchange in multilingual environments.

Summary

This chapter has provided us with a comprehensive understanding of various commands that are essential for converting and manipulating file content in a Linux environment. The chapter covered a range of important commands, including `tail`, `file`, `convert`, `dos2unix`, `unix2dos`, and `recode`. These commands offer powerful functionalities for working with files, performing format conversions, and ensuring compatibility between different systems. The `tail` and `file` commands enable us to extract specific portions of files and gather valuable information about file types and formats. The `convert` command proves to be a versatile tool for converting file formats, allowing us to transform files from one format to another.

In the next chapter, we will delve into Linux SWAP commands. These commands are essential for managing swap space, providing additional memory resources, initializing partitions or files for swap usage, and monitoring memory consumption. By understanding and utilizing these commands, system administrators can optimize memory management and enhance system performance in Linux environments.

8

Linux SWAP Commands

Linux SWAP commands are an integral part of Linux system administration, allowing administrators to effectively manage swap space within the operating system. Swap space serves as a crucial component of memory management, providing additional virtual memory when the physical RAM capacity is insufficient. These commands are widely utilized by Linux system administrators due to their importance in optimizing system performance and ensuring efficient memory utilization. The importance of Linux SWAP commands lies in their ability to enhance system stability and prevent issues related to memory exhaustion. By effectively managing swap space, administrators can alleviate memory constraints, allowing the system to handle memory-intensive tasks and prevent crashes or slowdowns. This is particularly valuable in scenarios where the system encounters high memory demands or when running multiple resource-intensive applications simultaneously. The purpose of these commands is to provide administrators with the necessary tools to control and monitor swap space. These commands enable the configuration and activation of swap devices or files, allowing administrators to fine-tune the system's memory management settings. Additionally, they provide insights into memory usage, allowing administrators to monitor swap space utilization and make informed decisions regarding memory allocation and optimization. They are highly valued by Linux system administrators due to their role in ensuring efficient memory utilization and system stability. By utilizing these commands, administrators can proactively manage and allocate memory resources according to the system's requirements. This, in turn, leads to improved system performance, reduced memory-related issues, and enhanced overall reliability.

With these commands, system administrators can effectively manage swap space and optimize memory utilization. Their significance lies in their ability to enhance system stability, prevent memory exhaustion, and allow efficient handling of memory-intensive tasks.

In this chapter, we are going to cover the following main topics:

- The swapon command
- The free command

The swapon command

The swapon command is a crucial utility in Linux that allows system administrators to activate and configure swap devices or files. Swap space serves as an extension to the physical memory (RAM) and provides additional virtual memory to the system. It is located on disk, typically in the form of a dedicated partition or a swap file. The operating system uses this disk space as an extension of the physical RAM, allowing it to move data between RAM and the swap space as needed to efficiently manage system memory. The swapon command plays a vital role in efficiently managing memory resources and optimizing system performance. One of the main reasons why the swapon command is of utmost importance is its ability to address situations where the system's physical memory is insufficient to handle the workload. By activating swap devices or files using the swapon command, administrators can effectively increase available memory resources, allowing the system to handle memory-intensive tasks without encountering memory exhaustion or performance degradation. This is particularly crucial in environments with limited physical memory or when running resource-intensive applications.

This command is widespread among Linux system administrators due to its versatility and flexibility. It enables administrators to configure swap devices or files according to their specific requirements. This includes specifying the location and size of the swap space, as well as defining swap priority levels for multiple swap devices. The swapon command empowers administrators to fine-tune the system's memory management settings, ensuring efficient utilization of available resources. The primary purpose of the swapon command is to enable efficient memory management and optimize system performance. By activating swap devices or files, the command expands the virtual memory of the system, allowing it to handle memory demands beyond the physical RAM capacity. This helps prevent memory-related issues such as **out-of-memory (OOM)** errors, system crashes, or sluggish performance. The swapon command is a critical tool for maintaining system stability and ensuring smooth operation, especially in environments where memory demands fluctuate or exceed physical memory limitations. Let's explore a few examples and leverage their practical applications:

- **Example 1**: The swapon command provides a means to obtain comprehensive details about active swap devices, offering valuable information such as the device path, type, size, and priority. This feature allows system administrators to gain insights into currently enabled swap devices and their associated properties. By executing the swapon command, users can retrieve a detailed summary of the active swap configuration, facilitating efficient monitoring and management of swap resources:

Figure 8.1 – Executing the swapon command to obtain details about active swap devices

In the example, the output displays the following columns:

- NAME: This column indicates the name or identifier of the swap device. In this case, it shows /dev/dm-1, which represents a swap partition on the /dev/dm-1 device.

- TYPE: This column indicates the type of the swap device. Here, it states that the device is a partition type, indicating that it is a dedicated partition specifically used for swap space.

- SIZE: This column displays the size of the swap device. In the example, the size is specified as 3G, indicating that the swap partition has a capacity of 3 GB.

- USED: This column indicates the amount of swap space that is currently being utilized. In the output, it shows 0B, indicating that none of the swap space is currently in use.

- PRIO: This column represents the priority assigned to the swap device. A higher priority value indicates a higher preference for utilizing that particular swap device. In the example, the priority is indicated as -2, suggesting that this swap device has a lower priority compared to others.

- **Example 2**: Now, let's explore a similar command that offers comparable functionality. We will discuss this specific command in detail in our upcoming topic. In this case, the free command is used to display information about the system's memory usage, including the total physical memory (RAM), used memory, free memory, and swap space. We will delve into the free command in our upcoming topic on monitoring memory usage, where we will explain how to interpret its output to assess the system's memory health:

```
[instructor@Instructor ~]$ free -h | grep 'Mem\|buffers/cache'
Mem:          8.0Gi       1.5Gi       5.3Gi       21Mi       1.2Gi       6.3Gi
```

Figure 8.2 – Displaying information about memory usage

The output of the free -h | grep 'Mem|buffers/cache' command provides information about the memory usage in the system. The line that starts with Mem: displays details about the physical memory (RAM) in the system. In this example, it shows that the total physical memory is 8.0Gi (GB). The next column indicates the amount of memory used, which is 1.5Gi. The following column represents the amount of memory allocated for buffers and cache, which is 5.3Gi. The subsequent columns provide information about other memory metrics, such as the amount of memory used for kernel purposes (21Mi) and the available memory (1.2Gi and 6.3Gi).

- **Example 3**: Check the available swap space:

```
[instructor@Instructor ~]$ swapon --summary | tail -n +2 |
awk '{sum += $3} END {print sum/1024 " MB"}'
3072 MB
[instructor@Instructor ~]$
```

Figure 8.3 – Checking the available swap space

The output of the `swapon --summary | tail -n +2 | awk '{sum += $3} END {print sum/1024 " MB"}'` command provides the total size of the swap space in MB.

Let's break down the command step by step:

- `swapon --summary` displays a summary of currently active swap devices and their respective sizes.
- `tail -n +2` filters the output and skips the first line, which is the header line, and displays only the subsequent lines containing information about the swap devices.
- `awk '{sum += $3} END {print sum/1024 " MB"}'` uses the awk command to calculate the sum of the third column (which represents the size of each swap device) and store it in the `sum` variable. The END block is executed after processing all the lines, and it prints the sum divided by 1,024 to convert it from KB to MB, followed by the MB unit.

In this example, the `3072 MB` output indicates that the total size of the swap space is 3,072 MB. This information is useful for monitoring and managing the available swap space in the system.

By combining these commands, you can get an overview of both the free memory in RAM and the available swap space in your Linux system. Additionally, the `swapon` command serves a crucial role in configuring and enabling specific files or devices to be used as swap space, expanding the virtual memory capacity of the system when needed. This enables efficient memory management and ensures that the system can handle tasks that exceed the physical RAM capacity. To sum up, the `swapon` command holds great significance for system administrators. Its primary function is to activate and configure swap devices or files, which adds extra virtual memory to the system. This capability is crucial for effectively managing memory resources, preventing memory depletion, and enhancing overall system performance. The `swapon` command offers a range of options and settings that empower administrators to fine-tune memory management parameters and maximize the utilization of available resources. As a result, it has become an indispensable tool in the arsenal of Linux system administrators, enabling them to optimize memory usage and maintain a well-performing system.

The free command

The `free` command is a powerful utility used in Linux systems to provide information about the system's memory usage. It plays a crucial role in monitoring and managing memory resources, allowing system administrators to optimize system performance and ensure efficient utilization of available memory. The command displays various metrics, including total memory, used memory, free memory, and memory allocated for buffers and cache. By analyzing the output of the `free` command, administrators can assess the memory status of the system, identify potential memory issues, and make informed decisions regarding memory allocation and optimization. The importance of the `free` command lies in its ability to provide real-time information about memory usage. Memory is a critical resource in any system, and monitoring its usage is essential for maintaining system stability and performance. The `free` command offers a comprehensive overview of memory utilization, enabling administrators to identify memory-hungry processes, detect memory leaks, and take appropriate actions to mitigate memory-related issues. It also allows administrators to gauge the impact of memory-intensive tasks on the system's overall performance and make necessary adjustments to optimize resource allocation.

The `free` command is extensively used by Linux system administrators for a variety of purposes. It helps in troubleshooting memory-related problems, such as identifying excessive memory usage or low available memory. Administrators can use the command to determine if a system is running low on memory and take appropriate actions to alleviate the situation, such as freeing up memory by terminating unnecessary processes or optimizing memory allocation for critical applications. Additionally, the `free` command aids in capacity planning, as administrators can gather information about memory usage trends over time to determine if additional memory resources are required to meet future demands. It serves as a valuable tool for monitoring system performance, ensuring optimal memory utilization, and maintaining a stable and efficient Linux environment. In our previous discussion, we explored the functionality of the `free` command. Now, let's further explore this command by examining additional flags and options that can be applied to it:

- Check memory usage:

```
[root@Instructor dev]# free -h
               total        used        free      shared  buff/cache   available
Mem:           8.0Gi       1.4Gi       5.5Gi        21Mi       1.2Gi       6.4Gi
Swap:          3.0Gi          0B       3.0Gi
```

Figure 8.4 – Using the free command to check memory usage

This will display the memory usage in a human-readable format, showing the total, used, and available memory.

- Check memory usage in continuous mode:

```
[root@Instructor dev]# free -s 5
               total        used        free      shared  buff/cache   available
Mem:         8438220     1437524     5759872       22124     1240824     6721836
Swap:        3145724           0     3145724

               total        used        free      shared  buff/cache   available
Mem:         8438220     1437832     5759528       22124     1240860     6721528
Swap:        3145724           0     3145724
```

Figure 8.5 – Using the free command to check memory usage in continuous mode

The `-s` flag specifies the interval in seconds for updating the displayed memory information. In this example, the command will continuously refresh the memory usage every 5 seconds, providing real-time updates.

Overall, the `free` command provides real-time information about memory usage and assists in troubleshooting memory-related problems. This makes it an essential component of memory management. By leveraging the insights provided by the `free` command, administrators can make informed decisions, enhance system performance, and ensure efficient resource allocation in their Linux systems.

Summary

This chapter delves into the realm of Linux SWAP commands, which are crucial for efficient memory management and performance optimization in Linux systems. The chapter highlights two key commands: `swapon` and `free`. The `swapon` command enables system administrators to activate and configure swap devices or files, thereby adding extra memory resources to the system. Lastly, the `free` command provides real-time information on memory usage, aiding in the identification of memory-related issues and assisting in capacity planning.

In the next chapter, we will explore a wide range of essential tools for monitoring system performance, troubleshooting issues, and debugging problems in Linux environments. These commands provide valuable insights into various aspects of the system, allowing administrators to identify and resolve issues efficiently. By mastering these commands, system administrators can maintain the stability, reliability, and performance of their Linux systems.

9

Linux Monitoring and Debugging Commands

Linux monitoring and debugging commands are a crucial set of tools widely employed by Linux system administrators for monitoring system performance, troubleshooting issues, and debugging problems in Linux environments. These commands provide real-time insights into the various components and processes of the system, enabling administrators to identify and address potential bottlenecks, errors, or performance issues promptly. The importance of these commands lies in their ability to ensure system stability, optimize resource utilization, and enhance overall system performance. By leveraging monitoring and debugging commands, administrators can proactively manage system health, mitigate risks, and maintain a reliable and efficient Linux environment. The primary objective of these commands is to equip system administrators with essential tools for effectively monitoring and diagnosing the status of their Linux systems. They can also provide valuable insights into critical system metrics, including CPU usage, memory utilization, disk I/O, network activity, and process information. By closely monitoring these metrics, administrators can proactively identify any unusual behavior, track system performance trends, and detect potential issues before they escalate into significant problems. Additionally, the debugging commands offer robust capabilities to investigate and resolve system errors, software bugs, and compatibility issues. They empower administrators to trace the execution of programs, capture error logs, analyze system logs, and perform troubleshooting steps to identify the underlying causes of issues and implement appropriate remedies.

These commands are among the most widely used tools by system administrators for several reasons. Firstly, these commands provide administrators with real-time and accurate insights into system performance and behavior, enabling them to make informed decisions and take proactive measures to optimize system resources. Secondly, the commands offer a wide range of functionalities, allowing administrators to monitor and analyze specific components or processes based on their requirements. This flexibility makes the commands adaptable to various use cases and scenarios. Additionally, the commands facilitate efficient troubleshooting and debugging processes by providing detailed information and diagnostic capabilities. This helps administrators save time and effort in identifying and resolving issues, leading to improved system stability and reduced downtime.

In this chapter, we are going to cover the following main topics:

- The top, ps, pstree, strace, watch, smartctl, and uptime commands
- The lsof, lsmod, last reboot, last, w, and vmstat commands
- The kill command
- The pkill command

As Linux gained popularity and became a prominent choice for server and enterprise environments, the need for robust monitoring and debugging tools became evident. The Linux community recognized the importance of having comprehensive tools that could provide insights into system performance, aid in troubleshooting, and enable efficient debugging of issues. Over time, numerous command-line utilities, software packages, and frameworks were developed to meet these needs. These tools aimed to provide administrators with real-time monitoring capabilities, detailed system information, and advanced debugging features. The continuous evolution of Linux monitoring and debugging commands has been driven by the ever-increasing complexity of modern systems, the demand for optimal performance, and the need to quickly identify and resolve issues. Today, Linux administrators have a vast array of powerful tools at their disposal to effectively monitor and debug their systems, ensuring the stability, reliability, and performance of their Linux environments.

The top command

The top command is a powerful Linux utility that provides real-time monitoring of system processes and resource usage. It is the go-to tool for system administrators to gain insights into the performance and health of their Linux systems. The primary purpose of the top command is to display a dynamic and interactive overview of system processes, CPU usage, memory utilization, load average, and other critical system statistics. By continuously updating this information, administrators can quickly identify resource-intensive processes, bottlenecks, or abnormalities that may impact system performance. The top command is a vital component of Linux monitoring, offering a comprehensive view of system activity and facilitating efficient troubleshooting.

One of the key reasons why the top command is widely used by system administrators is its versatility. It provides a wealth of information in a compact and easy-to-understand format, making it an invaluable tool for monitoring system health. Administrators can use the top command to observe real-time CPU usage, memory allocation, and process activity. This allows them to detect potential performance issues, identify processes consuming excessive resources, and take appropriate action to optimize system performance. Additionally, the top command provides information on the system load average, indicating the overall system workload and allowing administrators to determine if the system is under heavy utilization. The importance of the top command extends beyond monitoring system resources. It also serves as a diagnostic tool for troubleshooting system issues. Administrators can use the top command to investigate the behavior of specific processes, identify potential bottlenecks, and analyze resource consumption patterns. By understanding how system resources are allocated and utilized, administrators can make informed decisions to optimize system performance and resolve issues. The top command also supports interactive features, allowing administrators to dynamically adjust the display, sort processes based on various criteria, and send signals to individual processes for further analysis or control. This level of flexibility and control makes the top command an essential tool for Linux system administrators. Let's dive into exploring the top command on our CentOS terminal:

- **Viewing overall system statistics**:

   The top command provides real-time insights into system statistics, including CPU usage, memory utilization, and system load. This information is dynamically updated, offering a comprehensive overview of the system's performance and resource allocation:

```
top - 14:19:13 up 5 min,  2 users,  load average: 0.78, 1.84, 0.97
Tasks:       total,       running,      sleeping,      stopped,      zombie
%Cpu(s):       us,        sy,      ni,      id,      wa,      hi,      si,      st
MiB Mem :       total,           free,           used,           buff/cache
MiB Swap:       total,           free,           used.           avail Mem

    PID USER      PR  NI    VIRT    RES    SHR S  %CPU  %MEM     TIME+ COMMAND
   6073 instruc+  20   0 3992736 302952 129488 S   1.7   3.6   0:13.17 gnome-shell
   7269 instruc+  20   0  732720  38480  31640 S   0.7   0.5   0:00.69 vmtoolsd
    544 root      20   0       0      0      0 I   0.3   0.0   0:00.08 kworker/u256
   1474 root      20   0  771928  34340  17248 S   0.3   0.4   0:08.91 tuned
   2651 apache    20   0 2572772  18196   6944 S   0.3   0.2   0:00.30 httpd
   3117 root      20   0  100964   8648   6020 S   0.3   0.1   0:00.32 pmdaproc
   3120 root      20   0   99964   8164   6480 S   0.3   0.1   0:00.87 pmdalinux

      1 root      20   0  176336  14588   8868 S   0.0   0.2   0:07.00 systemd
      2 root      20   0       0      0      0 S   0.0   0.0   0:00.11 kthreadd
```

Figure 9.1 – Viewing overall system statistics

- **Sorting processes by CPU usage**:

   In addition to its regular functionalities, the top command also offers the capability to sort a displayed list of processes based on their CPU usage. This can be seen in the following screenshot:

```
%Cpu(s):       us,        sy,      ni,      id,      wa,      hi,      si,      st
MiB Mem :       total,           free,           used,           buff/cache
MiB Swap:       total,           free,           used.           avail Mem

    PID USER      PR  NI    VIRT    RES    SHR S  %CPU  %MEM     TIME+ COMMAND
   6073 instruc+  20   0 4271100 318288 129736 S   3.0   3.8   0:47.83 gnome-shell
   3120 root      20   0   99952   8168   6480 S   0.7   0.1   0:01.47 pmdalinux
   1127 root      20   0  562784  13380   9612 S   0.3   0.2   0:02.92 vmtoolsd
   1474 root      20   0  771928  34340  17248 S   0.3   0.4   0:12.15 tuned
   1817 root      20   0  265096  11352   8984 S   0.3   0.1   0:00.38 httpd
   3117 root      20   0  100752   8496   6020 S   0.3   0.1   0:01.13 pmdaproc
   6386 instruc+  20   0  589840  11012   8472 S   0.3   0.1   0:00.47 ibus-daemon
  10145 instruc+  20   0  747156  47352  35688 S   0.3   0.6   0:02.54 gnome-terminal-
      1 root      20   0  176336  14588   8868 S   0.0   0.2   0:07.15 systemd
      2 root      20   0       0      0      0 S   0.0   0.0   0:00.11 kthreadd
      3 root       0 -20       0      0      0 I   0.0   0.0   0:00.00 rcu_gp
      4 root       0 -20       0      0      0 I   0.0   0.0   0:00.00 rcu_par_gp
      5 root       0 -20       0      0      0 I   0.0   0.0   0:00.00 slub_flushwq
```

Figure 9.2 – Sorting processes by CPU usage

This feature allows you to quickly identify the process consuming the most CPU resources, as it will be listed at the top of the output. Such capability provides a convenient way to prioritize and monitor CPU-intensive processes. This, in turn, makes it easier for system administrators to identify potential performance bottlenecks and take appropriate actions to optimize system resources.

- **Monitoring memory usage**:

We use the -o %MEM option to monitor memory usage, as shown in the following screenshot:

Figure 9.3 – Command for monitoring memory usage

The result is as follows:

%Cpu(s):	us,	sy,	ni,	id,	wa,	hi,	si,	st
MiB Mem :	total,		free,		used,		buff/cache	
MiB Swap:	total,		free,		used.		avail Mem	

PID	USER	PR	NI	VIRT	RES	SHR	S	%CPU	%MEM	TIME+	COMMAND
6073	instruc+	20	0	4263900	318364	129736	S	3.3	3.8	0:57.23	gnome-shell
2921	root	20	0	870540	219828	25040	S	0.0	2.6	0:18.02	packagekitd
7217	instruc+	20	0	1331724	72248	42284	S	0.0	0.9	0:01.89	gnome-software
6404	instruc+	20	0	773344	63324	51300	S	0.0	0.8	0:00.33	ibus-x11
6225	instruc+	20	0	290004	51940	40196	S	0.0	0.6	0:00.33	Xwayland
10145	instruc+	20	0	747156	47436	35688	S	0.0	0.6	0:03.41	gnome-terminal-
1399	root	20	0	506332	43804	18568	S	0.0	0.5	0:01.53	firewalld
7013	root	20	0	400904	40040	8268	S	0.0	0.5	0:00.93	sssd_kcm
7269	instruc+	20	0	733120	39140	31976	S	0.0	0.5	0:02.78	vmtoolsd
6582	instruc+	20	0	1054536	36852	30032	S	0.0	0.4	0:00.38	goa-daemon
1474	root	20	0	771928	34596	17472	S	0.3	0.4	0:13.65	tuned
7330	instruc+	20	0	765076	32552	17516	S	0.0	0.4	0:00.39	tracker-store
6876	instruc+	20	0	1050160	31672	25228	S	0.0	0.4	0:00.15	evolution-calen
7036	instruc+	20	0	1325872	31288	24988	S	0.0	0.4	0:00.16	evolution-calen
7138	instruc+	20	0	1245372	30904	26508	S	0.0	0.4	0:00.13	evolution-addre
7092	instruc+	20	0	1036700	29160	24872	S	0.0	0.3	0:00.16	evolution-addre

Figure 9.4 – Monitoring memory usage

The top command will display a list of processes sorted by their memory usage, allowing you to monitor which processes are utilizing the most memory.

- **Filtering processes by user**:

For this, we will be replacing username with the actual username we want to filter:

Figure 9.5 – Command to filter processes by user

The result is as follows:

```
 PID USER       PR  NI    VIRT    RES    SHR S  %CPU  %MEM     TIME+ COMMAND
6073 instruc+   20   0 4555536 335892 129736 S   1.7   4.0   1:14.33 gnome-shell

6225 instruc+   20   0  290004  52032  40196 S   0.3   0.6   0:00.39 Xwayland
10145 instruc+  20   0  747156  47448  35688 S   0.3   0.6   0:04.40 gnome-terminal-
5577 instruc+   20   0   89680   9988   8388 S   0.0   0.1   0:00.31 systemd
5585 instruc+   20   0  235948   6020      4 S   0.0   0.1   0:00.00 (sd-pam)
5626 instruc+    9 -11 1457700  14652  11248 S   0.0   0.2   0:01.47 pulseaudio
5656 instruc+   20   0  517020   8100   4920 S   0.0   0.1   0:00.07 gnome-keyring-d
5695 instruc+   20   0  427608  10008   7112 S   0.0   0.1   0:00.05 gdm-wayland-ses
5700 instruc+   20   0   65248   6472   5096 S   0.0   0.1   0:00.46 dbus-daemon
5724 instruc+   20   0  868664  17580  14632 S   0.0   0.2   0:00.38 gnome-session-b
6153 instruc+   20   0  522800   9260   8120 S   0.0   0.1   0:00.05 gvfsd
6193 instruc+   20   0  379816   8668   7544 S   0.0   0.1   0:00.02 gvfsd-fuse
6254 instruc+   20   0  372256   8956   7860 S   0.0   0.1   0:00.04 at-spi-bus-laun
6259 instruc+   20   0   64432   5456   4932 S   0.0   0.1   0:00.04 dbus-daemon
```

Figure 9.6 – Using top to filter processes by user

The top command filters the displayed processes to show only those owned by the specified username.

Overall, the top command is a versatile and essential tool for monitoring system processes and resource usage in Linux environments. Its real-time insights into system performance, interactive features, and diagnostic capabilities make it a valuable asset for system administrators. By utilizing the top command, system administrators can effectively monitor system health, identify resource-intensive processes, troubleshoot issues, and optimize system performance. Its widespread use among Linux system administrators is a testament to its importance and effectiveness in maintaining the stability, reliability, and optimal functioning of Linux systems.

The ps command

The ps command is a powerful utility in Linux used to provide information about the running processes on a system. It stands for **process status** and plays a fundamental role in monitoring and managing processes. The command offers insights into the current state of processes, including their **process IDs (PIDs)**, CPU and memory usage, running time, and other attributes. By displaying this vital information, system administrators can gain a comprehensive view of processes running on their system and make informed decisions to optimize system performance, troubleshoot issues, and manage system resources effectively. The importance of the ps command lies in its ability to offer real-time visibility into the system's running processes. It is a valuable tool for monitoring the health and efficiency of a system, allowing administrators to identify any misbehaving or resource-intensive processes that may be affecting system performance.

The primary use of the ps command is for process monitoring and management. Administrators can use it to view a snapshot of active processes on the system, including their status, resource utilization, and relationships with other processes. This information is vital for troubleshooting system issues, identifying potential bottlenecks, and optimizing system performance.

For example, the ps command can be used for the following:

- **Viewing all running processes**:

    The ps command displays a list of all running processes in the system. It provides information about each process, including the PID, the terminal associated with the process, the CPU and memory usage since it was started, and the command that started the process:

```
[instructor@Instructor ~]$ ps -e
  PID TTY          TIME CMD
    1 ?        00:00:07 systemd
    2 ?        00:00:00 kthreadd
    3 ?        00:00:00 rcu_gp
    4 ?        00:00:00 rcu_par_gp
    5 ?        00:00:00 slub_flushwq
    7 ?        00:00:00 kworker/0:0H-events_highpri
   10 ?        00:00:00 mm_percpu_wq
   11 ?        00:00:00 rcu_tasks_rude_
   12 ?        00:00:00 rcu_tasks_trace
   13 ?        00:00:00 ksoftirqd/0
   14 ?        00:00:00 rcu_sched
   15 ?        00:00:00 migration/0
   16 ?        00:00:00 watchdog/0
```

Figure 9.7 – Using the ps command to view all running processes

- **Viewing processes owned by a specific user**:

    Executing the -e option with the ps command shows a list of processes owned by a specific user, where username is replaced with the actual username. It is useful for providing administrators an overview of processes belonging to a particular user:

```
[instructor@Instructor ~]$ ps -u instructor
  PID TTY          TIME CMD
 5577 ?        00:00:00 systemd
 5585 ?        00:00:00 (sd-pam)
 5626 ?        00:00:01 pulseaudio
 5656 ?        00:00:00 gnome-keyring-d
 5695 tty2     00:00:00 gdm-wayland-ses
 5700 ?        00:00:00 dbus-daemon
 5724 tty2     00:00:00 gnome-session-b
 6073 tty2     00:01:49 gnome-shell
 6153 ?        00:00:00 gvfsd
 6193 ?        00:00:00 gvfsd-fuse
 6225 tty2     00:00:00 Xwayland
 6254 ?        00:00:00 at-spi-bus-laun
```

Figure 9.8 – Viewing processes owned by a specific user

In summary, the ps command is a cornerstone tool for Linux system administrators, providing essential insights into running processes and facilitating process management and troubleshooting. Its real-time information about process status, resource utilization, and relationships enables administrators to ensure system stability, enhance performance, and efficiently allocate system resources. With its versatility and broad range of applications, the ps command remains an indispensable part of the Linux monitoring and management toolkit.

The pstree command

The pstree command is a Linux utility that displays a tree-like representation of running processes on the system. It provides a visual and hierarchical view of processes, showing their parent-child relationships. The command is particularly useful when trying to understand the process structure and how different processes are related to each other. By displaying processes in a tree format, administrators can quickly identify the parent process (init or system) and its descendants, helping them grasp the overall process hierarchy. This information is crucial for system debugging, performance analysis, and troubleshooting scenarios. The pstree command also aids in process management, as it allows administrators to visualize complex process structures and their dependencies, making it easier to identify potential issues and optimize system performance. Let's take a closer look at how it can be used:

- **Viewing a process tree**:

  - The command will display a process tree, showing the hierarchy of processes in a tree-like structure

  - Each process will be listed with its parent process and child processes, making it easy to visualize the relationships between different processes

  - Use the tree structure to analyze the process hierarchy and understand the relationships between different processes

The following output demonstrates the execution of the pstree command:

```
[instructor@Instructor ~]$ pstree  ◄────
systemd─┬─ModemManager───2*[{ModemManager}]
        ├─NetworkManager───2*[{NetworkManager}]
        ├─VGAuthService
        ├─3*[abrt-dump-journ]
        ├─abrtd───2*[{abrtd}]
        ├─accounts-daemon───2*[{accounts-daemon}]
        ├─alsactl
        ├─atd
        ├─auditd─┬─sedispatch
        │        └─2*[{auditd}]
        ├─avahi-daemon───avahi-daemon
        ├─bluetoothd
        ├─chronyd
        ├─colord───2*[{colord}]
        ├─crond
        ├─cupsd
        ├─dbus-daemon───{dbus-daemon}
        ├─dnsmasq───dnsmasq
        ├─firewalld───{firewalld}
```

Figure 9.9 – Viewing a process tree with the pstree command

- **Viewing a PID**:

    When you execute the `pstree -p` command in the terminal, it will show a hierarchical representation of all running processes on your system, similar to the standard `pstree` output, but with each process's PID displayed next to its name. The PID is a unique ID assigned to each process by the operating system:

```
[instructor@Instructor ~]$ pstree -p
systemd(1)──┬─ModemManager(1397)──┬─{ModemManager}(1441)
            │                      └─{ModemManager}(1459)
            ├─NetworkManager(1467)──┬─{NetworkManager}(1468)
            │                       └─{NetworkManager}(1469)
            ├─VGAuthService(1126)
            ├─abrt-dump-journ(1379)
            ├─abrt-dump-journ(1380)
            ├─abrt-dump-journ(1381)
            ├─abrtd(1125)──┬─{abrtd}(1235)
            │              └─{abrtd}(1376)
            ├─accounts-daemon(1140)──┬─{accounts-daemon}(1181)
            │                        └─{accounts-daemon}(1372)
```

Figure 9.10 – Viewing a PID with pstree

The `pstree -p` command can be particularly useful when troubleshooting or investigating processes on your system. It allows you to quickly identify the parent-child relationships between processes and their corresponding PIDs. This can aid in understanding the structure of the processes running on your system and help you identify specific processes that might be causing issues or consuming excessive resources.

The strace command

The `strace` command is a powerful Linux tool used for tracing and debugging system calls made by a process. It intercepts and records the system calls a process makes while running, providing detailed information about interactions between the process and the Linux kernel. This level of visibility is invaluable for diagnosing and resolving issues related to system calls, application behavior, and software errors. By analyzing the output of `strace`, administrators can identify issues such as file access problems, library dependencies, permission errors, or resource conflicts. It is particularly useful for debugging complex applications, troubleshooting crashes, and ensuring correct program execution. The `strace` command is widely used by system administrators, developers, and support teams as a fundamental tool for investigating low-level system interactions and understanding the root cause of various software and performance problems. Please note that `sudo` access is required when using `strace` to trace processes with elevated permissions or system-level access. Both `pstree` and `strace` commands are essential tools in the Linux administrator's arsenal. They provide valuable insights into the process hierarchy and system interactions, helping administrators understand system behavior, diagnose issues, and optimize performance. `pstree` facilitates a clear visualization of process relationships, enabling administrators to comprehend complex process structures and identify possible process bottlenecks. On the other hand, `strace` offers in-depth tracing of system calls, allowing administrators to monitor the interaction between processes and the kernel, thus aiding in debugging and identifying problems with software applications. The importance of these commands is evident in their ability to streamline the troubleshooting process, enhance system stability, and improve overall system performance, making them indispensable tools for Linux system administrators. We will explore illustrative examples of each of the commands:

- **Filtering system calls**:

  - The `strace` command will trace only open and read system calls made by the `ls` command

  - Filtering system calls allows focusing on specific operations and reduces the amount of output generated by `strace`

  - Analyze the filtered output to gain insights into how the `ls` command interacts with files by opening and reading them:

```
[root@Instructor instructor]# strace -e trace=open,read ls    ←
read(3, "\177ELF\2\1\1\0\0\0\0\0\0\0\0\0\3\0>\0\1\0\0\0\200z\0\0\0\0\0\0"..., 832) = 832
read(3, "\4\0\0\0\20\0\0\0\5\0\0\0GNU\0\2\0\0\300\4\0\0\3\0\0\0\0\0\0\0", 32) = 32
read(3, "\4\0\0\0\20\0\0\0\5\0\0\0GNU\0\2\0\0\300\4\0\0\3\0\0\0\0\0\0\0", 32) = 32
read(3, "\177ELF\2\1\1\0\0\0\0\0\0\0\0\0\3\0>\0\1\0\0\0340&\0\0\0\0\0\0"..., 832) = 832
read(3, "\4\0\0\0\20\0\0\0\5\0\0\0GNU\0\2\0\0\300\4\0\0\3\0\0\0\0\0\0\0", 32) = 32
read(3, "\4\0\0\0\20\0\0\0\5\0\0\0GNU\0\2\0\0\300\4\0\0\3\0\0\0\0\0\0\0", 32) = 32
read(3, "\177ELF\2\1\1\3\0\0\0\0\0\0\0\0\0\3\0>\0\1\0\0\0 \256\3\0\0\0\0\0"..., 832) = 832
read(3, "\4\0\0\0\20\0\0\0\5\0\0\0GNU\0\2\0\0\300\4\0\0\3\0\0\0\0\0\0\0", 32) = 32
read(3, "\177ELF\2\1\1\0\0\0\0\0\0\0\0\0\3\0>\0\1\0\0\0200#\0\0\0\0\0\0"..., 832) = 832
read(3, "\4\0\0\0\20\0\0\0\5\0\0\0GNU\0\2\0\0\300\4\0\0\3\0\0\0\0\0\0\0", 32) = 32
read(3, "\4\0\0\0\20\0\0\0\5\0\0\0GNU\0\2\0\0\300\4\0\0\3\0\0\0\0\0\0\0", 32) = 32
read(3, "\177ELF\2\1\1\0\0\0\0\0\0\0\0\0\3\0>\0\1\0\0\0p\16\0\0\0\0\0\0"..., 832) = 832
read(3, "\177ELF\2\1\1\0\0\0\0\0\0\0\0\0\3\0>\0\1\0\0\0360n\0\0\0\0\0\0"..., 832) = 832
'backup (1)'   backup.tar.gz   Documents   file.txt     output2.txt   Pictures    Public      Videos
'backup (2)'   Desktop         Downloads   Music        output.txt    projects    Templates
+++ exited with 0 +++
```

Figure 9.11 – Filtering system calls with strace

In conclusion, both the `pstree` and `strace` commands are indispensable tools for Linux system administrators, each serving unique purposes in system monitoring and debugging. The `pstree` command offers a clear and hierarchical view of running processes, simplifying the understanding of process relationships and dependencies. This visual representation aids in troubleshooting, performance analysis, and process management tasks, contributing to improved system stability and performance. On the other hand, the `strace` command excels in tracing system calls and providing detailed insights into process behavior, software errors, and low-level system interactions. This powerful level of visibility is crucial for diagnosing complex issues and identifying the root cause of software problems. System administrators and developers rely on `strace` for troubleshooting crashes, detecting permission errors, resolving library dependencies, and ensuring correct program execution.

The watch command

The watch command is a powerful utility in Linux that's used to execute a specified command repeatedly at defined intervals and display its output in the terminal. It is particularly useful for real-time monitoring and observing changes in system data over time. The command takes a command-line argument and refreshes the terminal screen at regular intervals to show the updated output of the given command. This continuous refresh provides a dynamic view of the data, making it easier for system administrators to track system metrics, analyze processes, or observe the behavior of certain commands. The watch command is valuable for monitoring tasks that require frequent updates, such as checking system resource usage, log file updates, or network activity. It streamlines the process of obtaining real-time information, allowing administrators to react promptly to any changes or anomalies, making it an essential tool in the Linux system administrator's toolkit.

We can monitor network traffic in real time using the watch command with the ifconfig command:

```
[root@Instructor instructor]# watch -n 1 ifconfig ens160
```

Figure 9.12 – Command to monitor network traffic in real time

The result is as follows:

```
Every 1.0s: ifconfig                                              Instru

        flags=4163<UP,BROADCAST,RUNNING,MULTICAST>  mtu 1500
        inet 192.           netmask 255.255.255.0  broadcast 192.
        inet6               prefixlen 64  scopeid 0x20<link>
        ether               txqueuelen 1000  (Ethernet)
        RX packets 21118  bytes 29836017 (28.4 MiB)
        RX errors 0  dropped 0  overruns 0  frame 0
        TX packets 14091  bytes 1023711 (999.7 KiB)
        TX errors 0  dropped 0  overruns 0  carrier 0  collisions 0
```

Figure 9.13 – Combining the watch and ifconfig commands

Let us now look at another command – the smartctl command.

The smartctl command

The smartctl command is a vital tool for Linux system administrators responsible for managing hard drives and storage devices. It is part of the **Self-Monitoring, Analysis, and Reporting Technology (S.M.A.R.T.)** suite, which is built into most modern hard drives and **solid-state drives (SSDs)**. The command enables administrators to access and interpret various attributes and health information of storage devices, providing insights into their overall health, performance, and potential issues. By using the smartctl command, administrators can proactively monitor the condition of their storage devices, detect signs of imminent failure, and take necessary action to prevent data loss and system downtime. This valuable information empowers system administrators to make informed decisions about storage maintenance, upgrade planning, and replacement strategies, ensuring data integrity and system stability.

We can retrieve the health and status of a storage device using the `smartctl` command:

```
[root@Instructor dev]# smartctl --all /dev/sda    ◄──
smartctl 7.1 2019-12-30 r5022 [x86_64-linux-4.18.0-500.el8.x86_64]
Copyright (C) 2002-19, Bruce Allen, Christian Franke, www.smartmont

=== START OF INFORMATION SECTION ===
Device Model:     VMware Virtual SATA Hard Drive
Serial Number:    00000000000000000001
LU WWN Device Id: 5 000c29 60170bcc6
Firmware Version: 00000001
User Capacity:    32,212,254,720 bytes [32.2 GB]
Sector Size:      512 bytes logical/physical
```

Figure 9.14 – Using smartctl to retrieve the health status of a storage device

The uptime command

The uptime command is a simple yet essential tool for Linux system administrators to quickly check the system's current uptime and load average. When executed, the command displays the current time, the system's running time since the last boot, the number of users currently logged in, and the load average for the last 1, 5, and 15 minutes. The load average represents the average number of processes in the system's run queue over the specified time intervals. The uptime command is invaluable for assessing system performance, resource utilization, and system responsiveness. By regularly monitoring the uptime and load average, administrators can identify periods of high system activity and potential bottlenecks, allowing them to make informed decisions about system optimization, capacity planning, and resource allocation. This tool is particularly useful when troubleshooting performance issues, as it provides a quick snapshot of system health and helps administrators detect anomalies or periods of heavy system load.

By further exploring the provided examples of the aforementioned command, we will delve into how it can be efficiently employed by system administrators:

- **Monitoring CPU usage:**

```
[root@Instructor instructor]# uptime    ◄──
 22:28:25 up 41 min,  2 users,  load average: 0.01, 0.06, 0.08
                                instructor@Instructor:~
File  Edit  View  Search  Terminal  Help
[instructor@Instructor ~]$ watch -n 1 uptime    ◄──
```

Figure 9.15 – Command for monitoring CPU usage

The result is as follows:

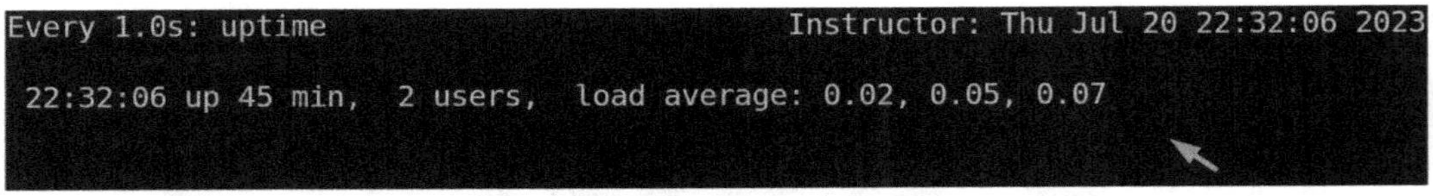

```
Every 1.0s: uptime                          Instructor: Thu Jul 20 22:32:06 2023

 22:32:06 up 45 min,  2 users,  load average: 0.02, 0.05, 0.07
```

Figure 9.16 – Monitoring CPU usage with uptime

In conclusion, the watch, smartctl, and uptime commands are indispensable tools for Linux system administrators, offering valuable capabilities for real-time monitoring, storage device management, and system performance evaluation.

The lsof command

The lsof command in Linux stands for **list open files**, and it is a powerful utility used by system administrators to display information about files currently opened by processes on the system. It provides a comprehensive view of all open files, directories, and network connections, along with the corresponding processes that have them open. This information is invaluable for troubleshooting purposes, as it allows administrators to identify processes that are holding file locks, investigate resource utilization, and diagnose issues related to file access. It aids in monitoring and managing files, network connections, and devices, enabling administrators to detect any abnormal behavior, track file access patterns, and identify potential security risks. Furthermore, the lsof command allows system administrators to perform various administrative tasks, such as killing processes that are holding locks on critical files or identifying processes associated with specific network connections.

The primary use of the lsof command lies in its versatility and flexibility. It can be used to examine various types of resources, such as regular files, directories, network sockets, and character/block devices. This makes it an essential tool for investigating network-related issues, analyzing disk usage, managing mounted filesystems, and checking for potential resource leaks. Overall, the lsof command empowers Linux system administrators with a wealth of information about file and process interactions, contributing to efficient system management and troubleshooting.

We will list all open files in the system using the following command:

```
[root@Instructor instructor]# lsof > file.txt
```

COMMAND	PID	TID TASKCMD	USER	FD	TYPE	DEVICE	SIZE/OFF	NODE	NAME
systemd	1		root	cwd	DIR	253,0	224	128	/
systemd	1		root	rtd	DIR	253,0	224	128	/
systemd	1		root	txt	REG	253,0	1609536	17404791	/usr/lib/systemd/systemd
systemd	1		root	mem	REG	253,0	1598824	491681	/usr/lib64/libm-2.28.so
systemd	1		root	mem	REG	253,0	658072	491821	/usr/lib64/libudev.so.1.6.11
systemd	1		root	mem	REG	253,0	735192	493589	/usr/lib64/libsepol.so.1
systemd	1		root	mem	REG	253,0	1805368	498240	/usr/lib64/libunistring.so.2.1.0
systemd	1		root	mem	REG	253,0	145984	493708	/usr/lib64/libgpg-error.so.0.24.2
systemd	1		root	mem	REG	253,0	66920	498262	/usr/lib64/libjson-c.so.4.0.0
systemd	1		root	mem	REG	253,0	371232	1397406	/usr/lib64/libdevmapper.so.1.02
systemd	1		root	mem	REG	253,0	26704	498327	/usr/lib64/libattr.so.1.1.2448
systemd	1		root	mem	REG	253,0	3083608	491275	/usr/lib64/libcrypto.so.1.1.1k
systemd	1		root	mem	REG	253,0	615744	491278	/usr/lib64/libssl.so.1.1.1k
systemd	1		root	mem	REG	253,0	99656	491111	/usr/lib64/libz.so.1.2.11
systemd	1		root	mem	REG	253,0	24928	498383	/usr/lib64/libcap-ng.so.0.0.0
systemd	1		root	mem	REG	253,0	33480	491106	/usr/lib64/libuuid.so.1.3.0
systemd	1		root	mem	REG	253,0	19128	491675	/usr/lib64/libdl-2.28.so
systemd	1		root	mem	REG	253,0	543304	383813	/usr/lib64/libpcre2-8.so.0.7.1
systemd	1		root	mem	REG	253,0	343680	491109	/usr/lib64/libblkid.so.1.1.0
systemd	1		root	mem	REG	253,0	119760	498477	/usr/lib64/liblz4.so.1.8.3

Figure 9.17 – Using lsof to list all open files in the system

Here's a breakdown of the command:

- `lsof`: The executed command is `lsof`. It provides information about files and processes currently open and in use by the system.

- `>`: This is the redirection operator in Linux. It is used to redirect the output of a command to a file instead of displaying it on the terminal.

- `file.txt`: This is the name of the file where the output of the `lsof` command will be saved. You can choose any desired filename, but `file.txt` is just an example.

The lsmod command

The `lsmod` command in Linux is used to display currently loaded kernel modules on the system. Kernel modules are small pieces of code that can be dynamically loaded or unloaded into the Linux kernel, adding or removing specific functionalities to the operating system. The `lsmod` command provides a concise and organized view of the kernel modules, showing their names, sizes, and the number of references or dependencies they have. The significance of the `lsmod` command lies in its capability to inspect the runtime configuration of the kernel. This command provides system administrators with the ability to confirm currently loaded and active modules in the kernel. This information holds immense importance when troubleshooting hardware-related problems, as kernel modules play a pivotal role in managing device drivers and other critical functionalities.

We will view currently loaded kernel modules using the following command:

```
[root@Instructor instructor]# lsmod
Module                Size  Used by
nls_utf8             16384  1
isofs                49152  1
uinput               20480  1
xt_CHECKSUM          16384  1
ipt_MASQUERADE       16384  3
xt_conntrack         16384  1
ipt_REJECT           16384  2
nft_compat           20480  16
nf_nat_tftp          16384  0
nft_objref           16384  1
nf_conntrack_tftp    16384  3 nf_nat_tftp
nft_counter          16384  33
bridge              294912  0
stp                  16384  1 bridge
llc                  16384  2 bridge,stp
nft_fib_inet         16384  1
```

Figure 9.18 – Using lsmod to view currently loaded kernel modules

Here's an explanation of the output:

- The header row provides the names of the columns in the output. The three main columns are Module, Size, and Used by.

- The Module column lists the names of the loaded kernel modules, and the Size and Used by columns indicate the size of each module in memory and the number of kernel components using each module, respectively.

- The output displays information for several kernel modules that are currently loaded and in use by the system.

- Each row corresponds to a specific kernel module, and the columns provide details about that module.

  For example, let's look at the first row:

  - The nls_utf8 module is loaded, and it occupies 16,384 bytes in memory

  - There is one kernel component using the nls_utf8 module

  Similarly, the other rows provide information about different modules that are currently loaded and their respective sizes and usage.

The last reboot command

The last reboot command in Linux is a simple yet crucial utility that provides information about the system's reboot history. It displays the timestamps of previous system reboots, along with the time since the last reboot. This information is helpful for system administrators to track system availability and uptime. By regularly checking the last reboot timestamps, administrators can quickly identify if the system experienced any unexpected shutdowns or reboots. This information can be vital for diagnosing potential hardware or software issues that may be causing system instability.

The primary use of the last reboot command is for historical analysis and tracking system availability. System administrators can utilize this information to calculate the system's **mean time between failures (MTBF)** and **mean time to repair (MTTR)**, which are essential metrics for evaluating system reliability.

To display the system's reboot history, we use the following command:

```
[root@Instructor instructor]# last reboot
reboot    system boot  4.18.0-500.el8.x Fri Jul 21 12:18    still running
reboot    system boot  4.18.0-500.el8.x Thu Jul 20 21:47 - 23:44  (01:57)
reboot    system boot  4.18.0-500.el8.x Thu Jul 20 21:17 - 21:46  (00:29)
reboot    system boot  4.18.0-500.el8.x Thu Jul 20 14:14 - 15:41  (01:27)
reboot    system boot  4.18.0-500.el8.x Wed Jul 19 22:13 - 22:40  (00:27)
reboot    system boot  4.18.0-497.el8.x Wed Jul 19 20:55 - 22:12  (01:16)
reboot    system boot  4.18.0-497.el8.x Thu Jul  6 21:45 - 23:14  (01:28)
reboot    system boot  4.18.0-497.el8.x Thu Jul  6 21:15 - 21:19  (00:04)
```

Figure 9.19 – Using last reboot to display the system's reboot history

The last command

The last command is a versatile and powerful tool used by Linux system administrators to view a history of user login activity on the system. It displays a list of previous login sessions, including the date, time, duration, and remote host from which the login occurred. This information is essential for monitoring user access to the system, identifying potential security breaches, and investigating unauthorized access attempts. The last command allows administrators to track user activities, detect unusual login patterns, and ensure the security and integrity of the system. Moreover, it facilitates auditing and compliance efforts by providing a comprehensive log of user login events, making it a crucial component of the system administrator's toolkit.

The following example shows the last logged-in users and system shutdown/reboot times:

```
[root@Instructor instructor]# last    ←
instruct tty2         tty2            Fri Jul 21 12:37   still logged in
instruct seat0        login screen    Fri Jul 21 12:37   still logged in
reboot   system boot  4.18.0-500.el8.x Fri Jul 21 12:18   still running
instruct tty2         tty2            Thu Jul 20 21:48 - down   (01:55)
instruct seat0        login screen    Thu Jul 20 21:48 - down   (01:55)
reboot   system boot  4.18.0-500.el8.x Thu Jul 20 21:47 - 23:44 (01:57)
instruct tty2         tty2            Thu Jul 20 21:37 - down   (00:09)
instruct seat0        login screen    Thu Jul 20 21:37 - down   (00:09)
```

Figure 9.20 – Viewing last logged-in users and system shutdown/reboot times

The w command

The w command is a valuable utility that provides real-time information about logged-in users and their activities on the system. When executed, the w command displays a list of currently logged-in users, along with details such as their username, terminal, login time, idle time, and current processes. This command enables system administrators to monitor user sessions, check system load, and assess resource utilization. The w command is particularly useful for managing system resources and ensuring fair distribution of resources among users. It helps administrators identify users who may be consuming excessive resources or causing system performance issues. By having access to this real-time data, administrators can take proactive measures to optimize resource allocation, improve system efficiency, and ensure a smooth and responsive user experience.

The following example displays information about currently logged-in users and their activities:

```
[root@Instructor instructor]# w    ←
 13:39:43 up  1:21,  2 users,  load average: 0.03, 0.08, 0.06
USER      TTY      FROM         LOGIN@   IDLE   JCPU    PCPU WHAT
instruct seat0    login-        12:37    0.00s  0.00s  0.01s /usr/li
instruct tty2     tty2          12:37    1:21m  2:29   0.02s /usr/li
```

Figure 9.21 – Using the w command to display information about
currently logged-in users and their activities

The vmstat command

The vmstat command is a powerful tool for monitoring system performance and analyzing resource usage. When executed, the vmstat command provides a detailed report on various system statistics, including CPU usage, memory usage, virtual memory, disk I/O, and system processes. This comprehensive overview allows system administrators to identify performance bottlenecks, detect potential issues, and make informed decisions about system optimization and resource allocation. The vmstat command is particularly valuable for performance tuning, capacity planning, and troubleshooting system slowdowns or resource constraints. It offers valuable insights into the system's health and performance, enabling administrators to proactively address any emerging issues and ensure the smooth operation of the Linux environment.

The following example is to monitor system memory, processor, and I/O statistics in real time:

```
[root@Instructor instructor]# vmstat  ←
procs ----------memory---------- ---swap-- -----io---- -system-- ------cpu-----
 r  b   swpd   free   buff  cache   si   so    bi    bo   in   cs us sy id wa st
 1  0      0 5510760   4284 1453552    0    0    65    11  103  119  1  2 96  1  0
[root@Instructor instructor]# █
```

Figure 9.22 – Monitoring system memory and processes with vmstat

This command is used for displaying information about virtual memory statistics, system processes, and CPU utilization.

Here is a breakdown of the command:

- procs: This displays information about processes and process states. The r column represents the number of processes in the running state, and the b column indicates the number of processes in the uninterruptible sleep or blocked state.

- memory: This provides details about memory usage. The swpd column shows the amount of virtual memory used (in KB) that has been swapped to the disk. The free column displays the amount of free memory (in KB) available for processes. The buff column shows the amount of memory (in KB) used as buffer cache by the kernel. The cache column displays the amount of memory (in KB) used as page cache by the kernel.

- swap: This displays information about swap space usage. The si column represents the amount of memory (in KB) swapped in from disk per second, and the so column represents the amount of memory (in KB) swapped out to disk per second.

- io: This provides information about I/O operations. The bi column shows the number of blocks received from a block device (such as a hard disk) per second, and the bo column shows the number of blocks sent to a block device per second.

- system: This section displays system-related statistics. The in column represents the number of interrupts per second, and the cs column represents the number of context switches per second.

- cpu: This section provides CPU utilization statistics. The us column represents the percentage of CPU time spent in user-level processes. The sy column represents the percentage of CPU time spent in system-level processes. The id column represents the percentage of idle CPU time. The wa column represents the percentage of CPU time spent waiting for I/O operations. The st column represents the percentage of CPU time stolen from a **virtual machine** (**VM**).

The kill command

The `kill` command is a fundamental and powerful utility in Linux used to terminate or send signals to running processes. In many cases, it requires superuser (`sudo`) privileges to terminate processes that belong to other users or are critical to system operation. Its primary purpose is to gracefully stop or forcibly terminate processes based on their PIDs. The `kill` command allows system administrators to manage and control the execution of processes, ensuring smooth system operation and resource management. One of the most common signals sent by the `kill` command is `SIGTERM` (signal 15), which politely asks a process to terminate, giving it a chance to perform cleanup tasks before exiting. Additionally, the `kill` command can send other signals such as `SIGKILL` (signal 9), which forcefully terminates a process without allowing it to perform any cleanup. This is useful in cases where a process is unresponsive or causing system instability. The `kill` command is crucial for handling unresponsive or problematic processes, preventing resource exhaustion, and maintaining system stability. Moreover, the `kill` command plays a vital role in process management, enabling administrators to prioritize certain processes over others. By sending different signals, administrators can alter the behavior of running processes. For example, sending the `SIGSTOP` signal suspends a process, while sending the `SIGCONT` signal resumes it. This capability is useful for pausing and resuming processes or controlling their execution based on specific conditions. The `kill` command is an essential tool for Linux system administrators when handling process-related issues, managing system resources, and ensuring efficient and reliable system performance.

Additionally, the `kill` command is integral to process coordination and **inter-process communication** (**IPC**). It allows processes to signal each other and synchronize their actions effectively. This feature is critical for complex system architectures, where multiple processes need to cooperate and interact with each other. By using the `kill` command, administrators can facilitate communication and coordination among processes, resulting in better overall system performance and functionality. The `kill` command is also commonly used in shell scripts and automation scripts to manage processes, making it a valuable tool for automating system tasks and maintenance.

The steps for killing a specific process with the `kill` command are set out here:

1. Find the PID of the target process using the `ps` command.

2. Use the `kill` command followed by the PID to terminate the process:

```
[instructor@Instructor ~]$ ps aux | grep vsftpd  <---
root        6939  0.0  0.0  27120   420 ?        Ss
instruc+    7112  0.0  0.0 221944  1144 pts/0    R+
[instructor@Instructor ~]$ kill 6939
bash: kill: (6939) - Operation not permitted
[instructor@Instructor ~]$ sudo kill 6939  <---
[instructor@Instructor ~]$ █
```

Figure 9.23 – Killing a specific process with the kill command

3.   We verify the process using the `systemctl` command, as demonstrated here:

```
[instructor@Instructor ~]$ systemctl status vsftpd   ←
● vsftpd.service - Vsftpd ftp daemon
   Loaded: loaded (/usr/lib/systemd/system/vsftpd.service; enabled; vendor preset: disabled)
   Active: inactive (dead) since Fri 2023-07-21 22:01:20 WAT; 6min ago
 Main PID: 6939 (code=killed, signal=TERM)   ←
```

Figure 9.24 – Verifying the kill process

The pkill command

The `pkill` command is a powerful utility in Linux used to terminate or signal processes based on their names or other criteria. Its primary purpose is to provide a more user-friendly and efficient way to kill processes compared to using their PIDs. One of the key reasons for its importance is its ability to simplify the process of terminating multiple instances of a process with the same name. This is particularly useful when dealing with applications that run multiple processes, such as web servers or database servers. The `pkill` command ensures that all relevant processes are terminated without the need to identify and input individual PIDs. Its ease of use makes it a valuable tool for system administrators in various scenarios, including troubleshooting, process management, and automation.

We can kill multiple processes with the `pkill` command.

Use the `pkill` command followed by the process name to terminate all processes with the same name:

```
[instructor@Instructor ~]$ systemctl status vsftpd
● vsftpd.service - Vsftpd ftp daemon
   Loaded: loaded (/usr/lib/systemd/system/vsftpd.service;
   Active: active (running) since Fri 2023-07-21 22:29:26 W
  Process: 9093 ExecStart=/usr/sbin/vsftpd /etc/vsftpd/vsft
 Main PID: 9094 (vsftpd)   ←
    Tasks: 1 (limit: 52372)
   Memory: 596.0K
   CGroup: /system.slice/vsftpd.service
           └─9094 /usr/sbin/vsftpd /etc/vsftpd/vsftpd.conf

Jul 21 22:29:26 Instructor systemd[1]: Starting Vsftpd ftp
Jul 21 22:29:26 Instructor systemd[1]: Started Vsftpd ftp d
[instructor@Instructor ~]$ sudo pkill vsftpd   ←
[instructor@Instructor ~]$ systemctl status vsftpd
● vsftpd.service - Vsftpd ftp daemon
   Loaded: loaded (/usr/lib/systemd/system/vsftpd.service;
   Active: inactive (dead) since Fri 2023-07-21 22:30:53 WA
  Process: 9093 ExecStart=/usr/sbin/vsftpd /etc/vsftpd/vsft
 Main PID: 9094 (code=killed, signal=TERM)   ←
```

Figure 9.25 – Killing multiple processes with the pkill command

In conclusion, Linux monitoring and debugging commands are indispensable tools for Linux system administrators. These commands empower administrators to monitor system performance, troubleshoot issues, and ensure the stability and reliability of their Linux systems. With a wide range of commands at their disposal, administrators can gain valuable insights into system behavior, identify problems, and implement effective solutions. By mastering these commands, administrators can optimize system performance, enhance security, and deliver a seamless user experience. Overall, Linux monitoring and debugging commands are essential for maintaining the health and functionality of Linux environments.

Summary

This chapter delves into a diverse range of crucial tools designed to empower Linux system administrators in efficiently monitoring system performance and identifying and resolving potential issues. The chapter covers a wide array of commands, each serving a specific purpose in gaining insights into various aspects of the system. From real-time monitoring using commands such as `top` and `vmstat` to analyzing process relationships with `pstree` and debugging software issues using `strace`, this chapter equips administrators with valuable tools to ensure the stability, reliability, and optimal performance of their Linux systems.

Additionally, the chapter explores commands such as `watch`, `smartctl`, `uptime`, `kill`, and `pkill` that aid in repetitive command execution, managing storage devices, terminating processes, and checking system uptime and load average, respectively. The combination of these monitoring and debugging commands equips system administrators with comprehensive visibility into system health, resource utilization, and user activity, enabling them to make informed decisions and proactively address potential issues.

In the next chapter, we will delve into a comprehensive array of indispensable tools designed to facilitate network management and enhance system performance in Linux environments. This chapter covers a diverse range of commands, each serving a specific purpose in configuring and monitoring network settings. From `iptables` for firewall management to commands such as `ifconfig` and `ip` for network interface configuration and more, this chapter equips system administrators with essential tools to ensure smooth network operations and secure communication.

10

Linux IPTABLES and Network Commands

Linux IPTABLES and network commands are essential tools for Linux system administrators to manage and control network traffic and security. IPTABLES is a powerful firewall tool that allows administrators to define rules for filtering, forwarding, and modifying network packets. It plays a crucial role in ensuring network security by blocking unauthorized access, preventing malicious traffic, and protecting sensitive data. Additionally, IPTABLES enables administrators to create complex network configurations, such as **network address translation (NAT)** and port forwarding, to optimize network performance and facilitate communication between internal and external networks, while the network commands in Linux offer a wide range of functionalities to monitor and manage network connections, interfaces, and network-related statistics. These commands provide insights into network performance, bandwidth usage, and active connections, enabling administrators to identify bottlenecks, diagnose network issues, and optimize network resources. Moreover, they facilitate troubleshooting network-related problems, such as DNS resolution, packet loss, and connectivity issues, by offering real-time information about network status and activity.

The importance of Linux IPTABLES and network commands lies in their ability to effectively secure and manage network communication. As Linux-based systems are widely used in various domains, including servers, routers, and IoT devices, the need for robust network security and efficient traffic control becomes paramount. By utilizing IPTABLES and network commands, administrators can implement customized network policies and access control lists, ensuring that only authorized traffic is allowed while blocking potential threats. This granular control over network traffic provides an additional layer of defense against cyberattacks, making these commands indispensable tools for Linux system administrators.

In this chapter, we will delve into the following main topics:

- iptables -t ACCEPT
- iptables -t DROP
- ifconfig, ip, route, and netstat
- hostname and nslookup
- host

Before we proceed, we must also recognize the significant contribution of IPTABLES and network commands in optimizing network performance and resource utilization. By analyzing network statistics and bandwidth usage, administrators can identify areas for improvement and make informed decisions about network architecture and capacity planning. This proactive approach ensures that network resources are used efficiently, enhancing overall network performance and minimizing downtime. IPTABLES and network commands offer versatile functionalities to safeguard network security, monitor network activity, and optimize network performance. Their flexibility and ability to configure custom network policies make them indispensable for managing and maintaining stable and secure network environments. As network security and efficient resource management are critical aspects of modern computing, Linux IPTABLES and network commands remain among the most widely used tools by Linux system administrators across diverse industries and environments.

iptables -t ACCEPT

In the realm of Linux networking and security, the `iptables` command with the `-t` option and the `ACCEPT` target is crucial. `iptables` is a powerful firewall utility in Linux that allows administrators to define rules for incoming and outgoing network packets, granting or denying access based on specified criteria. The `-t ACCEPT` part of the command is used to specify the target of the rule, which, in this case, is to accept the packet. The importance of `iptables` with the `-t ACCEPT` configuration lies in its ability to provide granular control over network traffic, allowing administrators to define rules that govern how data flows through the system. By using `iptables` with the `ACCEPT` target, administrators can explicitly permit packets to pass through the firewall, ensuring that authorized network communication is allowed while potentially harmful or unauthorized traffic is blocked. This capability is essential for network security as it enables administrators to define access rules tailored to their specific needs, protecting the system from malicious attacks and unauthorized access.

Next, we will delve into practical examples of utilizing the `iptables -t ACCEPT` command:

1. Check the current `iptables` rules to understand the existing configuration:

```
[root@Instructor instructor]# iptables -L  ◄───
Chain INPUT (policy ACCEPT)
target      prot opt source               destination
LIBVIRT_INP  all  --   anywhere             anywhere

Chain FORWARD (policy ACCEPT)
target      prot opt source               destination
LIBVIRT_FWX  all  --   anywhere             anywhere
LIBVIRT_FWI  all  --   anywhere             anywhere
LIBVIRT_FWO  all  --   anywhere             anywhere

Chain OUTPUT (policy ACCEPT)
target      prot opt source               destination
LIBVIRT_OUT  all  --   anywhere             anywhere
```

Figure 10.1 – Viewing current iptables rules

2. Allow incoming SSH connections from the specified IP address (`192.168.x.xxx`).

    When you use the `iptables` command, it will add a rule to the `INPUT` chain of the `iptables` firewall, allowing incoming TCP traffic from the source IP address, `192.168.x.xxx`, to the destination port, `22` (which is the default port for SSH), to be accepted and allowed through the firewall. However, if the rule is successfully added, no confirmation or message will be displayed in the Terminal.

3. To check the rules in the `iptables` firewall and verify that the new rule has been added, you can use the following command:

```
[root@Instructor instructor]# iptables -A INPUT -s 192              -p tcp --dport 22 -j ACCEPT
[root@Instructor instructor]# iptables -L  ◄───
Chain INPUT (policy ACCEPT)
target      prot opt source               destination
LIBVIRT_INP  all  --   anywhere             anywhere
ACCEPT      tcp  --   Instructor           anywhere             tcp dpt:ssh
ACCEPT      tcp  --   19                   anywhere             tcp dpt:ssh  ◄───

Chain FORWARD (policy ACCEPT)
target      prot opt source               destination
LIBVIRT_FWX  all  --   anywhere             anywhere
LIBVIRT_FWI  all  --   anywhere             anywhere
LIBVIRT_FWO  all  --   anywhere             anywhere
```

Figure 10.2 – Allowing SSH connections from specified IPs

iptables -t DROP

The `iptables` command in Linux is a fundamental tool for managing network traffic and enforcing security policies. It allows system administrators to define rules for incoming and outgoing network packets, granting or denying access based on specified criteria. The `-t` flag, used in conjunction with `iptables`, specifies the target table within which the rule will be defined. In the context of security, the DROP target is particularly significant. When combined with `-t`, as in `iptables -t DROP`, it signifies that incoming network packets matching the defined rule will be dropped or blocked, effectively denying access. In Linux, the `iptables` command allows administrators to manage and manipulate the **netfilter** firewall rules, which determine how the kernel handles network packets. Administrators can block malicious or suspicious traffic from entering the network by selectively dropping packets

For experts, `iptables -t DROP` provides fine-grained control over network traffic, enabling them to customize rules and mitigate complex security risks effectively. Moreover, by strategically using the DROP target, administrators can prevent certain types of attacks, such as **denial-of-service (DoS)** and **distributed denial-of-service (DDoS)** attacks, from overwhelming the system and disrupting its services or this command can be used to block specific IP addresses known for malicious activities, limit access to certain services, or protect vulnerable ports.

The primary use and purpose of the DROP action is to filter and control incoming network traffic based on defined criteria, such as source IP address, destination port, and protocol type. By specifying rules, administrators can determine which packets should be dropped, preventing them from reaching the intended destination. This command plays a crucial role in crafting network security policies as it allows administrators to define rules that align with their organization's security requirements and regulatory compliance. By efficiently managing network traffic with `iptables -t DROP`, Linux system administrators can create a robust and secure networking environment that safeguards their infrastructure from potential threats. Let's delve into practical examples of utilizing the `iptables -t DROP` command.

To block incoming traffic from the specified IP address, use the following command:

```
[root@Instructor instructor]# iptables -A INPUT -s 192.168.      -j DROP
[root@Instructor instructor]# iptables -L
Chain INPUT (policy ACCEPT)
target      prot opt source              destination
LIBVIRT INP all  --  anywhere            anywhere
ACCEPT      tcp  --  Instructor          anywhere            tcp dpt:ssh
ACCEPT      tcp  --                      anywhere            tcp dpt:ssh
DROP        all  --  loc                 anywhere
```

Figure 10.3 – Blocking incoming traffic

This command adds a new rule to the `INPUT` chain of `iptables`, which drops any incoming packets from the IP address, `192.168.x.xxx`.

ifconfig, ip, route, and netstat

The `ifconfig` command, short for **interface configuration**, is a powerful utility in Linux that's used to view, configure, and manage network interfaces on a system. It provides essential information about the network interfaces, such as IP addresses, subnet masks, MAC addresses, and link status. The `ifconfig` command remains a fundamental command for network management and advanced configurations. Experts can leverage `ifconfig` to manually configure network interfaces, set static IP addresses, enable or disable specific interfaces, and modify advanced network settings. It is particularly useful in server environments, where multiple network interfaces are present, and specific configurations are required. Additionally, `ifconfig` can be combined with other commands for network diagnostics and performance monitoring. While `ifconfig` is widely used and familiar to Linux administrators, it is worth noting that some Linux distributions are deprecating this command in favor of newer tools such as `ip`. Nonetheless, `ifconfig` remains relevant and valuable in many Linux environments, providing a simple yet effective means to manage network interfaces.

ip, route, and netstat

The `ip`, `route`, and `netstat` commands are essential Linux network tools that collectively offer a comprehensive set of functionalities for network configuration, routing, and monitoring. For both beginners and experts, these commands provide vital insights into network setup, traffic routing, and active network connections. `ip` is a versatile command that replaces many functionalities of `ifconfig`, providing advanced configuration options for network interfaces, routing tables, and tunnels. `route` allows users to view and modify the system's IP routing table, controlling how packets are forwarded between networks. `netstat` offers a detailed overview of network connections, open ports, and active network statistics. Note that mastering these commands is essential for understanding network setup and troubleshooting. The `ip` command offers a more modern and feature-rich alternative to `ifconfig`, providing a broader range of functionalities for network configuration and management. `route` assists beginners in grasping the concept of routing and how data packets are directed through the network. `netstat` helps beginners identify active network connections, monitor port usage, and diagnose network issues, such as identifying processes that are consuming network resources. As beginners explore Linux networking, these commands equip them with the necessary tools to comprehend and configure network settings effectively. These commands become indispensable in network administration and troubleshooting. For example, the `ip` command's advanced features enable experts to set up complex network configurations, create virtual interfaces, manage routing tables, and implement NAT. `route` allows experts to fine-tune routing rules, optimize traffic flow, and manage multiple network interfaces efficiently. `netstat` is a valuable tool for experts to monitor network performance, detect suspicious network activity, and identify potential security threats. In combination, these commands provide experts with comprehensive network visibility, enabling them to maintain a robust and secure networking environment. The depth and versatility of `ip`, `route`, and `netstat` make them indispensable tools for Linux network administrators, allowing them to optimize network performance, troubleshoot issues, and ensure smooth and reliable network connectivity. Now that we have gained an understanding of these commands, let's apply them in practical examples:

- To view the current network interfaces and their configurations, run the following commands:

```
[root@Instructor instructor]# ifconfig    ←
ens160: flags=4163<UP,BROADCAST,RUNNING,MULTICAST>  mtu 1500
        inet 192.:            netmask 255.255.255.0  broadcast 192.
        inet6 fe80::::                    prefixlen 64  scopeid 0x20<link>
        ether 00:0c            txqueuelen 1000  (Ethernet)
        RX packets 31653  bytes 39672335 (37.8 MiB)
        RX errors 0  dropped 0  overruns 0  frame 0
        TX packets 19166  bytes 1415493 (1.3 MiB)
        TX errors 0  dropped 0 overruns 0  carrier 0  collisions 0

lo: flags=73<UP,LOOPBACK,RUNNING>  mtu 65536
        inet 127.0.0.1  netmask 255.0.0.0
        inet6 ::1  prefixlen 128  scopeid 0x10<host>
        loop  txqueuelen 1000  (Local Loopback)
        RX packets 3318  bytes 200272 (195.5 KiB)
        RX errors 0  dropped 0  overruns 0  frame 0
        TX packets 3318  bytes 200272 (195.5 KiB)
        TX errors 0  dropped 0 overruns 0  carrier 0  collisions 0
```

Figure 10.4 – Viewing current network interfaces

- Let's utilize the `ip` command to view the network interface:

```
[root@Instructor instructor]# ip addr show    ←
1: lo: <LOOPBACK,UP,LOWER_UP> mtu 65536 qdisc noqueue state UNKNOWN
    link/loopback 00:00:00:00:00:00 brd 00:00:00:00:00:00
    inet 127.0.0.1/8 scope host lo
       valid_lft forever preferred_lft forever
    inet6 ::1/128 scope host
       valid_lft forever preferred_lft forever
2: ens160: <BROADCAST,MULTICAST,UP,LOWER_UP> mtu 1500 qdisc mq state
    link/ether 00:(             rd ff:ff:ff:ff:ff:ff
    altname enp3s0
    inet 192.             brd 192.          scope global dynamic nop
       valid_lft 72506sec preferred_lft 72506sec
    inet6 fe80::20c::                 scope link noprefixroute
       valid_lft forever preferred_lft forever
```

Figure 10.5 – Viewing current network interfaces

This will display a list of all network interfaces, along with their IP addresses, subnet masks, and other network configuration details.

- To add a static route to the routing and viewing network statistics, such as open network connections and listening ports, run the following command:

```
[root@Instructor instructor]# ip route add 192.168.   /24 via 192.168 .1
[root@Instructor instructor]# netstat -tuln
Active Internet connections (only servers)
Proto Recv-Q Send-Q Local Address          Foreign Address          State
tcp        0      0 192.                    0.0.0.0:*                LISTEN
tcp        0      0 0.0.0.0:22              0.0.0.0:*                LISTEN
tcp        0      0 127.0.0.1:631           0.0.0.0:*                LISTEN
tcp        0      0 127.0.0.1:44321         0.0.0.0:*                LISTEN
tcp        0      0 127.0.0.1:4330          0.0.0.0:*                LISTEN
tcp        0      0 0.0.0.0:111             0.0.0.0:*                LISTEN
tcp6       0      0 :::21                   :::*                     LISTEN
tcp6       0      0 :::22                   :::*                     LISTEN
```

Figure 10.6 – Routing and viewing network statistics

This command adds a route to the `192.168.x.0/24` subnet via the `192.168.x.x` gateway. Then, the next command displays a list of all active network connections and the corresponding ports.

The `-tuln` options in the `netstat` command are used to display a list of all open TCP and UDP ports on the system, in numerical format:

- `-t`: Show TCP connections
- `-u`: Show UDP connections
- `-l`: Show listening ports
- `-n`: Show numerical addresses instead of trying to determine symbolic hosts, ports, or usernames

What is the impact of the `ip route add` command?

The `ip route add` command is used to add a new route to the routing table. The routing table is a database that the kernel uses to determine how to route packets to their destinations.

The impact of the `ip route add` command is that it will allow the system to communicate with devices on the `192.168.x.x/24` network.

The `ip route add` command can be used to add routes to any network, not just local networks. This can be useful for configuring routing between different networks or for routing packets over VPNs.

Hostname and nslookup

The `hostname` command in Linux is used to view or set the system's hostname. The hostname is a unique identifier given to a device on a network, and it helps distinguish it from other devices. The hostname is essential for various networking tasks, such as accessing the device over a network and identifying it when communicating with other devices. The `hostname` command provides a simple and efficient way to manage the system's hostname, making it an indispensable tool for Linux administrators. The `hostname` command's importance lies in its role in networking and system identification. A meaningful hostname enhances the manageability and organization of systems within a network, simplifying administrative tasks and making it easier to locate and communicate with specific devices. Additionally, the hostname is often used in log files and system monitoring tools to provide context and identify the origin of events, aiding in troubleshooting and auditing. For servers hosting multiple services, setting a descriptive hostname helps users and administrators identify the purpose or function of each server, streamlining system management and reducing the risk of confusion. Overall, the hostname command plays a vital role in maintaining efficient network operations and effective system administration.

The nslookup command is a powerful tool that's used to query **domain name system (DNS)** servers to obtain information about domain names and IP addresses. DNS is the system that translates human-readable domain names (for example, www.example.com) into IP addresses (for example, 192.168.x.x) that computers can understand. The nslookup command provides a way to interactively query DNS servers, making it an invaluable utility for network administrators and developers. The importance of the nslookup command lies in its ability to troubleshoot DNS-related issues and validate DNS configurations. It allows administrators to verify DNS records, check if a domain is resolving to the correct IP address, and troubleshoot DNS resolution problems. By querying specific DNS servers with the nslookup command, administrators can ensure the accuracy of DNS information and diagnose DNS-related problems, such as incorrect DNS entries or misconfigured DNS servers. Additionally, the nslookup command can be used to test the response time of DNS servers, helping administrators identify potential bottlenecks in the DNS infrastructure and optimize DNS performance. Overall, the nslookup command is an indispensable tool for managing and troubleshooting DNS in Linux environments, ensuring the smooth functioning of network communication and internet connectivity.

Now, let's apply these commands in practical examples:

- To display the system's hostname, simply enter the following command:

```
[instructor@Instructor ~]$ hostname
Instructor   ←
[instructor@Instructor ~]$
```

Figure 10.7 – Displaying the system's hostname

This command will output the hostname of your Linux system. The hostname is a unique name that identifies the system on the network and is used for local and remote communication.

- To perform a DNS name resolution for a specific domain (for example, www.example.com), you can use the nslookup or host command. Here's an example:

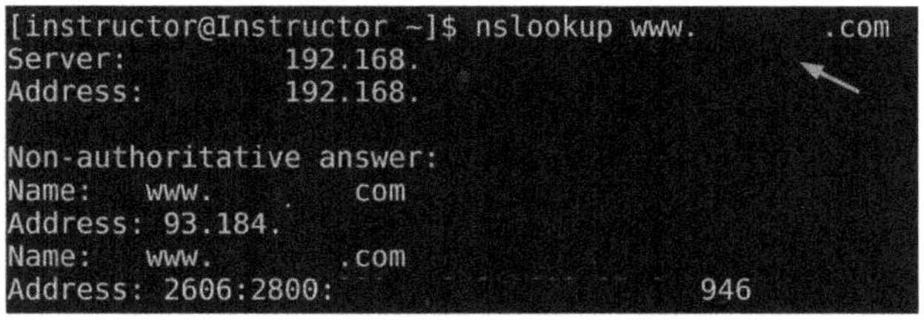

Figure 10.8 – Performing DNS name resolution

host

The host command is a powerful utility that's used for DNS-related tasks in Linux systems. It is primarily used to perform DNS lookups, translating domain names into IP addresses, and vice versa. The importance of the host command lies in its role as a versatile tool for network administrators and developers to resolve DNS queries and troubleshoot domain resolution issues. By using the host command, administrators can verify if a domain name is correctly mapped to an IP address and vice versa, ensuring proper communication between devices across the internet. Additionally, the host command provides information about DNS records, such as the authoritative name server for a domain, **time-to-live** (TTL) values, and **mail exchange** (MX) records, aiding in DNS configuration and debugging tasks. The host command is commonly used in various scenarios, such as checking DNS propagation after domain changes, diagnosing DNS resolution problems, and verifying domain name configurations. Its ease of use and ability to provide real-time DNS information make it an essential tool for both novices and experts in the field of networking and system administration. Now, let's delve into practical examples to better understand the usage of these commands:

- Like nslookup, we can also perform the same actions using the host command.

  Both commands will display the IP addresses associated with the domain name provided. The DNS is responsible for translating human-readable domain names into IP addresses that computers can understand. These commands allow you to check if DNS resolution is working correctly and retrieve the IP address of a specific domain:

Figure 10.9 – Checking DNS resolution with the host command

In summary, Linux IPTABLES and network commands play a vital role in a Linux system administrator's arsenal, providing essential functionalities to ensure network security, monitor network activity, and optimize overall performance.

Summary

In this chapter, we explored essential tools for Linux system administrators that provide them with powerful capabilities to manage network communication effectively and enhance network security. This chapter covered a wide range of commands, each serving a specific purpose in configuring network rules and gaining valuable insights into network activity. The `iptables` commands, such as `iptables -t ACCEPT` and `iptables -t DROP`, allow administrators to customize network policies, enabling authorized traffic while blocking potential threats. These commands play a critical role in safeguarding network resources and defending against cyberattacks, making them indispensable tools for Linux system administrators. This chapter also delved into network configuration and analysis commands, including `ifconfig`, `ip`, `route`, and `netstat`. These commands offer administrators the ability to view and manage network interfaces, configure IP addresses, inspect routing tables, and monitor network statistics. By using these commands, administrators can optimize network performance, troubleshoot connectivity issues, and ensure efficient resource utilization. Additionally, this chapter explored the `hostname`, `nslookup`, and `host` commands, which provide insights into DNS resolution and hostname-related information. These commands are valuable for verifying DNS configurations, resolving domain names, and identifying network connectivity problems. The seamless integration of these network commands equips Linux system administrators with the necessary tools to maintain stable, secure, and high-performing network environments.

In the next chapter, we will explore a set of crucial tools that enable seamless file transfer, efficient downloading, and effective log file management in Linux environments. We will cover a range of commands, each serving a specific purpose in streamlining file transfers and ensuring log file accessibility. From using `netcat` and `socat` for copying files into remote systems to leveraging `wget`, `curl`, `axel`, and more for efficient file downloads, this will equip system administrators with essential techniques to handle various file-related tasks effectively.

11

File Transfer, Downloading, and Managing Log Files

File transfer, downloading, and managing log files are crucial aspects of managing a Linux system effectively, enabling system administrators to efficiently handle data exchange, retrieve essential software or content, and maintain a robust record of system activities. This multifaceted topic encompasses a variety of commands and utilities, each serving distinct purposes and collectively supporting seamless file operations and log management. Understanding and mastering these tools is vital for administrators to ensure smooth system functioning, troubleshoot issues, and maintain data integrity.

The significance of file transfer, downloading, and managing log file commands lies in their essential role in day-to-day system administration tasks. File transfer commands such as `netcat`, `socat`, `wget`, `curl`, and `axel` facilitate seamless data exchange between local and remote systems. These tools are critical for sharing files, backups, and configurations, both within an internal network and across the internet. Similarly, downloading commands such as `wget`, `curl`, and `axel` empower administrators to efficiently retrieve files, software packages, and updates from remote servers or repositories. These commands are indispensable for obtaining the necessary resources efficiently and ensuring the system remains up to date and well-equipped. Equally important is managing log files, which plays a pivotal role in system analysis, performance monitoring, and troubleshooting. Log files are records that contain critical information about system activities, errors, and events. By exploring common log files, administrators can gain valuable insights into the system's health, identify potential issues, and take preventive measures. This level of visibility is essential for maintaining system stability, ensuring security, and complying with regulatory requirements.

In this chapter, we will delve into the following main topics:

- Copying files into remote systems using `netcat` and `socat`

- Downloading files with `wget` and `curl`

- Exploring common log files

The purpose of mastering file transfer, downloading, and managing log file commands is to equip system administrators with the ability to perform a wide array of tasks effectively. By understanding these tools, administrators can confidently perform file transfers, secure content exchange, and retrieve essential data. They can also analyze and interpret log files to gain valuable information about the system's performance and diagnose any underlying issues. These commands provide the flexibility and control needed to handle diverse file operations and maintain a well-organized log management system. As such, file transfer, downloading, and managing log file commands remain essential and are widely used by Linux system administrators, empowering them to efficiently manage their systems and deliver optimal performance and security.

Copying files into remote systems using netcat and socat

Copying files into remote systems using the `netcat` and `socat` commands is a crucial aspect of file transfer and system administration in Linux environments. Both `netcat` and `socat` are versatile networking utilities that offer powerful capabilities for transferring data between systems over the network. These commands provide a simple and efficient way to securely send files, directories, or streams from one host to another, making them indispensable tools for Linux system administrators. They operate at the network level, allowing data to be transmitted over TCP or UDP connections, making them ideal for transferring large files or backups across the network. Unlike traditional file transfer methods, such as **File Transfer Protocol (FTP)** or **Secure Copy Protocol (SCP)**, `netcat` and `socat` provide a more lightweight and flexible approach. FTP and SCP are well-established methods for transferring files over networks, but they come with certain limitations. For instance, FTP requires a dedicated FTP server setup, which can be resource-intensive and less flexible in ad hoc network scenarios. SCP, while secure, relies on SSH and might not be available or practical in all situations. `netcat` and `socat`, on the other hand, are lightweight and versatile tools that allow for direct network communication, making them ideal for quick and ad hoc file transfers. They don't require dedicated servers or complex configurations to be set up, making them valuable tools in various network administration and troubleshooting tasks. Moreover, they can be used in various scenarios, including data replication, system backups, remote administration, and even tunneling encrypted communication. These commands provide administrators with greater control over the data transfer process, making it easier to customize and automate file transfer tasks.

The use of netcat and socat in copying files into remote systems is highly practical and efficient. Administrators can quickly transfer files by piping the content through netcat or socat to the destination system. The process is relatively simple, involving a single line of command, reducing the need for complex setups or additional software installations. Additionally, netcat and socat support various options that allow administrators to specify data streams, handle multiple connections, and control the transfer speed, providing greater flexibility and control over the file transfer process. Overall, the netcat and socat commands provide efficient and reliable solutions for copying files into remote systems, streamlining file transfer tasks, and enhancing the overall efficiency of system administration. Now, let's delve into practical examples of how these commands can be effectively utilized by system administrators:

- Transferring files using netcat (CentOS machine):

  - The first command, ls -l /bin/wget, lists detailed information about the wget file located in the /bin directory. The output includes various attributes such as permissions, owner, group, size, modification date, and the name of the file. In this case, the wget file is an executable with -rwxr-xr-x permissions, indicating that it is readable, writable, and executable by the owner, and executable by others.

  - The second command, nc -nv 192.168.x.xxx 4444 < wget, involves the use of the nc (netcat) command for network communication. Here, the user is attempting to send the content of the wget file to a remote machine at IP address 192.168.x.xxx, port 4444. The < symbol is used for input redirection, indicating that the content of the wget file will be provided as input to the nc command.

  - The -n flag ensures that no DNS resolution is performed for the IP address, 192.168.x.xxx, and -v provides verbose output about the connection process.

  - The subsequent lines show the output of the netcat command. It starts by displaying the version of Ncat (a modern reimplementation of netcat) being used. Then, it reports that a connection has been established to the specified IP address and port:

```
[root@Instructor bin]# ls -l wget          ◄──
-rwxr-xr-x. 1 root root 533936 Dec 15  2022 wget       ✦
[root@Instructor bin]# nc -nv 192.168.    4444 < wget
Ncat: Version 7.92 ( https://nmap.org/ncat )
Ncat: Connected to 192.168.    4444.
Ncat: 533936 bytes sent, 0 bytes received in 0.07 seconds.
[root@Instructor bin]# █
```

Figure 11.1 – File transfer with netcat

- Remote machine:

  - The first command that's executed is nc -nlvp 4444 > wget. This command uses the nc (netcat) utility to listen for incoming network connections on port 4444. The output of the incoming connection is redirected to a file named wget in the current directory. The

> symbol is used for output redirection. The output indicates that the system is now listening on port 4444. Note that when sending a file via nc, no progress bar will be displayed in the Terminal.

- The second command that's executed is ls -l wget. This command lists detailed information about the wget file in the current directory. The output includes attributes such as permissions, owner, group, size, modification date, and the name of the file.

- The third command that's executed is sudo chmod +x wget. This command uses chmod to change the permissions of the wget file. The +x argument adds the executable permission to the file.

- The concluding command that's issued is wget --help. This command aims to verify the successful transfer of the file, as evidenced by the output, which demonstrates that it was executed successfully:

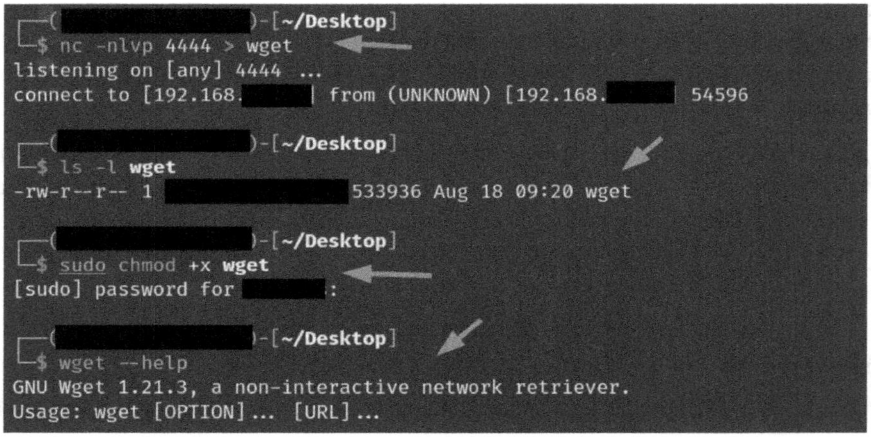

Figure 11.2 – Receiving an incoming file using nc

- Transferring files using socat (remote machine):

On the remote machine, the socat TCP4-LISTEN:4444,fork file:shadow.txt command is executed. This command sets up a TCP listener on port 4444. When a connection is established to this port, socat reads the content of the local shadow.txt file and sends it to the connected client. The fork option allows socat to handle multiple incoming connections independently. In this example, the shadow.txt file contains text stating file file, as shown here:

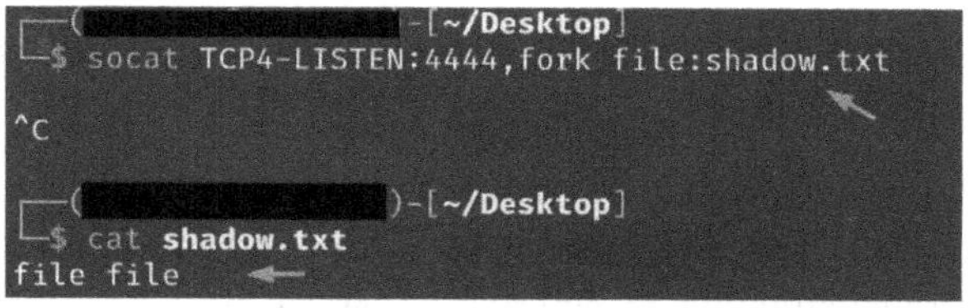

Figure 11.3 – Sending a file with socat on a remote machine

- CentOS machine:

  On the CentOS machine, the socat TCP4:192.168.x.xxx:4444 file:shadow.txt, create command is executed. This command initiates a TCP connection to the remote machine at IP address 192.168.x.xxx on port 4444. Once connected, socat reads the contents of the local shadow.txt file and sends it to the remote machine. The create option instructs socat to create the shadow.txt file on the remote machine if it doesn't already exist. After the transfer is complete, the local shadow.txt file is created or overwritten with the received data. The ls -l shadow.txt command confirms the creation of the file, and the cat shadow.txt command displays its content, which is file file:

Figure 11.4 – Receiving and verifying the transferred file

While both Netcat and Socat are used for networking tasks and data transfer, Netcat is a simpler utility that's primarily used for basic networking tasks, whereas Socat offers more advanced capabilities and options, making it suitable for a wider range of networking scenarios, including complex data manipulation, encryption, and proxying.

Downloading files with wget and curl

Downloading files is a fundamental task in system administration, and tools such as wget and curl play a pivotal role in simplifying and optimizing this process. These commands are designed to fetch files from remote servers, repositories, or URLs and bring them to the local system. Their importance stems from the need to keep systems updated with the latest software versions, retrieve critical data, and efficiently manage resources. The significance of these commands lies in their versatility and ease of use. wget, for instance, is a robust and feature-rich tool capable of handling various protocols, such as HTTP, HTTPS, and FTP. Its ability to recursively download files and mirror entire websites is particularly valuable for administrators managing large-scale systems or websites. curl, on the other hand, is equally powerful, supporting a wide range of protocols and enabling administrators to not only download files but also perform various other network-related tasks, such as sending data to servers and handling authentication.

These commands are indispensable for system administrators due to their role in maintaining up-to-date software, retrieving critical data, and ensuring the smooth operation of a system. Their ease of use, flexibility in handling different protocols, and ability to accelerate downloads make them essential tools in the toolkit of every Linux system administrator. Let's make use of these commands practically on our Linux machine:

- Using `wget`:

    The `wget http://192.168.x.xxx:80/file.txt` command is used to download a file from a remote web server. Here's a breakdown of what each part of the command does:

    - `http://192.168.x.xxx:80/file.txt`: This is the URL of the file we want to download. Here `http` specifies the protocol to use for the download – in this case, HTTP

    When we execute the command, `wget` establishes an HTTP connection to the provided IP address and port, sends an HTTP GET request for the specified file (`/file.txt`), and receives the file's content in response. The downloaded file will be saved in the current working directory on our local machine with the same name as on the server (in this case, `file.txt`):

```
[instructor@Instructor ~]$ wget http://192.168.    :80/file.txt
--2023-08-18 20:25:06--  http://192.168.    /file.txt
Connecting to 192.168.    :80... connected.
HTTP request sent, awaiting response... 200 OK
Length: 0 [text/plain]
Saving to: 'file.txt.1'

file.txt.1              [ <=>                    ]       0  --.-KB/s

2023-08-18 20:25:06 (0.00 B/s) - 'file.txt.1' saved [0/0]
```

Figure 11.5 – File download with wget

- Using `curl`:

    The `curl -O http://192.168.x.xxx:80/file.txt` command is used to download a file from a remote web server using the `curl` command-line tool. Here's a breakdown of what each part of the command does:

    - `curl`: This is a command-line utility that stands for **client for URLs**. It is used to transfer data to or from a server and supports various protocols, including HTTP, HTTPS, FTP, and more.

    - `-O`: This option tells `curl` to save the downloaded file using the same name as on the remote server. It's used to preserve the original filename.

- `http://192.168.x.xxx:80/file.txt`: This is the URL of the file you want to download, similar to the previous explanation:

  - `http`: This specifies the protocol to use for the download – in this case, HTTP

When we execute this command, `curl` establishes an HTTP connection to the provided IP address and port, sends an HTTP GET request for the specified file (`/file.txt`), and receives the file's content in response. The downloaded file will be saved in the current working directory on the local machine with the same name as on the server (`file.txt`):

```
[instructor@Instructor ~]$ curl -O http://192.168.    80/file.txt  ⟵
  % Total    % Received % Xferd  Average Speed   Time    Time     Time  Current
                                 Dload  Upload   Total   Spent    Left  Speed
  0     0    0     0    0     0      0      0 --:--:-- --:--:-- --:--:--     0
[instructor@Instructor ~]$ ls -l file.txt
-rw-rw-r--. 1 instructor instructor 0 Aug 18 20:35 file.txt
[instructor@Instructor ~]$ 
```

Figure 11.6 – File download with curl

By offering options for batch downloads, resumable transfers, and detailed progress reporting, `wget` and `curl` streamline the process of obtaining files from remote sources, enhancing efficiency and productivity for administrators across various domains and industries.

Exploring common log files

System administrators check log files for various reasons due to their critical importance in maintaining system health, diagnosing issues, and ensuring security. These logs provide a comprehensive record of system activities, errors, and events, allowing administrators to gain valuable insights into the system's behavior. For instance, the `/var/log/messages` log is a goldmine for general system-wide events, which assists in troubleshooting issues that might affect the entire system. This log's significance lies in its ability to offer a holistic view of the system's health and performance, aiding administrators in detecting anomalies early on and addressing potential bottlenecks or threats.

Moreover, log files such as `/var/log/secure` and `/var/log/auth.log` are pivotal in upholding system security. System administrators continuously monitor these logs to track authentication and authorization activities, helping them identify unauthorized access attempts or breaches. The importance of such logs cannot be overstated as they provide the necessary trail to investigate security incidents, enforce access controls, and mitigate potential security risks. Additionally, logs related to web servers such as `/var/log/httpd/` hold the key to identifying unauthorized access attempts, suspicious activities, or web server errors, which are crucial for maintaining the integrity and security of web applications. Regularly checking these logs empowers administrators to proactively identify and rectify security vulnerabilities, keeping sensitive data and systems safeguarded.

In CentOS 8, several common log files are located in various directories that record system events, application activities, and errors. Here is a list of some of the common log files, along with their paths:

- `/var/log/messages`:

  This log file contains general system messages generated by various processes. It's a catch-all location for different log messages, including those from daemons, services, and the kernel.

- `/var/log/dmesg`:

  The kernel ring buffer messages are stored here. These messages provide information about the kernel's interactions with hardware during boot and while the system is running.

- `/var/log/boot.log`:

  This file contains messages related to the boot process and startup information. It's useful for diagnosing boot issues.

- `/var/log/secure`:

  Authentication and security-related events, including successful and failed login attempts, are logged here. Monitoring this file helps in tracking unauthorized access attempts.

- `/var/log/wtmp`:

  This log file records the user's login and logout history. It maintains a record of user sessions and their durations.

- `/var/log/yum.log` and `/var/log/dnf.rpm.log`:

  These logs contain package management activities. Entries include package installations, updates, and removals performed using YUM or DNF package managers.

- `/var/log/httpd/`, `/var/log/mariadb/`, `/var/log/nginx/`:

  These directories contain logs specific to Apache, MariaDB, and nginx servers, respectively. They include access logs, error logs, and other server-related events.

- `/var/log/maillog`:

  Tailored for email-related activities, this log tracks email sending, receiving, and errors for mail server configurations, helping in troubleshooting email communication problems.

- `/var/log/cron`:

  Focused on scheduled tasks, this log records the execution of cron jobs and their outcomes. It's indispensable for ensuring that automated tasks run as expected.

- `/var/log/audit/audit.log`:

  The audit log is a treasure trove for security teams. It contains records of system activities and security events, aiding in identifying suspicious activities and policy violations.

- `/var/log/auth.log`:

  Like `/var/log/secure`, this log concentrates on authentication and authorization activities. It's a window into user access, password changes, and privilege modifications.

- `/var/log/kern.log`:

  Kernel messages and hardware-related events are logged here. When troubleshooting hardware issues or kernel-level problems, this log can be instrumental.

- `/var/log/udev`:

  This directory contains logs related to device management and device events. It's helpful for understanding device-related problems.

- `/var/log/sssd/` and `/var/log/avahi-daemon/`:

  These logs pertain to **System Security Services Daemon (SSSD)** and Avahi Daemon, respectively. SSSD handles authentication and identity resolution, while Avahi focuses on local network service discovery.

- `/var/log/firewalld`:

  `firewalld` logs provide information about firewall rules and activities, aiding in monitoring and managing network security.

- `/var/log/audit/`:

  This directory stores SELinux audit logs. It helps in tracking security-related incidents and identifying policy violations.

- `/var/log/sa/`:

  The system accounting (`sa`) logs help monitor system performance metrics such as CPU, memory, and disk usage over time.

- `/var/log/cloud-init.log`:

  Cloud initialization logs contain information about the initialization process on cloud instances, aiding in tracking cloud-based system setups.

- `/var/log/libvirt/`:

  Libvirt logs include events and activities related to virtualization using the Libvirt framework.

In essence, the regular scrutiny of these log files by system administrators is indispensable. These logs serve as a vital toolset for troubleshooting, performance optimization, and security enhancement. By harnessing the insights embedded in these logs, administrators can ensure seamless system operation, prompt issue resolution, and robust security posture, ultimately contributing to the overall stability and reliability of the Linux environment.

Summary

This chapter provided a comprehensive exploration of crucial techniques and tools tailored for Linux system administrators. This chapter should empower administrators with the proficiency to efficiently manage file transfers, execute seamless downloads, and effectively handle log files, all of which are integral aspects of maintaining robust and secure Linux systems. We began by learning how to copy files into remote systems while leveraging the capabilities of `netcat` and `socat`. These utilities facilitate secure and efficient file transfers, providing administrators with the means to exchange data across networks with confidence. Subsequently, we delved into the art of downloading files by utilizing the `wget` and `curl` commands. These commands empower administrators to seamlessly fetch content from the web or other remote locations, simplifying the process of acquiring essential resources for system management and enhancement. This chapter further enriched its content by delving into the significance and diverse array of log files, which constitute a fundamental component of effective system administration. Logging serves as an indispensable practice for monitoring system activities, diagnosing potential issues, and safeguarding security protocols. By delving into the intricacies of common log files, Linux system administrators can attain a comprehensive grasp of system health and performance indicators. Proficiency in comprehending log files proves pivotal for troubleshooting errors, promptly identifying security breaches, and optimizing overall system functionality. This comprehensive exploration equips administrators with the expertise to proactively address challenges, maintain system integrity, and drive efficient operations.

In the next chapter, we'll delve into crucial security measures for Linux systems. We will show you how to utilize enforcing and permissive modes in SELinux, manage SELinux Boolean values, strategies to secure **Secure Shell (SSH)** access, methods for locking user accounts, and techniques for enhancing system booting security.

Part 4:
Linux Security and the Cloud

In this part, we dive into Linux security, a critical duty for administrators of production systems. Linux features powerful security tools such as SELinux, integrated firewalls, and standard system permissions. This section offers a clear overview of Linux security measures and guides you through setting up CentOS 8 on AWS.

This section contains the following chapters:

- *Chapter 12, Exploring Linux Security*
- *Chapter 13, Linux in the Cloud*

12
Exploring Linux Security

In the ever-evolving landscape of information technology, the security of systems and data stands as an unwavering priority. As the backbone of countless infrastructures, Linux operating systems have solidified their presence in various domains, from servers to embedded devices. Within this realm, this chapter embarks on a comprehensive journey, delving into the realm of Linux security. This exploration isn't just an exercise in fortifying digital fortresses; it's a pivotal pursuit that safeguards sensitive information, guarantees operational integrity, and upholds user trust. In the contemporary digital era, where interconnectedness dominates, the importance of Linux security cannot be overstated. Organizations of all sizes rely on Linux-based systems to manage databases, power websites, and orchestrate complex networks. These systems contain troves of sensitive information, from proprietary algorithms to personal user data. Ensuring the security of this data is imperative not only to maintain the competitive edge but also to safeguard the reputation of the entity in question. Breaches in security can lead to dire consequences, including financial losses, legal ramifications, and the erosion of customer confidence.

The purpose of this exploration transcends the realm of routine system administration. It's a proactive stance against potential threats that could exploit vulnerabilities and wreak havoc. Linux administrators, armed with a profound understanding of security mechanisms, can erect potent defenses against a multitude of cyber threats, from malware and ransomware to data breaches and denial-of-service attacks. By comprehending the intricacies of Linux security, administrators can effectively mitigate risks, respond swiftly to emerging threats, and prevent security incidents that could otherwise cripple operations.

Linux security isn't just a technical checklist – it's an integral component of responsible administration. First and foremost, Linux is an open source ecosystem, meaning that its source code is publicly accessible. While this fosters collaboration and rapid development, it also exposes the system to potential scrutiny and exploitation. Hence, understanding Linux security is paramount to identify and rectify vulnerabilities that might otherwise go unnoticed. Moreover, the diverse applications of Linux, from personal computing to corporate servers, demand a nuanced approach to security. Administrators must navigate this spectrum while factoring in the unique security requirements of each scenario. This necessitates a deep comprehension of Linux security mechanisms, such as access controls, encryption, authentication protocols, and intrusion detection systems. By harnessing these tools effectively, administrators can customize security strategies that align with specific needs.

In essence, this chapter serves as a compass in the labyrinth of Linux administration. It equips administrators with the knowledge and strategies needed to uphold the resilience and integrity of Linux-based systems, fostering a digital landscape where security stands as an unwavering pillar of operational success.

In this chapter, we will delve into the following main topics:

- Utilizing enforcing and permissive modes
- Enabling or disabling SELinux Boolean values
- Locking user accounts
- Securing SSH

Utilizing enforcing and permissive modes

In the realm of access control and security management, the concepts of **enforcing** and **permissive** modes assume crucial roles, particularly within the context of operating systems such as Linux. These modes pertain to the behavior of security mechanisms, such as **Mandatory Access Control** (**MAC**) frameworks. For instance, RHEL and Fedora Linux use **Security-Enhanced Linux** (**SELinux**) as their MAC framework, while Ubuntu employs AppArmor for similar purposes. Enforcing mode signifies a state where strict adherence to security policies is upheld, disallowing any actions that contravene these rules. On the other hand, permissive mode adopts a more lenient stance, allowing actions that would typically be denied under "enforcing." The purpose of these modes lies in striking a balance between maintaining system integrity and facilitating essential operations without undue hindrance. These modes are essential for system administrators aiming to enhance system security while ensuring the smooth operation of their systems. By utilizing enforcing mode, administrators can ensure that all actions, whether initiated by users or applications, adhere rigidly to established security policies. This prevents unauthorized access, reduces the potential attack surface, and mitigates the risks associated with breaches, malware infiltration, and unauthorized data manipulation. Conversely, permissive mode proves invaluable in scenarios where the immediate implementation of strict security measures might disrupt critical operations or lead to unintended consequences. Administrators can temporarily switch to the permissive mode to identify potential issues that would arise under enforcing mode. This approach aids in fine-tuning security policies without causing system-wide disruptions. Additionally, permissive mode allows administrators to understand the scope and impact of security policy changes before fully committing to them.

A short introduction to Linux hardening and the role of SELinux's enforcing and passive modes

In the ever-evolving landscape of cybersecurity, the term **Linux hardening** emerges as a critical practice to enhance the security posture of Linux-based systems. Linux hardening refers to the systematic process of fortifying the security of a Linux operating system by minimizing vulnerabilities, reducing attack surfaces, and implementing robust defense mechanisms. At its core, Linux hardening seeks to create an environment that withstands a broad spectrum of threats, ranging from cyberattacks to unauthorized data breaches. In this intricate dance between technology and security, the roles of SELinux's enforcing and permissive modes stand out as pivotal players, shaping the defense strategies adopted by system administrators.

The role of enforcing mode

In the realm of MAC, SELinux stands as a pioneering framework that enforces fine-grained security policies within a Linux system. SELinux's enforcing mode assumes a role akin to an unyielding guardian, allowing only actions that align with meticulously defined security rules. When operating in enforcing mode, SELinux rigidly enforces access controls and security contexts, thereby confining potentially malicious actions and reducing the likelihood of unauthorized intrusion. This mode ensures that even if an attacker gains access, their ability to maneuver and exploit vulnerabilities is severely curtailed, thereby enhancing the overall resilience of the system to enable enforcing mode:

```
[instructor@Instructor ~]$ sudo setenforce 1
[sudo] password for instructor:
[instructor@Instructor ~]$ getenforce
Enforcing
```

Figure 12.1 – SELinux's enforcing mode

Let's take a closer look:

- The setenforce command is used to modify SELinux's enforcing mode. By running sudo setenforce 1, you are instructing SELinux to switch to enforcing mode. In this mode, SELinux will strictly enforce the defined security policies, denying actions that violate those policies.

- To verify that SELinux is in enforcing mode, you can use the getenforce command. The getenforce command provides a simple way to query the status of SELinux and determine whether it's currently operating in enforcing mode or permissive mode.

The role of permissive mode

In contrast, SELinux's permissive mode serves as an insightful observer in the security landscape. When switched to permissive mode, SELinux refrains from blocking actions that breach security policies, but it actively logs these incidents. This mode serves as an essential tool for system administrators seeking to fine-tune their security policies without abruptly disrupting operations. By analyzing the logs generated in permissive mode, administrators can identify potential issues that would arise if the system were operating in enforcing mode. This invaluable feedback loop empowers administrators to iteratively refine security policies, ensuring they strike an optimal balance between stringent security and operational functionality to enable SELinux's permissive mode:

```
[instructor@Instructor ~]$ sudo setenforce 0
[sudo] password for instructor:
[instructor@Instructor ~]$ getenforce
Permissive
```

Figure 12.2 – SELinux's permissive mode

Let's take a closer look:

- This time, by running `sudo setenforce 0`, you are instructing SELinux to switch to permissive mode. In permissive mode, SELinux does not actively block actions that violate security policies. Instead, it logs these actions for later analysis.

- To verify that SELinux is in enforcing mode, you can use the `getenforce` command to verify whether it's switched to permissive mode.

To summarize, the dynamic interplay of SELinux's enforcing and permissive modes exemplifies the delicate art of Linux hardening. These modes offer administrators a granular approach to security, allowing them to choose between airtight enforcement and pragmatic observation. By judiciously deploying these modes, administrators can navigate the labyrinthine world of Linux security, creating fortified environments that confidently withstand the evolving landscape of cyber threats.

Enabling or disabling SELinux Boolean values

In the intricate landscape of Linux security, SELinux emerges as a dynamic framework that empowers administrators to finely tune access controls and enforce security policies. At the heart of SELinux's configurational arsenal lie Boolean values, encapsulating binary settings that enable or disable specific security features. These Boolean values serve as cryptographic keys that can unlock a multitude of security configurations, allowing administrators to sculpt the behavior of the system with precision. From enabling network connectivity for web servers to permitting specific user interactions, Boolean values offer a nuanced approach to tailoring security protocols, ensuring that the system operates within the desired security boundaries. The importance of enabling or disabling SELinux Boolean values transcends the realm of mere customization. It plays a pivotal role in aligning system security with the ever-evolving operational demands of the digital landscape. A tangible example of their significance is found in web server scenarios. When deploying a web application, certain functionalities might require network connectivity, such as sending emails or accessing remote databases. By manipulating Boolean values, administrators can enable specific network-related permissions for the web server process while keeping other potentially vulnerable actions locked down. This granular control not only mitigates risks but also ensures that security is an enabler, not an inhibitor, of functionality.

The use of SELinux Boolean values extends to scenarios where system administrators need to balance security and usability. For instance, when introducing a new software package, it might demand unconventional access rights to function optimally. Rather than compromising the overall system security, administrators can modify Boolean values to grant temporary permissions. This empowers administrators to evaluate the software's behavior in a controlled environment while preserving the integrity of the larger system. Moreover, the ability to enable or disable specific Boolean values facilitates the implementation of security policies that are congruent with organizational policies and regulatory requirements. This not only enhances security posture but also streamlines compliance efforts by allowing administrators to cater to unique operational needs. Now, let's take a look at the current values for all SELinux Boolean settings and understand the output:

```
[instructor@Instructor ~]$ getsebool -a
abrt_anon_write --> off
abrt_handle_event --> off
abrt_upload_watch_anon_write --> on
antivirus_can_scan_system --> off
antivirus_use_jit --> off
auditadm_exec_content --> on
authlogin_nsswitch_use_ldap --> off
authlogin_radius --> off
authlogin_yubikey --> off
awstats_purge_apache_log_files --> off
```

Figure 12.3 – Output of current Boolean values

The provided outputs are the results of running the `getsebool -a` command. This command is used to display the current values of all SELinux Boolean settings. SELinux Boolean values are binary settings that determine whether a specific security feature or permission is enabled (on) or disabled (off). These Boolean values allow administrators to finely control the behavior and security policies enforced by SELinux. Let's break down the output and explain each line:

- `abrt_anon_write --> off`: This indicates that the SELinux Boolean value for allowing the **Automatic Bug Reporting Tool (ABRT)** to write to anonymous memory is currently disabled.

- `abrt_handle_event --> off`: This Boolean value controls whether ABRT can handle events is disabled. ABRT handles system events such as crashes or abnormal terminations.

- `abrt_upload_watch_anon_write --> on`: This means that the Boolean value that allows ABRT to watch for uploads with anonymous write access is enabled.

- `antivirus_can_scan_system --> off`: This states that the Boolean value that permits antivirus software to scan the entire system is currently disabled.

- `antivirus_use_jit --> off`: The Boolean value controlling whether antivirus software can use **Just-In-Time (JIT)** scanning is disabled.

- `auditadm_exec_content --> on`: This indicates that the Boolean value allowing the `auditadm` user to execute content is enabled.

- `authlogin_nsswitch_use_ldap --> off`: The Boolean value that determines whether the `authlogin` program should use the **Network Security Services** (**NSS**) LDAP module is disabled.

- `authlogin_radius --> off`: The Boolean value that controls whether the `authlogin` program can use the `radius` protocol for authentication is disabled.

- `authlogin_yubikey --> off`: This means that the Boolean value permitting the `authlogin` program to use YubiKey for authentication is disabled.

- `awstats_purge_apache_log_files --> off`: The Boolean value that decides whether `awstats` should be allowed to purge Apache log files is disabled.

Each of these lines represents a specific SELinux Boolean value and its current status. The value next to the arrow (that is, `on` or `off`) indicates whether the Boolean is enabled or disabled. These Boolean values allow system administrators to tailor the security policies of their systems to match their specific operational requirements while maintaining a robust security posture.

Searching for a Boolean and getting its information

Follow these steps:

1. If you're not sure about the exact name of a Boolean but want to search for it, you can use the `semanage boolean -l` command:

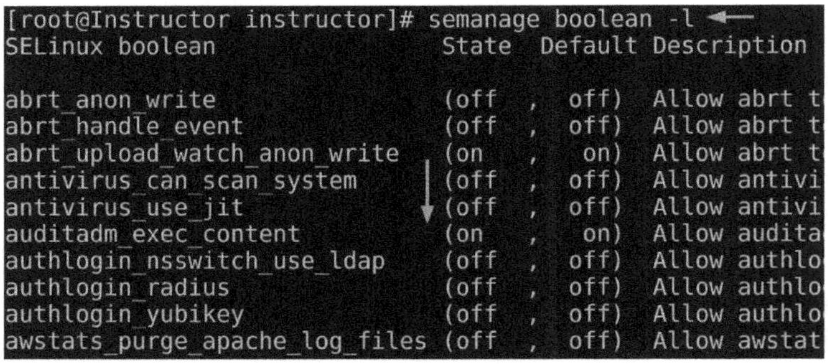

Figure 12.4 – Searching for Booleans

2. To check the status of a specific SELinux Boolean, use the `getsebool` command followed by the name of the Boolean. For example, to check its status, you can run the following command:

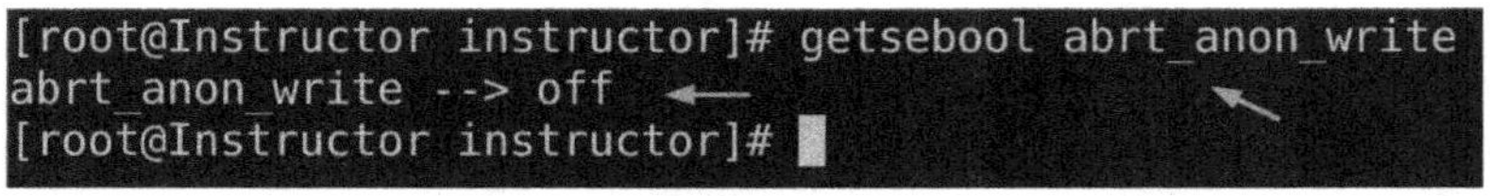

Figure 12.5 – Checking a specific Boolean's status

3. Now, let's run a command to get information about a Boolean:

```
[root@Instructor instructor]# semanage boolean -l | grep xguest_connect_n
etwork
xguest_connect_network          (on  ,   on) Allow xguest to connect net
work
[root@Instructor instructor]#
```

Figure 12.6 – Getting information about a Boolean

The preceding command searches through the list of SELinux Booleans, finds the one named xguest_connect_network, and displays its current status as on, indicating that network connections are allowed for the xguest user or process. The comment provides additional context about why this particular Boolean exists and what it controls.

Now, let's enable and disable a Boolean value.

Enabling a SELinux Boolean value

To enable a SELinux Boolean value, you can use the setsebool command with the -P option (which makes the change permanent), followed by the name of the Boolean and 1 to indicate on. For instance, if you want to enable the xguest_use_bluetooth Boolean, you can run the following code:

```
[root@Instructor instructor]# setsebool -P xguest_use_bluetooth 1
[root@Instructor instructor]# semanage boolean -l | grep xguest_use_bluet
ooth
xguest_use_bluetooth            (on  ,   on) Allow xguest to use bluetoo
th
[root@Instructor instructor]#
```

Figure 12.7 – Enabling Boolean values

After executing this command, we used the semanage command to get information about the changes that were made. This command sets the xguest_use_bluetooth Boolean to on and makes the change permanent across system reboots.

Disabling a SELinux Boolean value

To disable an SELinux Boolean value, use the setsebool command with the -P option, followed by the name of the Boolean and 0 to indicate off. For example, to disable the mount_anyfile boolean, follow these steps:

1. Query the current state:

   semanage boolean -l | grep mount_anyfile: This command lists all SELinux Boolean values and filters the output using grep to find the line containing mount_anyfile. This line shows that the mount_anyfile Boolean is currently enabled, as indicated by (on, on). Additionally, it provides a description, Allow mount to anyfile, which explains the purpose of this Boolean.

2. Disable the Boolean:

    `setsebool -P mount_anyfile 0`: This command uses `setsebool` to change the status of the `mount_anyfile` Boolean. The `-P` flag makes this change permanent (persisting across reboots), and `0` signifies `off`. After running this command, SELinux is configured to disallow the `mount` command to mount any file as a filesystem.

3. Verify the change:

    `semanage boolean -l | grep mount_anyfile`: This command is used to query the status of the `mount_anyfile` Boolean after it has been modified. Now, it shows (`off`, `off`) for this Boolean, confirming that it has been disabled. The description remains the same, indicating that the `mount` command is not allowed to mount any file as a filesystem:

```
[root@Instructor instructor]# semanage boolean -l | grep mount_anyfile
mount_anyfile                    → (on  ,    on)  Allow mount to anyfile
[root@Instructor instructor]# setsebool -P mount_anyfile 0 ←
[root@Instructor instructor]# semanage boolean -l | grep mount_anyfile
mount_anyfile                      (off ,   off)  Allow mount to anyfile
[root@Instructor instructor]#
```

Figure 12.8 – Disabling Boolean values

This command sets the `mount_anyfile` Boolean to `off` and ensures that the change persists after the system reboots.

In summary, the command checks the status of the `mount_anyfile` SELinux Boolean, disables it, and verifies that the change took effect. SELinux Booleans allow administrators to finely control access and permissions within the system, and modifying them should be done with a clear understanding of the security implications for the system's operation.

Locking user accounts

In SELinux, the concept of locking user accounts is often associated with standard Linux account management practices, such as using the `passwd` command. SELinux itself does not directly handle account locking; rather, it relies on Linux's account management tools to lock and unlock user accounts. Here are some Terminal examples of how to lock and unlock a user account:

*   Locking a user account:

    To lock a user account, you typically disable the account by changing the account's password. This can be achieved by using the `passwd` command with the `-l` (lock) option:

```
[root@Instructor instructor]# passwd -l intruder
Locking password for user intruder.
passwd: Success
[root@Instructor instructor]# passwd -S intruder
intruder LK 2023-09-01 0 99999 7 -1 (Password locked.)
```

Figure 12.9 – Locking a user account

- Unlocking a user account:

    To unlock a user account that has been locked, you can use the passwd command again, with -u to unlock and f for the force option:

```
[root@Instructor instructor]# passwd -u intruder -f
Unlocking password for user intruder.
passwd: Success
[root@Instructor instructor]# passwd -S intruder
intruder PS 2023-09-01 0 99999 7 -1 (Password set, SHA512 crypt.)
```

Figure 12.10 – Unlocking a user account

The first command unlocks the password for the intruder user, and the output confirms that the account was unlocked successfully. The second command provides information about the user's current password status, indicating that they have a password set and it is securely encrypted using SHA-512. This scenario ensures that the intruder user can now access their account with their password.

Securing SSH

Secure Shell (SSH) is a widely used protocol for secure remote access and secure file transfers over an insecure network. It plays a pivotal role in modern IT infrastructures, enabling administrators, developers, and users to access remote systems securely. However, to harness the full potential of SSH and maintain the confidentiality and integrity of data during remote connections, it's paramount to implement robust security measures.

The primary purpose of securing SSH is to protect sensitive information and prevent unauthorized access to remote systems. SSH achieves this by encrypting data during transmission and employing strong authentication mechanisms. By utilizing cryptographic protocols, SSH ensures that data that's exchanged between the client and server remains confidential and is not susceptible to eavesdropping by malicious actors. Furthermore, SSH's public-key authentication and password-based authentication mechanisms enhance the security of remote access, reducing the risk of unauthorized logins. The ability to securely tunnel various network services through SSH, known as SSH tunneling, also extends its use beyond remote access, making it a versatile tool for secure data transfer and network management. In essence, securing SSH is integral to safeguarding sensitive data, protecting against malicious intrusions, and ensuring the trustworthiness of remote connections. The importance of SSH security is underscored by its ubiquity in enterprise environments and the critical role it plays in securing remote access to servers, networking devices, and cloud infrastructure. Inadequate SSH security can lead to devastating consequences, including data breaches, unauthorized system access, and exposure to confidential information. This underscores the necessity of implementing best practices, such as enforcing strong password policies, using multi-factor authentication, and configuring SSH servers to allow only trusted users and hosts. SSH security also aligns with compliance requirements and regulatory standards, making it indispensable for organizations subject to data protection regulations such as GDPR or HIPAA. Here are some examples:

- Change the default SSH port:

  Changing the default SSH port (22) to a non-standard port can help deter automated scanning and brute-force attacks.

  To change the SSH port to 2222, edit the SSH configuration file, /etc/ssh/sshd_config, located in the corner of the shell, as shown in the following screenshot:

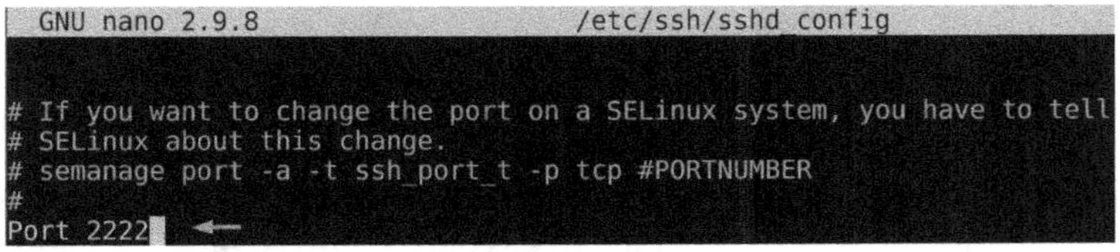

Figure 12.11 – Changing the default port

  Inside the file, locate the line with Port 22 and change it to Port 2222 or any other port number of your choice. Save the file.

- Update SELinux rules:

  When SELinux is enabled, it's important to note that SELinux policies are designed to enhance system security by enforcing strict rules and restrictions on various system resources, including network ports. These policies might initially prevent SSH traffic on a new port that you've configured.

  To ensure that SSH traffic can flow smoothly on the new port, you'll need to update the SELinux policy to allow it. You can achieve this using the semanage command, which is a powerful tool for managing SELinux policies. Specifically, you'll need to use semanage to modify the SELinux port policy to permit SSH communication on the new port.

  Once you've made the necessary policy adjustments, it's crucial to apply these changes and then restart the SSH service to put the new configuration into effect. This ensures that SSH connections on the modified port are allowed as per the updated SELinux policy. Here's how you can accomplish this:

Figure 12.12 – Updating SELinux rules and restarting sshd

We can verify this by running the following command:

```
[instructor@Instructor ~]$ sudo systemctl status sshd
● sshd.service - OpenSSH server daemon
   Loaded: loaded (/usr/lib/systemd/system/sshd.service; enabled; vendor pres
   Active: active (running) since Fri 2023-09-01 23:06:31 WAT; 2min 23s ago
     Docs: man:sshd(8)
           man:sshd_config(5)
 Main PID: 6541 (sshd)
    Tasks: 1 (limit: 52280)
   Memory: 1.1M
   CGroup: /system.slice/sshd.service
           └─6541 /usr/sbin/sshd -D -oCiphers=aes256-gcm@openssh.com,chacha20

Sep 01 23:06:31 Instructor systemd[1]: Starting OpenSSH server daemon...
Sep 01 23:06:31 Instructor sshd[6541]: Server listening on        port 2222.
Sep 01 23:06:31 Instructor sshd[6541]: Server listening or        port 2222.
```

Figure 12.13 – Verifying the changes

- Disable password authentication:

Disabling password-based authentication in favor of public key authentication enhances security by eliminating the risk of password-guessing attacks.

Edit the SSH configuration file, /etc/ssh/sshd_config, located in the corner of the shell, as shown in the following screenshot:

```
  GNU nano 2.9.8                          /etc/ssh/sshd_config

# For this to work you will also need host keys in /etc/ssh/ss
#HostbasedAuthentication no
# Change to yes if you don't trust ~/.ssh/known_hosts for
# HostbasedAuthentication
#IgnoreUserKnownHosts no
# Don't read the user's ~/.rhosts and ~/.shosts files
#IgnoreRhosts yes

# To disable tunneled clear text passwords, change to no here!
#PasswordAuthentication yes
#PermitEmptyPasswords no
PasswordAuthentication no
```

Figure 12.14 – Disabling password authentication

Find the line with PasswordAuthentication yes and change it to Password Authentication no. Save the file and restart SSH:

```
[root@Instructor instructor]# nano /etc/ssh/sshd_config
[root@Instructor instructor]# systemctl restart sshd
[root@Instructor instructor]# █
```

Figure 12.15 – Restarting sshd

Ultimately, securing SSH is not only a matter of technological implementation but a fundamental component of comprehensive cybersecurity strategies, contributing to the resilience and trustworthiness of IT systems.

Summary

This chapter provided Linux administrators with a deep understanding of SELinux modes and how they influence system security. We explored the concepts of enforcing and permissive modes and their significance in the context of Linux administration. Administrators need to learn to leverage these modes to strike a balance between security and system functionality, ensuring that SELinux policies are effectively enforced. This chapter also covered the crucial topic of *enabling or disabling SELinux Boolean values*. We delved into the reasons, importance, and practical use of SELinux Boolean values, demonstrating how they allow administrators to fine-tune security policies to meet specific system requirements. By enabling or disabling Boolean values, administrators gain flexibility in tailoring SELinux policies to their system's needs while maintaining a high level of security. Another essential aspect of system security that we explored in this chapter was *locking user accounts in SELinux security*. Here, you discovered the reasons for locking user accounts, the importance of doing so, and the methods to achieve it within the SELinux framework. This knowledge should have equipped you to effectively manage user access and enhance the overall security posture of your system.

Finally, we delved into securing SSH, a critical component of remote system administration. Administrators learn best practices for securing SSH, including changing the default SSH port, disabling password authentication in favor of public key authentication, and limiting SSH access to specific users or groups. By implementing these security measures, administrators bolster the security of remote access to their Linux systems.

In the next chapter, we'll explore the world of cloud computing and how Linux plays a pivotal role in it. This chapter will take you on a journey through running Linux machines on the cloud, creating Linux instances, and various administrative tasks within a cloud-based Linux environment. By the end, you will have the knowledge and skills to thrive in the cloud computing era.

13
Linux in the Cloud

The advent of cloud computing has revolutionized the world of IT infrastructure, and Linux has been at the forefront of this transformative journey. Linux's integration into the cloud ecosystem has not only reshaped the way businesses and organizations manage their computing resources but has also empowered system administrators with a dynamic and scalable environment. This introduction delves into the pivotal role of Linux in the cloud and how it has redefined the landscape of system administration. Linux, renowned for its open source nature and versatility, has seamlessly adapted to the cloud environment. In doing so, it has provided a stable and flexible foundation for cloud-based solutions. One of the key reasons for Linux's prominence in the cloud is its ability to offer various distributions tailored to specific cloud service providers, such as **Amazon Web Services** (**AWS**), Microsoft Azure, and Google Cloud Platform. For system administrators, this means they can harness the power of Linux in a way that aligns perfectly with the chosen cloud infrastructure, streamlining resource management and deployment.

One of the major roles Linux plays in the cloud is enabling system administrators to create and manage virtual instances effortlessly. Linux distributions such as CentOS offer robust and secure platforms for administrators to deploy a wide array of cloud services, from web hosting to data analytics. While CentOS is known for its stability, compatibility, and strong community support, it's important to note that Ubuntu and various other Linux-based servers are widely utilized in the cloud as well. When conducting an internet search, you'll find diverse opinions on these platforms' suitability for your specific needs. This not only simplifies the process of launching virtual machines but also allows administrators to scale resources up or down as needed, providing a responsive and cost-effective solution for businesses.

Linux also offers a wide range of features and tools that are essential for system administration in the cloud, such as the following:

- **Resource virtualization**: Linux allows system administrators to create and manage **virtual machines** (**VMs**), which are isolated computing environments that can run multiple operating systems and applications on a single physical server. This enables efficient utilization of resources and facilitates dynamic scaling of cloud-based services.

- **Containerization**: Linux is also a popular platform for containerization, which is a lightweight virtualization technology that allows applications to be packaged and deployed in isolated environments called containers. Containers are highly portable and scalable, making them ideal for running cloud-native applications.

- **Security**: Linux is known for its security features, such as **Security-Enhanced Linux** (**SELinux**), which provides granular control over system access and permissions. This makes Linux a secure platform for running cloud-based workloads, even in multi-tenant environments.

- **Automation**: Linux offers a wide range of tools and frameworks for automating system administration tasks, such as configuration management, deployment, and monitoring. This enables system administrators to manage large and complex cloud environments efficiently and effectively.

Additionally, Linux distributions such as CentOS prioritize security and stability in the cloud environment. System administrators rely on Linux's rigorous security protocols and prompt updates to protect cloud-based assets from threats. The open source nature of Linux further empowers administrators to tailor security configurations to meet specific organizational requirements, ensuring the safety of data and applications hosted in the cloud.

In this chapter, we will delve into the following main topics within the scope of AWS services:

- Creating EC2 instances on AWS

- Connecting to a created EC2 instance using PuTTY

- Working on our EC2 instance

Creating EC2 instances on AWS

Creating **Elastic Compute Cloud** (**EC2**) instances on AWS represents a foundational step in building and deploying scalable and flexible computing resources in the cloud. An EC2 instance can be thought of as a virtual server in the AWS cloud, and understanding how to create one is crucial for harnessing the full power of AWS. The importance of this skill lies in the unparalleled agility and cost-efficiency it offers to businesses and organizations. By creating EC2 instances, users can provision computing capacity on-demand, scale resources vertically or horizontally to meet changing workloads, and achieve operational efficiencies by paying only for what they consume. The primary reason for creating EC2 instances is the flexibility and versatility they bring to the cloud computing landscape. EC2 instances can be customized to meet specific application requirements, whether it's running a web server, hosting a database, performing data analytics, or running machine learning workloads. The ability to choose from a wide range of instance types, each optimized for different use cases, allows users to tailor their virtual servers to the exact needs of their applications. Additionally, users can select the operating system, configure network settings, and choose storage options, providing an unparalleled level of control over their cloud infrastructure.

The use of creating EC2 instances extends beyond mere resource allocation; it encompasses high availability, fault tolerance, and scalability. EC2 instances can be integrated with AWS services such as **Elastic Load Balancing** (**ELB**), Auto Scaling, and Amazon RDS to build resilient and scalable applications. The flexibility to start, stop, and terminate instances at will ensures optimal resource utilization and cost management. Moreover, EC2 instances are the foundation of many cloud-based solutions, including web hosting, data processing, and content delivery, making them a fundamental component of AWS's vast ecosystem. In summary, mastering the creation of EC2 instances is pivotal for anyone seeking to leverage AWS's cloud capabilities fully. It empowers users with the ability to design and deploy robust, scalable, and cost-effective cloud solutions that meet the unique demands of modern businesses and organizations.

Before creating an instance, visit the AWS website (`https://aws.amazon.com/`) to create your account. Please note that initial account activation may take up to 24 hours, so it's essential to plan accordingly. In the context of AWS Free Tier, it's important to understand that it offers users the opportunity to explore AWS services at no cost with specific usage limitations. You can find further information in the FAQ section as shown in the following screenshot:

General

Q: What is the AWS Free Tier?

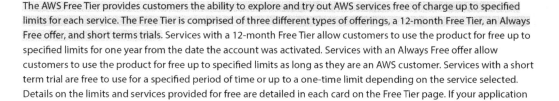

The AWS Free Tier provides customers the ability to explore and try out AWS services free of charge up to specified limits for each service. The Free Tier is comprised of three different types of offerings, a 12-month Free Tier, an Always Free offer, and short terms trials. Services with a 12-month Free Tier allow customers to use the product for free up to specified limits for one year from the date the account was activated. Services with an Always Free offer allow customers to use the product for free up to specified limits as long as they are an AWS customer. Services with a short term trial are free to use for a specified period of time or up to a one-time limit depending on the service selected. Details on the limits and services provided for free are detailed in each card on the Free Tier page. If your application use exceeds the free tier limits, you simply pay standard, pay-as-you-go service rates (see each service page for full pricing details). Restrictions apply; see offer terms for more details.

Figure 13.1 – AWS Free Tier information

Next, we can proceed to log into our AWS account and initiate the creation of EC2 instances on the AWS platform:

1. We can locate EC2 on our dashboard, as illustrated in the screenshot provided:

Figure 13.2 – Searching for EC2 virtual servers

This action will take us to the EC2 Dashboard. In the **Resources** section, we currently have zero instances running, zero dedicated hosts, and zero instances, as depicted in the next screenshot:

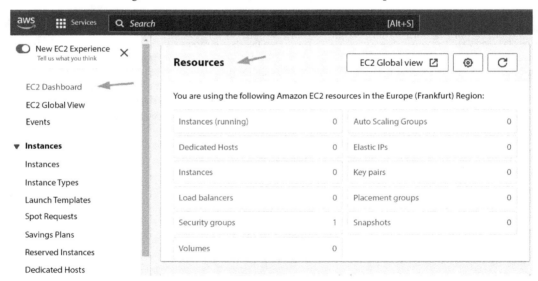

Figure 13.3 – The EC2 Dashboard and Resources panel

2. The AWS console offers a user-friendly interface for handling your EC2 instances. Clicking the **Instances** button grants access to a page displaying your active EC2 instances. From here, you can perform various actions such as halting or terminating running instances and establishing connections to them. On the other hand, the **Launch Instances** button directs

you to a dedicated page for creating new EC2 instances. Here, you can choose from a variety of instance types and customize the instance with your preferred operating system, applications, and other necessary settings:

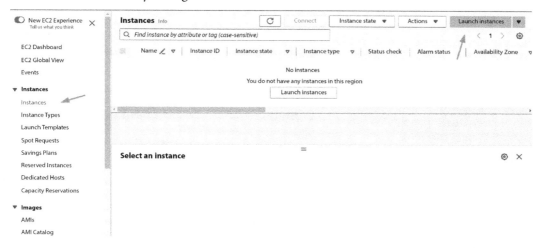

Figure 13.4 – Viewing active EC2 instances

3. First, we give our instance a name. Then, we click the **Browse more AMIs** link:

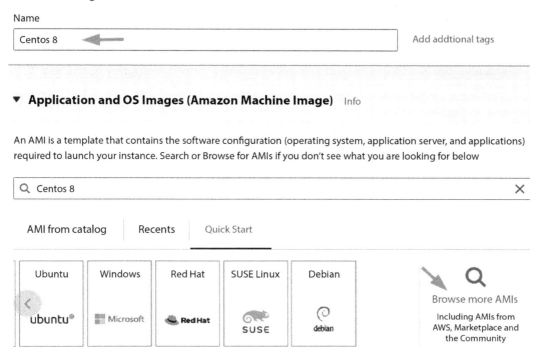

Figure 13.5 – Selecting an AMI (1)

4. Next, we will navigate to the **Amazon Machine Images** (**AMIs**) section. For this walkthrough, we will search for `CentOS 8` in the Marketplace area and choose the one shown in the following screenshot:

Figure 13.6 – Selecting an AMI (2)

The AMIs within AWS serve as ready-made templates or virtual machine images. They encompass the essential components, such as the operating system, application server, and other necessary software, required for launching a virtual instance. These AMIs simplify and expedite the process of creating virtual machines by eliminating the need for manual installation and setup. Furthermore, AMIs are versatile, available in diverse configurations, and compatible with various operating systems, making them a cornerstone for rapidly deploying virtual instances in the AWS cloud. For more in-depth information about AMIs, visit `https://docs.aws.amazon.com/AWSEC2/latest/UserGuide/AMIs.html?tag=buylocal0e8-20`.

5. Next, we are presented with a pop-up showing the CentOS 8 information and a **Continue** button. Click it:

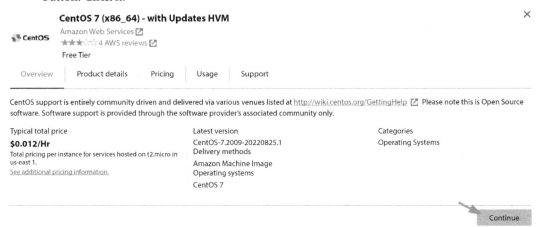

Figure 13.7 – Selecting an AMI (3)

6. Next is **Key pair (login)**.

A key pair consists of two cryptographic keys: a public key and a private key. The public key is employed to encrypt data, while the private key is employed to decrypt data. When a key pair is utilized to log in to an instance, the instance employs the public key to encrypt your login credentials. Subsequently, you utilize the private key to decrypt the login credentials.

Additional information about the key pair login screen includes the following:

*   The **Select a key pair** drop-down menu displays a list of all key pairs linked to your account

*   The **Create a new key pair** button enables you to generate a new key pair

*   The **Download your key pair** button permits you to download the private key associated with the selected key pair

> **Note**
> It is important to keep your private key secret. If someone else gains access to your private key, they will be able to log in to your instances and access your data.

▼ **Key pair (login)** Info

You can use a key pair to securely connect to your instance. Ensure that you have access to the selected key pair before you launch the instance.

Key pair name - *required*

| Select ▼ | ↻ *Create new key pair*

Figure 13.8 – The Key pair (login) window

7. Let's create a new key pair. You will have to click on the **Create new key pair** link.

The **Create key pair** page includes the following fields:

*   **Key pair name**: This field is for specifying the name of the key pair. Key pair names can be up to 255 ASCII characters in length and should not contain leading or trailing spaces. For this example, we'll be using the name connect.

*   **Key pair type**: This field allows you to choose the type of key pair you want to create. You have two options: **RSA** or **ED25519**. RSA is the more common key pair type and is supported by all AWS services. ED25519 is a newer and more secure key pair type compared to RSA, but we'll make use of the RSA.

- **Private key file format**: In this field, you can select the format in which you want to save the private key. You have two choices: **.pem** or **.ppk**. **.pem** is the standard format for private keys and is supported by all SSH clients. **.ppk** is a format specific to the PuTTY SSH client. We'll select the **.ppk** option and then click the **Create key pair** button:

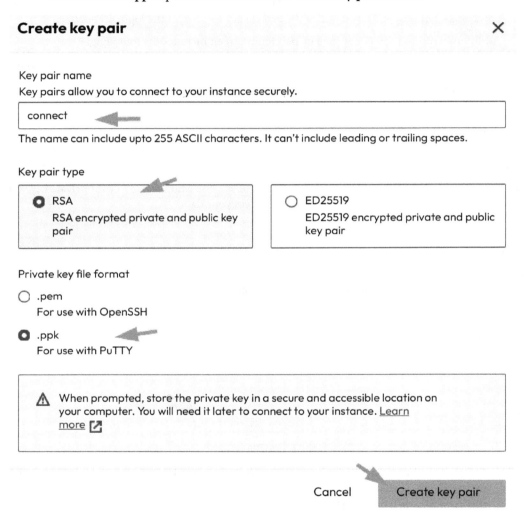

Create key pair   ✕

Key pair name
Key pairs allow you to connect to your instance securely.

connect   ⬅

The name can include upto 255 ASCII characters. It can't include leading or trailing spaces.

Key pair type

◉ RSA
RSA encrypted private and public key pair

○ ED25519
ED25519 encrypted private and public key pair

Private key file format

○ .pem
For use with OpenSSH

◉ .ppk   ⬅
For use with PuTTY

⚠ When prompted, store the private key in a secure and accessible location on your computer. You will need it later to connect to your instance. Learn more 🗗

Cancel   Create key pair

Figure 13.9 – Create key pair

After clicking on the **Create key pair** button, the key will be automatically downloaded in the Downloads folder:

Figure 13.10 – The downloaded .ppk key

Next, we will do the network settings. The Security Groups page provides a comprehensive view of all security groups associated with your AWS account. Each security group entry on this page includes information such as the security group name, description, and its **virtual private cloud** (**VPC**) association. On the Security Groups page, you have the flexibility to perform various actions, including creating new security groups, modifying existing ones, and deleting those no longer needed.

Let's delve into what a VPC is.

A VPC is a fundamental component of AWS and similar cloud computing platforms. It is a virtual network environment that allows users to create and manage a logically isolated section of the AWS cloud infrastructure. VPCs provide an additional layer of security and control over the cloud resources, allowing users to design their own network architecture, define IP address ranges, create subnets, and configure routing tables.

Within a VPC, users can launch and manage a wide range of cloud-based resources, including virtual machines (EC2 instances), databases, load balancers, and more. By segmenting the cloud environment into VPCs, organizations can establish isolated networks that mimic traditional data center infrastructures with the added flexibility and scalability of the cloud. This isolation enables users to implement fine-grained security policies, ensuring that only authorized traffic can access resources within the VPC. VPCs also support the creation of VPNs and direct connections to on-premises data centers, facilitating secure hybrid cloud deployments. In summary, VPCs are a cornerstone of cloud networking, offering a flexible and controlled environment for deploying and managing cloud resources while enhancing security and network segmentation.

8. To initiate the creation of a new security group, click the **Edit** button on the **Network settings** page:

Figure 13.11 – Editing security groups (1)

9. On the next page, click the **Create Security Group** button to create a new security group.

To edit an existing security group, click on the respective security group name:

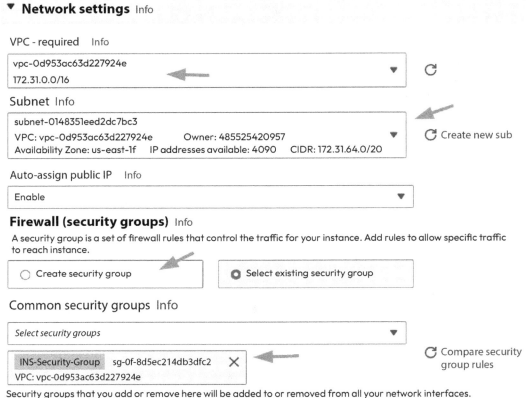

Figure 13.12 – Editing security groups (2)

10. If you wish to remove a security group, click on the security group name and follow it up by clicking the **Delete Security Group** button.

Here are some valuable tips for effectively utilizing security groups:

- **Keep restrictive rules**: Maintain your security groups with the principle of least privilege in mind. Only permit the traffic that is essential for the functionality of your EC2 instances.

- **Isolate traffic**: Create distinct security groups for different types of traffic. For instance, separating security groups for web servers and database servers can enhance your network security.

- **Review regularly**: Periodically assess your security groups to ensure they align with your evolving needs and security requirements.

11. Lastly, we take a look at the rules. They permit SSH traffic from any source on the internet to connect to port 22 on the specified security group:

Inbound Security Group Rules

▼ Security group rule 1 (TCP, 22, 0.0.0.0/0)   [Remove]

Type Info	Protocol Info	Port range Info
ssh ▼	TCP	22

Source type Info	Source Info	Description - *optional* Info
Anywhere ▼	🔍 *Add CIDR, prefix list or securit*	*e.g. SSH for admin desktop*
	0.0.0.0/0 ✕	

Figure 13.13 – Inbound Security Group Rules

Let's break down the various components of this rule:

- **Type**: This indicates the type of traffic allowed by the rule. In this instance, it's **ssh**.

- **Protocol**: This is the protocol to which the rule applies. In this case, it's TCP.

- **Port range**: This is the range of ports covered by the rule. Here, it's port 22.

- **Source type**: This specifies the source of the allowed traffic. In this case, it's 0.0.0.0/0, signifying that traffic from anywhere on the internet is permitted.

- **Description**: This is a brief description of the rule, which, in this case, is SSH access.

12. Next, we will configure the storage.

The root volume type pertains to the storage used for an instance's root device, which houses the operating system and essential files.

There are two primary root volume types:

- **Elastic Block Store (EBS)**: EBS volumes are block storage devices attached to EC2 instances. They offer persistence, ensuring data remains intact even if the instance is terminated.

For the purposes of this book, we'll be increasing the size to 30 GB:

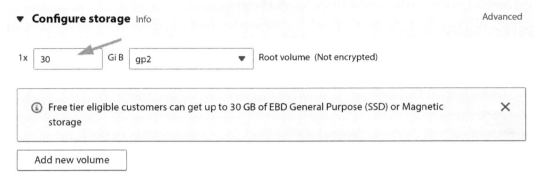

Figure 13.14 – Configuring the storage

- **Instance Store**: These volumes provide temporary storage for EC2 instances but lack persistence. Data on instance store volumes is not retained when the instance is terminated.

Selection of the root volume type for an EC2 instance is made during the instance's launch. While it is possible to change the root volume type post-launch, doing so necessitates stopping the instance.

The majority of EC2 instances opt for EBS volumes as their root storage due to the following advantages:

- **Persistence**: EBS volumes retain data even after instance termination, making them ideal for storing crucial data such as operating system files and application data.

- **Scalability**: EBS volumes can be adjusted in size, accommodating applications with varying storage requirements.

- **Performance**: EBS volumes offer multiple performance options, such as **General Purpose (SSD)**, **Provisioned IOPS (SSD)**, and **Magnetic**, enabling users to select the appropriate performance level for their applications.

13. After making these selections, we move to the summary area to launch our instance. The summary includes the following information (see also *Figure 10.15*):

- **Number of instances: 1**
- **Software Image (AMI): CentOS-7-2111-20220825_1.x86_64 ami-002070d43b0a4f171**
- **Virtual server type (instance type): t2.micro**
- **Firewall (security group): INS-Security-Group**
- **Storage (volumes): 1 volume(s) - 30 GB**

The summary also shows that the instance is eligible for the AWS Free Tier. This means that you can use the instance for free for up to 750 hours per month in your first year.

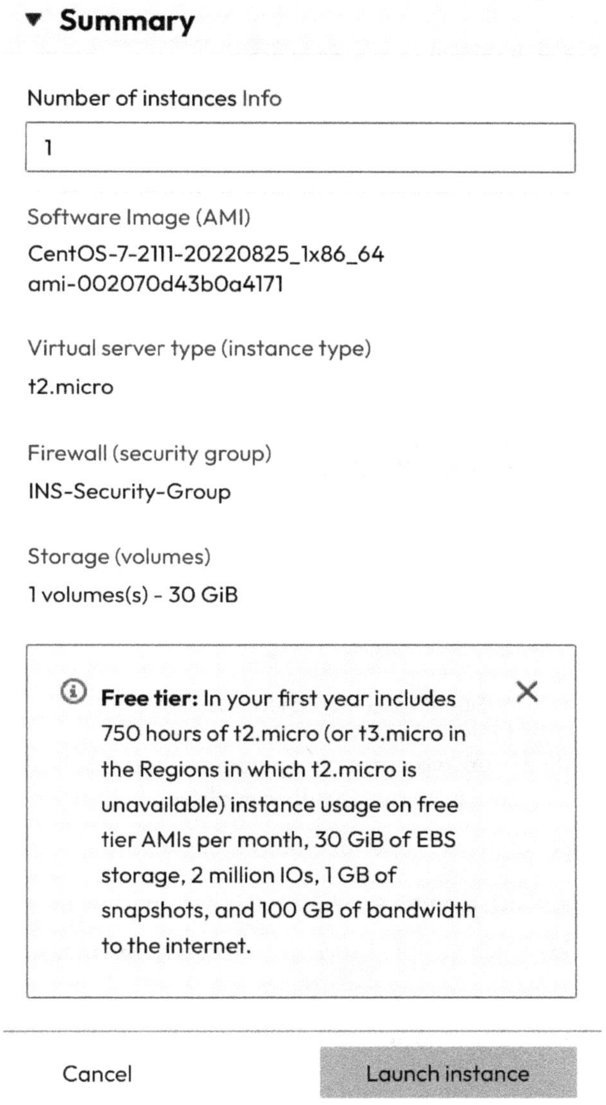

▼ **Summary**

Number of instances Info

1

Software Image (AMI)
CentOS-7-2111-20220825_1x86_64
ami-002070d43b0a4171

Virtual server type (instance type)
t2.micro

Firewall (security group)
INS-Security-Group

Storage (volumes)
1 volumes(s) - 30 GiB

ⓘ **Free tier:** In your first year includes   ✕
750 hours of t2.micro (or t3.micro in
the Regions in which t2.micro is
unavailable) instance usage on free
tier AMIs per month, 30 GiB of EBS
storage, 2 million IOs, 1 GB of
snapshots, and 100 GB of bandwidth
to the internet.

Cancel   Launch instance

Figure 13.15 – Summary

14. Click on **Launch instance**. When you see that the launching instance progress was successful, click **EC2** beside **Instances**:

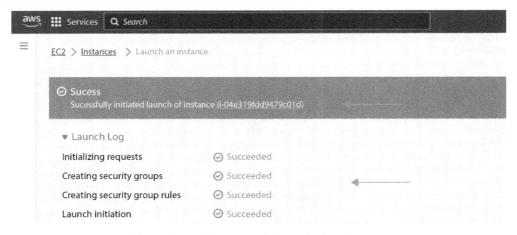

Figure 13.16 – The successful launch of an instance

15. After clicking **EC2** in the preceding step, we'll be redirected to the **EC2 Dashboard** page. The following screenshot displays an AWS EC2 instance with a **Running** status and a **2/2 checks passed** status check:

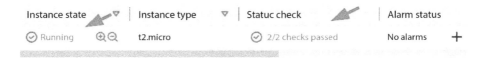

Figure 13.17 – 2/2 checks passed

This indicates that the instance is currently operational and that both of the status checks conducted by AWS EC2 have been successfully completed.

AWS EC2 conducts two types of status checks for each running instance:

- System status checks, which monitor the AWS systems supporting the instance
- Instance status checks, which identify issues within the EC2 instance itself

If one of these status checks fails, the overall status of the instance is marked as **Impaired**. In such cases, the instance may not function as expected.

The **Impaired** status indicates that there might be issues with the instance's health, but it doesn't automatically mean that the instance is irreparably damaged.

Depending on the nature of the issue, you may be able to troubleshoot and resolve it without recreating the entire AMI. The specific steps to take to resolve the issue would depend on the nature of the failure. Here are examples of types of issues:

- **System status check fails**: If this check fails, it often indicates problems with the underlying infrastructure. AWS may automatically attempt to recover the instance. In some cases, you might need to stop and start the instance or you may need to contact AWS support for assistance.

- **Instance status check fails**: When this check fails, it generally points to issues within the instance itself, such as software or configuration problems. You can usually access the instance, identify the problem, and apply fixes without creating a new AMI.

In the context of the previous screenshot, a **2/2 checks passed** status confirms that both system and instance checks have been successfully cleared, signifying that the instance is in a healthy and fully operational state.

Connecting to a created EC2 instance using PuTTY

Establishing a connection to an EC2 instance within AWS is a fundamental step in harnessing the capabilities of cloud computing. It involves creating a remote link to a virtual server hosted in the AWS cloud infrastructure. This connection allows users to access, manage, and configure the virtual server, taking advantage of the adaptability, scalability, and cost-efficiency provided by AWS.

The primary motivation for connecting to an EC2 instance is to gain secure and efficient remote access to a cloud-based server environment. This connectivity is invaluable for system administrators, developers, and DevOps practitioners, empowering them to perform critical tasks relating to server setup, software installation, real-time monitoring, troubleshooting, and routine maintenance. It enables the seamless administration of server resources and file transfers and the timely implementation of system updates, all without any physical presence at the server's location. Connecting to an EC2 instance is crucial for deploying and managing web applications, databases, and other cloud-native services. It streamlines collaborative efforts and ensures that cloud resources are accessible from any location, making it an essential component of modern cloud infrastructure management.

The purpose of connecting to an EC2 instance is multifaceted. System administrators use remote access to oversee server configurations, apply security patches, and monitor performance metrics. Developers leverage these connections for deploying and testing applications, debugging procedures, and managing development environments in the cloud. DevOps teams rely on remote connections to streamline server provisioning, configure extensive server fleets, and efficiently orchestrate complex **continuous integration/continuous deployment (CI/CD)** pipelines. Organizations embracing **Infrastructure as Code (IaC)** principles depend on remote access for programmatically managing their cloud infrastructure systematically and efficiently.

Before we can connect to our created instance, please visit `https://www.chiark.greenend.org.uk/~sgtatham/putty/latest.html` to download PuTTY. Depending on your system's architecture, you can choose either the 64-bit or 32-bit version:

Package files

You probably want one of these. They include versions of all the PuTTY utilities (except the new

(Not sure whether you want the 32-bit or the 64-bit version? Read the FAQ entry.)

We also publish the latest PuTTY installers for all Windows architectures as a free-of-charge dow

MSI ('Windows Installer')

64-bit x86:	`putty-64bit-0.79-installer.msi`	(signature)
64-bit Arm:	`putty-arm64-0.79-installer.msi`	(signature)
32-bit x86:	`putty-0.79-installer.msi`	(signature)

Unix source archive

`.tar.gz`:	`putty-0.79.tar.gz`	(signature)

Figure 13.18 – PuTTY 64-bit version or 32-bit version

After installing PuTTY, we can proceed to check our created Linux instance. We will examine the instance summary, which includes the public IPv4 address, as well as details related to security, networking, storage, status checks, monitoring, tags, and private IPv4 addresses:

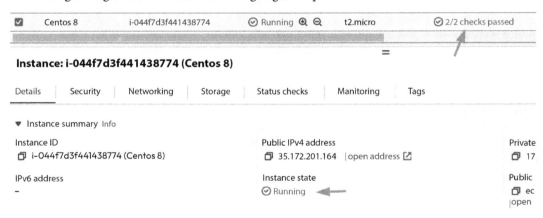

Figure 13.19 – View of the instance summary

We can try quickly connecting to our instance using PuTTY:

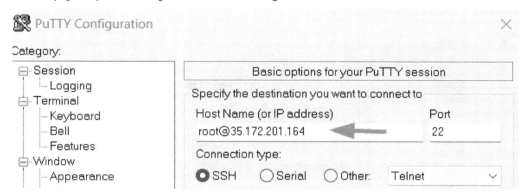

Figure 13.20 – PuTTY Configuration

Enter the public IP address from your instance summary into the **Host Name (or IP address)** field shown in the screenshot. Keep the port at the default setting of 22 and click **Open**. Subsequently, you'll receive a PuTTY output. The information in the screenshot shows that our user is attempting to log into the EC2 instance as the root user using a public key. This is because, by default, root login is disabled on EC2 instances:

Figure 13.21 – PuTTY output

The user is prompted to log in as the user centos instead, but first, let's check how to load our .pkk key on PuTTY. Locate the key:

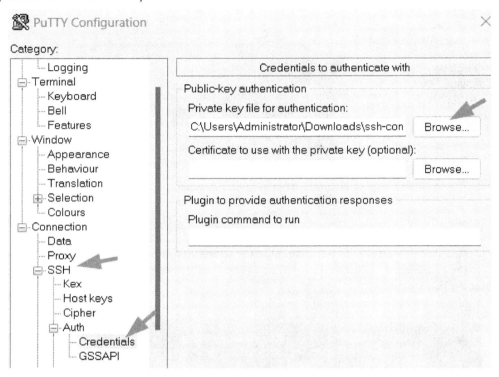

Figure 13.22 – Adding the .pkk key to PuTTY

We can call it any name. Have a look at the following example:

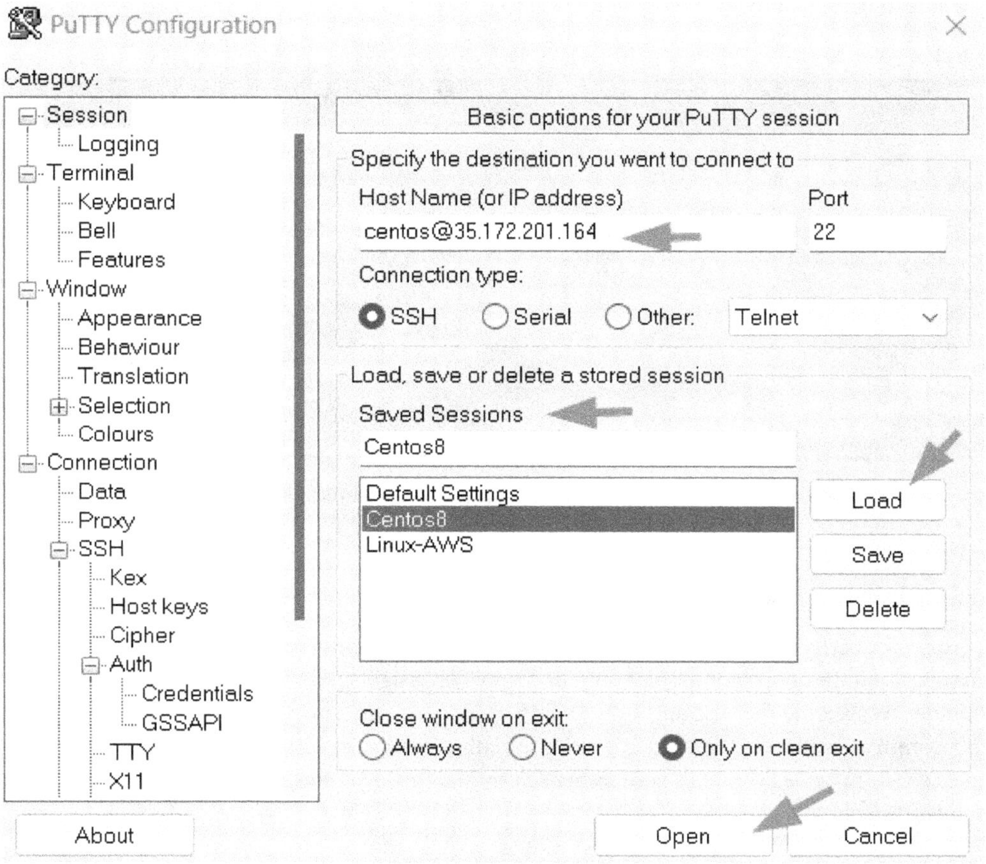

Figure 13.23 – Saved session settings

The arrows in the image are pointing to the default settings for a PuTTY session. They are located in the following places:

- **Host Name (or IP address)**: This is the address of the server that you want to connect to. In the image, the default setting is `centos@35.172.201.164`.

- **Saved Sessions**: This button allows you to save the current PuTTY session settings to a file. This can be useful if you connect to the same server on a regular basis, as you can simply load the saved session settings instead of having to enter them each time like with **Linux-AWS** in the image.

- **Load**: This button allows you to load a saved PuTTY session. To do this, simply select the session file that you want to load and click the **Load** button.

- **Open**: This button allows you to open a PuTTY session using the current settings, and this will lead us into authenticating with our .pkk key:

```
centos@ip-172-31-16-157:~                                          —    □    ×
Using username "centos".
Authenticating with public key "ssh-connect2"
[centos@ip-172-31-16-157 ~]$ df
Filesystem      1K-blocks     Used Available Use% Mounted on
devtmpfs           480972        0    480972   0% /dev
tmpfs              506468        0    506468   0% /dev/shm
tmpfs              506468    13184    493284   3% /run
tmpfs              506468        0    506468   0% /sys/fs/cgroup
/dev/xvda1       31445996  1480476  29965520   5% /
tmpfs              101296        0    101296   0% /run/user/0
tmpfs              101296        0    101296   0% /run/user/1000
[centos@ip-172-31-16-157 ~]$ whoami && hostname && uname -a
centos
ip-172-31-16-157.ec2.internal
Linux ip-172-31-16-157.ec2.internal 3.10.0-1160.76.1.el7.x86_64 #1 SMP Wed Aug 10 16:21
:17 UTC 2022 x86_64 x86_64 x86_64 GNU/Linux
```

Figure 13.24 – Authenticating with the public key

After successfully establishing a connection, you'll gain access to a terminal window, allowing you to efficiently manage the instance.

In the process of verifying available free space on the system, we employ the df command to display information about the file systems. This command provides insights into disk usage and available space. Additionally, we execute the whoami && hostname && uname -a command sequence. The whoami command retrieves the current user's username, hostname displays the system's hostname, and uname -a provides you with comprehensive system information, including the kernel version and architecture.

In summary, connecting to an EC2 instance is a pivotal step that unlocks the full potential of cloud computing, facilitating server administration, cloud-native application development, and infrastructure automation, all seamlessly integrated within the AWS cloud environment.

Working on our EC2 instance

In this section, we are going to make use of some commands similar to those used in CentOS and apply them to perform some short tasks. So, let's begin:

- **Updating and upgrading**:

    You've just launched your CentOS 8 Linux instance on AWS. To ensure it's up to date, use the following commands:

```
[centos@ip-172-31-16-157 ~]$ sudo yum update && sudo yum upgrade
Loaded plugins: fastestmirror
Loading mirror speeds from cached hostfile
 * base: download.cf.centos.org
 * extras: download.cf.centos.org
 * updates: download.cf.centos.org
Resolving Dependencies
--> Running transaction check
---> Package bind-export-libs.x86_64 32:9.11.4-26.P2.el7_9.9 will be updated
---> Package bind-export-libs.x86_64 32:9.11.4-26.P2.el7_9.14 will be an update
---> Package ca-certificates.noarch 0:2021.2.50-72.el7_9 will be updated
---> Package ca-certificates.noarch 0:2022.2.54-74.el7_9 will be an update
---> Package cronie.x86_64 0:1.4.11-24.el7_9 will be updated
---> Package cronie.x86_64 0:1.4.11-25.el7_9 will be an update
---> Package cronie-anacron.x86_64 0:1.4.11-24.el7_9 will be updated
---> Package cronie-anacron.x86_64 0:1.4.11-25.el7_9 will be an update
```

Figure 13.25 – Updating and upgrading

Here's the transaction summary:

```
Transaction Summary
==================================================
Install    1 Package
Upgrade   42 Packages

Total download size: 110 M
Is this ok [y/d/N]: y
```

Figure 13.26 – Transaction summary

The summary indicates that one package is in the process of being installed, 42 packages are undergoing updates, and the cumulative download size amounts to 110 MB. The user is prompted to decide whether to continue with the installation process.

When it comes to updating software packages, package managers serve as essential tools for users to effortlessly manage software installation, updates, and removal on their systems. These utilities offer the flexibility to install software from diverse sources, encompassing official repositories, third-party repositories, and local files, providing users with versatile options for software management.

- **Package installation**:

   The following shows the installation of an Apache web server on a CentOS 8 instance:

```
[centos@ip-172-31-16-157 ~]$ sudo yum install httpd   <---
Loaded plugins: fastestmirror
Loading mirror speeds from cached hostfile
 * base: download.cf.centos.org
 * extras: download.cf.centos.org
 * updates: download.cf.centos.org
Resolving Dependencies
--> Running transaction check
---> Package httpd.x86_64 0:2.4.6-99.el7.centos.1 will be installed
--> Processing Dependency: httpd-tools = 2.4.6-99.el7.centos.1 for pack
```

Figure 13.27 – Installing a package

- **Service management:**

    The following is how to start the Apache service and enable it to start on boot:

```
[centos@ip-172-31-16-157 ~]$ sudo systemctl status httpd  ←
● httpd.service - The Apache HTTP Server
   Loaded: loaded (/usr/lib/systemd/system/httpd.service; disabled; vendor preset: disabled)
   Active: inactive (dead)
     Docs: man:httpd(8)
           man:apachectl(8)
[centos@ip-172-31-16-157 ~]$ sudo systemctl start httpd  ←
[centos@ip-172-31-16-157 ~]$ sudo systemctl enable httpd  ←
Created symlink from /etc/systemd/system/multi-user.target.wants/httpd.service to /usr/lib/syste
[centos@ip-172-31-16-157 ~]$ sudo systemctl status httpd  ←
● httpd.service - The Apache HTTP Server
   Loaded: loaded (/usr/lib/systemd/system/httpd.service; enabled; vendor preset: disabled)
   Active: active (running) since Mon 2023-10-16 23:10:21 UTC; 19s ago
     Docs: man:httpd(8)
           man:apachectl(8)
 Main PID: 24635 (httpd)
   Status: "Total requests: 0; Current requests/sec: 0; Current traffic:    0 B/sec"
   CGroup: /system.slice/httpd.service
           ├─24635 /usr/sbin/httpd -DFOREGROUND
           ├─24636 /usr/sbin/httpd -DFOREGROUND
           ├─24637 /usr/sbin/httpd -DFOREGROUND
           ├─24638 /usr/sbin/httpd -DFOREGROUND
           ├─24639 /usr/sbin/httpd -DFOREGROUND
           └─24640 /usr/sbin/httpd -DFOREGROUND

Oct 16 23:10:21 ip-172-31-16-157.ec2.internal systemd[1]: Starting The Apache HTTP Server...
Oct 16 23:10:21 ip-172-31-16-157.ec2.internal systemd[1]: Started The Apache HTTP Server.
```

Figure 13.28 – Starting Apache on boot

Here's a breakdown of the command:

- `sudo systemctl status httpd`: This command checks the status of the Apache HTTP Server (`httpd`). It displays information about the service, such as its description, whether it's loaded or active, and its related documentation. In this case, it shows that the service is loaded but inactive (dead).

- `sudo systemctl start httpd`: This command starts the Apache HTTP Server. It initiates the service, making it active and running.

- `sudo systemctl enable httpd`: This command enables the automatic start of the Apache HTTP Server at boot. It creates a symbolic link from the multi-user target to the httpd service, ensuring that the service starts when the system boots up.

- `sudo systemctl status httpd`: After starting and enabling the service, this command checks the status of the Apache HTTP Server again. Now, it shows that the service is loaded, enabled, and active (running). It provides additional details about the service, including its main **process ID (PID)** and current status.

- **Logging and monitoring**:

  journalctl is used to access and view the systemd journal on a Linux system. The systemd journal is a system log that contains various log entries and messages generated by the system and its components. The output of journalctl displays a chronological list of log entries, providing information about the system's activities and events.

  In the provided output, we can observe the following details:

  - The command shows logs that can begin at a specific timestamp (e.g., Mon 2023-10-16 21:22:47 UTC) and end at another timestamp (e.g., Mon 2023-10-16 23:15:01 UTC) with the understanding that the timestamps may vary.

  - The logs display various system events, including messages from systemd components and kernel-related activities.

  - These events may include system initialization, SELinux policy loading, hardware and kernel configuration, virtualization detection, hostname configuration, and more.

  - The log entries also include details about systemd processes and their status, such as whether they started successfully or encountered issues.

  - The journalctl command provides a comprehensive view of system activities, aiding in system administration, debugging, and troubleshooting.

```
[centos@ip-172-31-16-157 ~]$ journalctl
-- Logs begin at Mon 2023-10-16 21:22:47 UTC, end at Mon 2023-10-16 23:15:01 UTC. --
Oct 16 21:22:47 localhost.localdomain systemd-journal[389]: Runtime journal is using 6.1M (max allowed
Oct 16 21:22:47 localhost.localdomain systemd-journald[99]: Received SIGTERM from PID 1 (systemd).
Oct 16 21:22:47 localhost.localdomain kernel: type=1404 audit(1697491366.731:2): enforcing=1 old_enforc
Oct 16 21:22:47 localhost.localdomain kernel: SELinux: 2048 avtab hash slots, 112730 rules.
Oct 16 21:22:47 localhost.localdomain kernel: SELinux: 2048 avtab hash slots, 112730 rules.
Oct 16 21:22:47 localhost.localdomain kernel: SELinux:  8 users, 14 roles, 5046 types, 316 bools, 1 sen
Oct 16 21:22:47 localhost.localdomain kernel: SELinux:  130 classes, 112730 rules
Oct 16 21:22:47 localhost.localdomain kernel: SELinux:  Completing initialization.
Oct 16 21:22:47 localhost.localdomain kernel: SELinux:  Setting up existing superblocks.
Oct 16 21:22:47 localhost.localdomain kernel: type=1403 audit(1697491366.957:3): policy loaded auid=429
Oct 16 21:22:47 localhost.localdomain kernel: random: crng init done
Oct 16 21:22:47 localhost.localdomain systemd[1]: Successfully loaded SELinux policy in 361.888ms.
Oct 16 21:22:47 localhost.localdomain kernel: ip_tables: (C) 2000-2006 Netfilter Core Team
Oct 16 21:22:47 localhost.localdomain systemd[1]: Inserted module 'ip_tables'
Oct 16 21:22:47 localhost.localdomain systemd[1]: Relabelled /dev, /run and /sys/fs/cgroup in 14.357ms.
```

Figure 13.29 – Tracking system activities

`journalctl` is a valuable tool that helps system administrators monitor system health and diagnose issues. The provided output represents a portion of the system log with events and timestamps, allowing users to track system activities and diagnose problems effectively.

- **Directory management**:

  The `sudo find / -size +100M` command is used to search the entire filesystem (`/`) for files that are larger than 100 megabytes (+100 MB). It begins at the root directory and searches through all directories and subdirectories. The output displays the paths of any files found that meet the size criteria:

```
centos@ip-172-31-16-157:~
[centos@ip-172-31-16-157 ~]$ sudo find / -size +100M
/proc/kcore
find: '/proc/24949/task/24949/fd/5': No such file or directory
find: '/proc/24949/task/24949/fdinfo/5': No such file or directory
find: '/proc/24949/fd/6': No such file or directory
find: '/proc/24949/fdinfo/6': No such file or directory
/var/cache/yum/x86_64/7/updates/gen/primary_db.sqlite
/usr/lib/locale/locale-archive
```

Figure 13.30 – Finding files (1)

The provided output shows that it has located several files that are larger than 100 megabytes, including the following:

- `/proc/kcore`: This file represents the core memory of the kernel, which is a virtual file and not an actual file on disk

- `/var/cache/yum/x86_64/7/updates/gen/primary_db.sqlite`: This file is a database used by the YUM package manager to store information about available packages and updates

- `/usr/lib/locale/locale-archive`: This file contains system locale information used for internationalization and localization

The error messages following the file paths indicate that the `find` command couldn't access certain directories within the `/proc` directory, which is expected because `/proc` is a virtual filesystem that doesn't contain actual files on disk. The errors can be safely ignored in this context.

The `sudo find / -user root -o -group root | less` command is used to search the entire filesystem (`/`) for files and directories that either belong to the `root` user or the `root` group:

Figure 13.31 – Finding files (2)

The | less part of the command pipes the output to the less command, which allows for easier navigation and viewing of the results one screen at a time.

The provided output shows that it has located various files and directories within the /dev directory that either have the owner set to root or belong to the root group. These include the following:

- /dev/vhci: This is a virtual host controller interface

- /dev/vfio: This is a virtual function I/O interface

- /dev/vfio/vfio: This is a subdirectory under /dev/vfio

- /dev/ppp: This is related to **Point-to-Point Protocol (PPP)** devices

- /dev/uinput: This is a virtual input device

- /dev/mqueue: These are message queue devices

- /dev/hugepages: These are files related to huge pages in memory management

- /dev/initctl: This is a **First In, First Out (FIFO)** special file used for communication with the init process

The command is helpful for system administrators when identifying files and directories with specific ownership or group membership, which can be useful for managing system security and access control. The less command is used to make the output more readable and navigable, especially when dealing with large sets of search results.

Summary

In this chapter, you were guided through the comprehensive process of creating Amazon EC2 instances on AWS. The chapter explores the key steps required to establish virtual servers in the cloud while delving into the multitude of instance types and configurations available on AWS. With a focus on practicality, you also gained valuable knowledge of configuring instance details, changing their storage, and setting up security groups for both performance and security. This chapter equipped you with the knowledge and skills to manage EC2 instances in a cloud environment. It provided a step-by-step guide on establishing secure connections to AWS EC2 instances following successful creation. This chapter also introduced PuTTY, a widely used SSH client, and elaborated on its effective use in connecting to Linux-based EC2 instances. The journey begins with an overview of PuTTY and the essential concept of SSH key pairs for secure authentication. Furthermore, you were provided with detailed guidance on installing and configuring PuTTY, including setting up a session, configuring credential locations, and loading the session. Finally, in the *Working on our EC2 Instance* section, we explored hands-on administrative tasks users can perform on AWS EC2 instances. The chapter underscored the importance of updating and upgrading EC2 instances to ensure that they run optimally and have the latest software packages installed. It offered step-by-step guidance on leveraging package managers for effective software installation, updates, and upgrades. You were also introduced to service management, enabling you to start and manage services using `systemd`. The chapter then introduced you to `journalctl`, a powerful tool for accessing system logs to monitor activities, troubleshoot issues, and gather essential system health information. It concluded with insights into directory management using the `find` command, rounding out your comprehensive understanding of EC2 instance administration in a dynamic cloud environment.

Index

Symbols

www.packtpub.com

Subscribe to our online digital library for full access to over 7,000 books and videos, as well as industry leading tools to help you plan your personal development and advance your career. For more information, please visit our website.

Why subscribe?

- Spend less time learning and more time coding with practical eBooks and Videos from over 4,000 industry professionals

- Improve your learning with Skill Plans built especially for you

- Get a free eBook or video every month

- Fully searchable for easy access to vital information

- Copy and paste, print, and bookmark content

Did you know that Packt offers eBook versions of every book published, with PDF and ePub files available? You can upgrade to the eBook version at www.packtpub.com and as a print book customer, you are entitled to a discount on the eBook copy. Get in touch with us at customercare@packtpub.com for more details.

At www.packtpub.com, you can also read a collection of free technical articles, sign up for a range of free newsletters, and receive exclusive discounts and offers on Packt books and eBooks.

Other Books You May Enjoy

If you enjoyed this book, you may be interested in these other books by Packt:

Fedora Linux System Administration

Alex Callejas

ISBN: 978-1-80461-840-0

- Discover how to configure a Linux environment from scratch
- Review the basics of Linux resources and components
- Familiarize yourself with enhancements and updates made to common Linux desktop tools
- Optimize the resources of the Linux operating system
- Find out how to bolster security with the SELinux module
- Improve system administration using the tools provided by Fedora
- Get up and running with open container creation using Podman

Cloud Penetration Testing for Red Teamers

Kim Crawley

ISBN: 978-1-80324-848-6

- Familiarize yourself with the evolution of cloud networks
- Navigate and secure complex environments that use more than one cloud service
- Conduct vulnerability assessments to identify weak points in cloud configurations
- Secure your cloud infrastructure by learning about common cyber attack techniques
- Explore various strategies to successfully counter complex cloud attacks
- Delve into the most common AWS, Azure, and GCP services and their applications for businesses
- Understand the collaboration between red teamers, cloud administrators, and other stakeholders for cloud pentesting

Packt is searching for authors like you

If you're interested in becoming an author for Packt, please visit `authors.packtpub.com` and apply today. We have worked with thousands of developers and tech professionals, just like you, to help them share their insight with the global tech community. You can make a general application, apply for a specific hot topic that we are recruiting an author for, or submit your own idea.

Share your thoughts

Now you've finished *Essential Linux Commands*, we'd love to hear your thoughts! Scan the QR code below to go straight to the Amazon review page for this book and share your feedback or leave a review on the site that you purchased it from.

`https://packt.link/r/1803239034`

Your review is important to us and the tech community and will help us make sure we're delivering excellent quality content.

Download a free PDF copy of this book

Thanks for purchasing this book!

Do you like to read on the go but are unable to carry your print books everywhere?

Is your eBook purchase not compatible with the device of your choice?

Don't worry, now with every Packt book you get a DRM-free PDF version of that book at no cost.

Read anywhere, any place, on any device. Search, copy, and paste code from your favorite technical books directly into your application.

The perks don't stop there, you can get exclusive access to discounts, newsletters, and great free content in your inbox daily

Follow these simple steps to get the benefits:

1. Scan the QR code or visit the link below

https://packt.link/free-ebook/9781803239033

2. Submit your proof of purchase
3. That's it! We'll send your free PDF and other benefits to your email directly

www.ingramcontent.com/pod-product-compliance
Lightning Source LLC
Chambersburg PA
CBHW080637060326
40690CB00021B/4968